WOMEN'S SECRETS

SUNY Series in Medieval Studies
Paul E. Szarmach, Editor

WOMEN'S SECRETS

A Translation of Pseudo–Albertus Magnus's *De Secretis Mulierum* with Commentaries

HELEN RODNITE LEMAY

State University
of New York
Press

Published by
State University of New York Press, Albany

For information, address State University of New York Press,
90 State Street, Suite 700, Albany, NY 12207

Production by Susan Geraghty
Marketing by Dana Yanulavich

Library of Congress Cataloging-in-Publication Data

De secretis mulierum. English.
      Women's secrets : a translation of Pseudo-Albertus Magnus' De
secretis mulierum with commentaries / Helen Rodnite Lemay.
      p.   cm.
    Sometimes attributed to Albertus Magnus.
    Includes bibliographical references and index.
    ISBN 0-7914-1143-5 (alk. paper) : $49.50. — ISBN 0-7914-1144-3
(pbk. : alk. paper) : $16.95
    1. Medicine, Medieval. 2. Medicine, Magic, mystic, and spagiric-
-Early works to 1800. I. Lemay, Helen Rodnite. II. Albertus,
Magnus, Saint, 1193–1280. III. Title.
R128.S3913   1992
610—dc20
                                             91–30690
                                              CIP

10 9 8 7 6 5 4 3 2 1

For
Roslyn Schwartz

CONTENTS

ACKNOWLEDGMENTS

This book represents a project begun about fifteen years ago, abandoned for some time, and taken up again with the encouragement of Peggy Gifford, formerly of the State University of New York Press. Although I am a more mature scholar now than I was when I first began to work with the *De secretis mulierum,* I found, to my surprise, that my research methods haven't changed at all over the years. I originally planned to write a "popular" introduction to the text; I have spent years studying medical writings on gynecology and obstetrics, and I thought I would simply incorporate the results of this research into my discussuon of the *Secrets,* and set the treatise into the context of women's issues in medieval science. Although I have done this, the book reflects much more my training with Paul Oskar Kristeller at Columbia University. I felt compelled to search out the sources, examine contemporary texts, consult manuscripts, take down variants—to apply to a "popular" text the methods of serious scholarship. Although Professor Kristeller has not seen the book, and is in no way responsible for any of the errors, he continues to inspire me in my work.

I am grateful to Richard Lemay for numerous corrections and suggestions, for reading the entire manuscript, and for supplying me with computer assistance. John Riddle of North Carolina State University graciously answered all my questions on medicinal herbs. The librarians at the rare book rooms of the New York Academy of Medicine and the National Library of Medicine in Bethesda, Maryland, have been particularly helpful in my research. Dean Andrew Policano of the State University of New York at Stony Brook was responsible for the award of a faculty travel research grant, making possible the trip to Bethesda in 1989.

This book is dedicated to Roslyn Schwartz, who provided me with inspiration and support over a period of four years.

INTRODUCTION

AUTHORS, DATES OF COMPOSITION, AND THE TEXT

The *De secretis mulierum* was composed in the late thirteenth or early fourteenth century by a disciple of the eminent thirteenth-century philosopher, theologian, and scientist Albertus Magnus. Although many manuscripts and editions name Albertus as the author, Lynn Thorndike has shown that the *Secrets of Women** is partly drawn from his genuine writings and partly modeled, somewhat faultily, after them.[1] Scholars have devoted much effort to discovering the identity of the author of this treatise. Besides Albertus, the names of Thomas of Brabant and Henry of Saxony have figured in a lengthy discussion about the correct attribution of this writing. Although Thomas and Henry have been ruled out, the question has not as yet been settled.

Brigitte Kusche has introduced another element into the debate: uncertainty over the text itself. Kusche has pointed out that the *De secretis mulierum* exists in a number of versions, and that scholars' different conclusions about authorship result from the differences in the texts they are analyzing. For Kusche the first question to address is not who wrote the *Secrets of Women*, but which text version is closest to the archetype, and indeed can an archetype be reconstructed from the many manuscripts that are available.[2]

The most recent study of the *De secretis*, Margaret Schleissner's 1987 dissertation, has identified 13 more manuscript copies of this treatise, bringing the count up to 83. The complicated codicological situation is matched by variations in the editions, of which over 50 were printed in the fifteenth century and over 70 in the sixteenth century.[3] Some of the variant readings from these printed versions are found in the notes to this translation.

---

* The English title *Secrets of Women* and the Latin *De secretis mulierum* will be used interchangeably in this discussion.

1

Although close, textual study is certainly a priority before drawing conclusions about the author or date of composition, this volume does not deal with these questions. Presented here is a working text of the *De secretis mulierum,* a work that sets forth ideas about women and science that were part of the thirteenth- and fourteenth-century scholastic milieu. As the large number of manuscripts and editions demonstrates, the treatise was immensely popular and we can therefore conclude that the ideas it expressed were highly influential.[4]

The text used as the basis of this translation is the Lyons, 1580, edition. This edition presents a clear Latin text, which is an example of the most frequently published version of the *Secrets,* and, from spot checking, correlates well with other witnesses to this redaction. Further, as I shall demonstrate, the text is of interest as evidence of a widely circulating epitome of the sixteenth-century view of women that resulted in witch hunting. The Lyons edition is selected, then, for its clarity and for its influence.

In the present translation, passages that were unclear have been corrected by references to other editions and to the manuscripts. These are all indicated in the notes. Vocabulary has occasionally been modernized: the most significant example is the Latin word *vulva* which has been translated by the anatomical term indicated by the context.[5] The last chapter, on sperm, is largely missing from this edition and is incomplete in some other editions. In this case, the text was established from two Munich manuscripts and corresponds, for the most part, with that of the Venice, 1508, edition.

In addition to the text of the *De secretis mulierum,* this volume contains selections from two commentaries by unknown authors.[6] They were frequently printed with the text and exist in many of the manuscripts. Commentary A is based on the Lyons, 1580, edition, and Commentary B on the Venice, 1508, edition. It should be noted that there is also confusion in the manuscript tradition between text and commentary. For example, MS Paris B.N. lat 7148, which does not contain a formal commentary, nevertheless incorporates into the text material that is printed as part of Commentary B.[7]

The selections have been chosen to illustrate further ideas about women's "secrets" current among some thirteenth- and fourteenth-century clerics. The commentaries are not translated in entirety, because large sections repeat the text, and others are filled with tedious scholastic disputation on matters largely unrelated to its central topic. For the most part, however, once a selection is made, everything in that section is included, even if it is not germane to the subject matter.

Nature of the Treatise and Commentaries

Natural Philosophy versus Medicine. Pseudo-Albert, as the author will be referred to (whereas the Latin form "Albertus" will indicate the Swabian doctor), states in the beginning of the *De secretis mulierum* that "its style is partly philosophical, partly medical, just as seems to fit the material." By "philosophical" the author refers to natural philosophy, or natural science. Pseudo-Albert believed, as a follower of Albertus Magnus, that the study of nature as perceived through sense experience and then analyzed in a rational manner forms a single discipline through which we come to comprehend the universe in its corporeal aspects.[8] Human reproduction, a main subject of this treatise, is one of these aspects, that nevertheless has repercussions for our understanding of the entire cosmos.

This becomes evident particularly in the treatment given to astrological influences on the developing fetus. Pseudo-Albert begins his discussion by outlining how the sphere of the fixed stars confers upon the fetus various virtues, and moves back and forth from particular celestial effects to a general treatment of prime matter and the intelligences. Natural philosophy, then, involves the study of all parts of the natural world, although in this treatise (as in the authentic writings of Albertus) we see the emphasis placed upon investigation of living things. In the *De secretis mulierum*, the author treats human nature, the influence of the planets on the developing fetus, spontaneous generation, monsters in nature, and the generation of sperm.[9]

Medicine is the other discipline included in this treatise. We come upon evidence of the author's awareness of the distinction between philosophy and medicine in his first chapter, where he sets down without comment the differing opinions of Aristotle and "the doctors" on the participation of male and female seed in generation of the embryo.[10] Although pseudo-Albert goes on to raise a number of properly medical topics—nature of the menses, period of gestation, birth complications, signs of conception, etc.—he treats most of these in a cursory manner. The menses are dealt with by posing and answering a few questions on their nature, and the signs of conception, of whether a male or female is in the uterus, of corruption of virginity, and of chastity are listed in a very abbreviated fashion. Pseudo-Albert gives slightly fuller treatment to suffocation of the womb and to impediments to conception, but in none of these cases does he present us with anything like his in-depth discussion of how celestial bodies influence terrestrial events.

Pseudo-Albert's sources are also more philosophical than medical. Besides Aristotle, his main authority, our author relies heavily on Avicenna and Averroes, but, for the most part, he chooses their metaphysical and not their medical works. The development of the embryo is one of the main topics in the *De secretis mulierum*, and natural philosophy was much more significant than medicine in the embryological tradition from which pseudo-Albert drew.[11] To give just one example, Giles of Rome, writing on the same subject in the *De formatione corporis humani in utero*, perceived himself as working in a specialized branch of what he called *philosophia naturalis*, and instead of using Latin versions of Arabic translations of Galen, other Greek medical writers, and commentaries on them, drew upon Aristotle on most occasions.[12]

It is significant that one of pseudo-Albert's commentators also perceived this distinction. Explicating the chapter on infertility, Commentator B attempts to make clear the reasons why tests for whether a woman is carrying a male or female child work. Before he begins his exposition, however, he states, "Now it is time to bring up the topic of how to assist a mother in childbirth, but this subject is a medical one, and so is omitted here."[13] It is clear to the commentator that information that the blood and milk of a woman carrying a boy are well digested and thickened is appropriate to the treatise, for it addresses the question of the composition of the natural world, while directions for the midwife belong in a properly medical writing.

Pseudo-Albert's command of medicine is also less than impressive; on more than one occasion we see him demonstrate his ignorance of some basic medical facts. In his exposition on the menstrual period, for example, he explains that menses is superfluous food that is purged monthly, and that the amount and time of the flow vary from woman to woman. He then goes on to pose and to answer some questions on the nature of the menses, one of these being whether they flow out through the anus with solid waste, or through the vulva, with the voiding of urine. Although he asserts correctly that the menses flow through the vulva, he clearly thinks that urine does, as well. It is true that ignorance of body parts was characteristic of the middle ages, however medical writers normally had a better idea of basic anatomy than pseudo-Albert demonstrates here.[14]

Another example of unorthodox, and somewhat inept, discussion of a medical topic is found in pseudo-Albert's passage on a problem faced by one of his comrades. The author states that he was asked during confession why a young man should have found himself covered with blood after sexual intercourse. Instead of an explanation of what might cause this discharge in the woman—menstruation, or a humoral imbalance—as one would be likely to find in a medical text, pseudo-Albert says simply that the flow was excess seed.

A good illustration of the difference between the *De secretis mulierum* and a properly medical text may be found in the chapter entitled, "On a Defect of the Womb." This defect, known as suffocation in the medical literature, has a long medical history. Dating back at least to the Egyptian papyri, the idea that a woman deprived of sexual intercourse suffers "suffocation" in which the womb either wanders around the body in search of moisture or stays put and poisons the other organs is standard in medieval medical literature.[15] Pseudo-Albert introduces the topic, and takes the position that the womb actually becomes displaced. He then repeats a story from Galen about a woman who was suffering from this disorder, but he leaves out the graphic description of how manual manipulation of the patient's genitals led to orgasm and an abundant flow of poisonous sperm.[16] The most pseudo-Albert can bring himself to do is to recommend that young women have regular sexual intercourse in order to avoid this malady, and he quickly tells his readers that this practice (presumably, sex outside of marriage) is against the custom of the time.

If we look at a typical medical treatise, such as the *Treatise on the Womb* by the fifteenth-century Italian physician Anthonius Guainerius, we see a much more detailed, treatment-oriented approach.[17] The Italian doctor explains that suffocation is caused by the retention of menses or of sperm, and that the vapors produced by this corrupt matter compress the heart, deprive the woman of sense and motion, and sometimes cause death. Signs of the malady are pain in the head, vertigo, difficulty in breathing, weakness in the legs, and pain in the umbilicus. The physician should determine whether retention of menses or of sperm is causing the malady; and Guainerius outlines the signs of each. Among the indications of suffocation caused by retention of sperm is the absence of male companionship in the life of a woman who was accustomed to it.

The cure for this malady is also treated in detail. The extremities should be rubbed with salt and vinegar; the woman should be bound up with cloth, and a foul-smelling substance should be applied to her nose. The reasoning here is that a horrible odor will excite the animal spirit within her which the illness has put to sleep. The author includes a prescription for the suggested foul-smelling substance. Another procedure is to anoint the mouth of the vulva with a different odiferous material, for which the prescription is also included, and to rub it into the neck of the womb as well. The rubbing, which should be done with the midwife's finger, will cause the womb to expel the sperm or corrupt humors and free the patient from disease.

Although there are no substantial disagreements in the two treatises, Anthonius Guainerius' chapter is obviously written for physicians. He is concerned with identifying the illness, noting its cause, and prescribing a cure. The author of the *De secretis mulierum*, on the other hand, describes suffocation of the womb as a phenomenon that occurs in nature. His aim is simply to tell us about one of the "accidents" that a womb might suffer; he is not attempting to make diagnosis possible, nor is he prescribing any cure more specific than that women should have intercourse regularly. Although the treatise is "partly philosophical, partly medical," then, medicine actually plays a minor role in pseudo-Albert's method.

Intended Audience. The intended audience of the *De secretis mulierum* remains almost as much a puzzle as the identity of the author. Of the many theories that have been advanced, the one that has the most evidence behind it is that the treatise was associated in some way with the monastic milieu. The *Secrets* is dedicated to a *dilecto in Christo socio et amico...clerico* and contains more than one reference to *fratres* and *socii*.[18] As noted above, pseudo-Albert tells us about his experience hearing confession from one of his companions, and his awareness of theological matters is made evident throughout the treatise. For example, our author states that he will refrain from giving too many details about how evil women set out to harm male organs because he fears his creator, evidently indicating that he believes it would be a sin to do so.[19] The commentators are also aware of the necessity to keep theological truth in mind. In the chapter on astrology, discussed below, we find a clear consciousness of doctrinal correctness, and a remark like Commentator A's statement that "we read that a universal flood took place because of the evil of men, however this has nothing to do with our subject because we are speaking in a natural manner" signals to us that religion is always in the back of the writer's mind.[20]

The thirteenth century was, of course, dominated by theology, and religious awareness does not demonstrate a writer's monastic affiliation. Nor, indeed, do references to "brothers," and "companions" constitute definitive proof that the author inhabited a Dominican cloister. Lynn Thorndike has warned that similar allusions in the *Alkiminia minor* ascribed to Albertus Magnus name the Dominican order (*frater ordinis praedicatorum*), and we find none of that specificity here.[21] Nevertheless, origin in a religious community is likely for this text, given the internal evidence.

Giovanni Romagnoli has analyzed the *De secretis* in terms of its Dominican affiliation, comparing it to three other writings on female matters emanating from the order: the works of Thomas of Cantimpré (also known as Thomas of Brabant), Bartholomaeus Anglicus, and the French cardinal Vital du Four. According to Romagnoli, it is significant that all four treatises present gynecological material useful in actual practice. Thomas of Cantimpré, he points out, sets forth practical chapters on obstetrics taken from the sixth-century translator Muscio, which are important here particularly because Thomas was a Dominican and Albertus Magnus's disciple.[22] Bartholomaeus Anglicus, Romagnoli claims, was well informed on anatomy and physiology, and therefore makes a valuable contribution to gynecological and obstetrical questions. Vital du Four's treatise is encyclopedic in nature, with gynecological material contained in an alphabetical arrangement of subjects. Finally, Romagnoli sees pseudo-Albert's treatise as belonging to the genre of popular medicine; he claims that it is a practical work designed for use by midwives.[23]

I have discussed above the medical content of the *De secretis mulierum*; it seems to me impossible to maintain that pseudo-Albert has written a practical medical treatise. Similarly, I shall demonstrate below that the *Secrets* has little to do with the encyclopedic tradition. Nevertheless, the connection between medicine and the cloister is not to be dismissed lightly, nor is Romagnoli's contention that popular medicine has an important place in the treatise. With regard to the first point, Monica Green, in her 1985 dissertation, demonstrates that male monastic culture was primarily responsible for the transmission of gynecological literature, and asserts that this material was actually being used, although, as she states, "we cannot tell if 'used' means to satiate monkish curiosity about female nature or to serve as the basis of real medical practice."[24]

Similarly, Romagnoli's point that pseudo-Albert's chapter on the signs of whether a male or female is in the uterus has some connection with popular medicine is well taken, although he perhaps does not realize to what extent these signs had become incorporated into learned medical texts.[25] Further evidence of popular material in the treatise is found in MS Paris B.N. lat. 7148 of the *De secretis mulierum* where the author tells a story about a good and honest woman relating to him in "social confession" that she observed on more than one occasion that if a man ejects his urine under the rays of the moon and then has sexual intercourse with a woman, she will conceive a fleshy mass instead of a human being, and she will labor just as much as with a normal fetus.[26] Traces of popular conceptions are found throughout the *De secretis mulierum*, although the overall character of this treatise is scholastic.

If we survey the various genres of learned writings to which the *Secrets* has been compared, we find that although it shares much material and some methodology with all of them, pseudo-Albert's book cannot be placed neatly into a single category. Our author draws on "question," "secrets," and "problem" literature, and many of the topics he handles are found as well in medieval encyclopedias. Yet despite an affinity of style and content when he writes about the female body, pseudo-Albert distinguishes himself from contemporaries by his treatment of celestial influences on the developing fetus. The *De secretis mulierum* attempts seriously to grapple with some of the philosophical issues involved with astrological determinism. It is true that the treatise does not reach the level of philosophical sophistication that we find in his Arabic astrological sources, and the overall level of discourse in no way approaches that of contemporaries like Giles of Rome or, indeed, Albertus Magnus himself. Nevertheless, pseudo-Albert's extended treatment of planetary effects on the developing embyo, and his attempt in this section to transcend formulaic statements and to address the mechanism of celestial influence sets him apart from other thirteenth-century compilers.

Let us look further at some of these compilers, especially the Dominicans discussed by Romagnoli. Thomas of Cantimpré has the greatest significance here, for the authorship of the *De secretis mulierum* has been attributed to him. Christoph Ferckel, the editor of gynecological sections from Thomas's encyclopedic writing *De naturis rerum*, completed in 1240, maintains that the two works are not connected, although they treat much of the same subject matter.[27] We do find in the *De naturis rerum* similar, brief discussion of topics like female breasts, the penis, and the impregnation of the woman; in this sense, the writings are similar because identical subjects are dealt with in the same cursory fashion. However, Thomas provides some recommendations for treatment for retention of menses and for suffocation of the womb in the form of medical recipes, and he inserts as well a short chapter on childbirth and the obstetrical art, both of these in the manner of properly medical writings. Similarities between Thomas and pseudo-Albert have little significance beyond the possibility of their sharing a common source, or of pseudo-Albert engaging in direct borrowing from Thomas.

Bartholomaeus Anglicus's *De proprietatibus rerum* is even less likely to emanate from the same tradition as the *Secrets*. This encyclopedic writing, composed in the 1230s, treats everything from God and the angels down to stones, plants, colors, and smells. The author includes a chapter on the creation of the infant (Book 6, Chapter 3), which gives a brief account of human generation, citing Galen, Constantine, Aristotle and Hippocrates.[28] As we shall see below, pseudo-Albert's treatment of this topic does not rely primarily on medical sources and is of a different nature.

In order to examine properly the thirteenth-century encyclopedic tradition in relation to the *De secretis mulierum*, we must look at the *Speculum naturale*, composed by another Dominican, Vincent of Beauvais, in the mid thirteenth century.[29] This majestic opus gives full treatment to aspects of the natural world, and therefore provides us with enough material for a more extended comparison between the two genres.

Vincent of Beauvais deals at great length with human sexual reproduction; he includes chapters on the definitions of male and female seed, causes of erection of the penis, nocturnal pollution, and sterility. His treatment is more extensive than pseudo-Albert's, and he uses medical sources much more freely. However, pseudo-Albert and the encyclopedists have very different approaches to nature. While pseudo-Albert separates natural philosophy from theology, Vincent, like Bartholomew, integrates the two. The thirty-first book of the *Speculum*, "On Human Generation," begins with a discussion of Cain and Abel; chapter one is entitled "Glossa super Genesim." In his second chapter, "On the Nature of Coitus Which Brings About Human Generation," Vincent begins by quoting Augustine's *City of God* and moves right into Constantinus Africanus, Hippocrates, Galen and other medical sources. For Vincent, theology and science are one and the same.

Although this encyclopedist may identify sacred and profane science in his discussion of human nature, however, he is aware of differences of orthodoxy among the scientists, points them out to his reader, and takes a conservative stand. He is also completely open about his sources. Unlike pseudo-Albert, Vincent names the Arab astrologer Albumasar as his source when presenting his opinion on the influence of the constellations on the developing fetus, drawing his information from the twelfth-century poet

Helinandus. The *Speculum naturale* states, nevertheless, that authority and reason, Augustine and the natural philosophers, contradict Albumasar's opinion that the gender and other properties of the fetus are determined by the constellations.[30] Pseudo-Albert, as we shall see below, conceals his use of Albumasar but accepts the Arab's opinions on planetary influence.

Another difference in methodology between Vincent and pseudo-Albert is that although pseudo-Albert's treatment of many topics may be abbreviated, Vincent's own discussion is even less extended. The *Speculum naturale* is mostly an extensive collection of quotations from authorities, with a short paragraph interspersed here and there by the author himself. Pseudo-Albert, on the other hand, writes his own treatise, and, in doing so, allows us to glimpse his weaknesses and some of his personal experiences.

Therefore, although pseudo-Albert and the encyclopedists overlap in their subject matter, they belong to very different traditions. Encyclopedists give a sweeping view of the world, including God and the angels in their purview. They draw indiscriminately from theological, philosophical, and medical sources, and have no sense of writing within a specific discipline. Pseudo-Albert, on the other hand, is clearly a natural philosopher who deals with other disciplines only peripherally. Although he is interested in doctrinal correctness, he is writing later than the others and must therefore keep in mind the condemnations of 1277 (in which 219 propositions, based largely on Aristotelian ideas and Arab astrology, were censured by Etienne Tempier, the bishop of Paris). Because of this concern, he is much more circumspect in his treatment of Arabic astrological source material.

Another genre with which the *De secretis mulierum* shares some affinity is the "questions" and "problems" literature. Brian Lawn has pointed out that Aristotle was the first to systematize the question and response method and used it for demonstrating all kinds of scientific and medical problems, many of which have survived in the pseudo-Aristotelian *Problemata*. The thirteenth- and fourteenth-century scholastic *quaestio* or disputation eventually supplanted the older question-and-answer technique, but the traditional material continued to form the basis for this form of scientific instruction.[31] The "question" literature, therefore, has a long history, and pseudo-Albert undoubtedly was familiar with this tradition.

The *De secretis mulierum* treats two subjects by means of these *dubia*: the menstrual period and the effects of lightning on the developing fetus. These topics are included in the Salernitan material described by Lawn, and it is certainly possible that pseudo-Albert drew on this source in these chapters.[32] The pseudo-Aristotelian *Problems*, composed in the first century B.C. and translated by Bartholomew of Messina around 1260 also belong to this genre.[33] The author of the *Problems* poses and answers questions about different parts of the body, and, once again, deals with many topics treated in the *Secrets*.[34] Although pseudo-Albert may have engaged in direct borrowing when discussing these two topics, however, the bulk of his treatise bears no relation to Salernitan or later questions.

The menstrual period and other topics related to human generation are also treated in a question-and-answer format in Albertus Magnus's *Quaestiones super De animalibus*. This writing treats many of the same topics as the *De secretis mulierum*, but here the questions are posed and responded to in a lengthy, scholastic manner with the author presenting all possible objections and resolving them in line with Aristotle's doctrines. The *Quaestiones* by Albertus are relatively sophisticated examples of this genre, and ask about the menstrual period, for example, whether it is necessary for generation, whether only women suffer it, whether the moon dominates it, whether it is a sudden flow, whether it causes infection, and whether it accelerates old age.[35] Many of the same topics are treated in the *Secrets*, although those presented in the *dubia* format center around very basic knowledge of the female cycle.

Judging simply from its title, we would expect the *De secretis mulierum* to belong to the genre of medieval "secrets" literature, represented by the pseudo-Aristotelian *Secretum secretorum* and Michael Scot's *De secretis naturae*, among others.[36] The first of these is an Arabic writing cast in the form of a supposed letter from Aristotle to Alexander. It is designed to present scientific information which the young prince should know, and concentrates on medicine and physiognomy.[37] The text gives a little bit of everything: qualities of kings, the four seasons of the year, how to eat and sleep, pharmaceutical recipes.[38] Like the treatises described above, the *Secretum secretorum* resembles the *Secrets of Women* only insofar as it gives summary treatments to many overlapping subjects.

Michael Scot's *De secretis naturae* is closer to pseudo-Albert's treatise, and, indeed, shares the same volume in the Lyons, 1580, edition. Like the *Secretum secretorum*, Michael's writing contains medicine, natural philosophy, and physiognomy, although the medicine is much more like pseudo-Albert's: descriptive instead of prescriptive. The *De secretis naturae* contains extensive information on the harmful effects of menses, and ties them in with the motion of the moon. Michael Scot also recognizes the value of astrology, stating that a woman ought to take care to note the exact time of coitus so that the astrologer can make accurate judgments about the nature of the offspring, and he traces the effects of the planets on the developing fetus.[39]

What sets the *De secretis mulierum* apart from the *De secretis naturae*, and, indeed, from all the thirteenth-century writings discussed so far, is pseudo-Albert's approach to the science of the stars. The *Secrets of Women* not only sets down standard astrological information (e.g., Saturn coagulates the matter of the fetus; the child born under Jupiter is beautiful and of fine temperament), but it attempts to explain how this happens and to relate this explanation to the philosophical ideas of Aristotle, Avicenna, and Averroes. Vincent of Beauvais and Michael Scot may note some of the celestial effects, but pseudo-Albert addresses himself seriously to the problem of how they come about, and this effort forms the major thrust of his writing. Although the *De secretis mulierum* names women's secrets as its subject matter, if we weigh the length and the level of discourse we can almost consider this to be an astrological treatise.

Pseudo-Albert's philosophical passages on the effects of the celestial bodies, although impressive in relation to the earlier popularizers of science whom we have just examined, in no way reach the level of his contemporaries. The *Secrets of Women* raises a few metaphysical issues, but the author's philosophical skills fall far below those of his master, Albertus Magnus, or of other late-thirteenth-century natural philosophers like Giles of Rome. Both of these writers also quote Aristotle, Avicenna, and

Averroes, but they are able truly to penetrate the thought of these authorities, and to grapple with problems raised by them. Pseudo-Albert's philosophy is less sophisticated; he has learned some important concepts and introduces them into his treatise, but does not take his discussion as far as it might go.

The *De secretis mulierum*, then, contains a mixture of scientific vulgarization and serious speculation. Although the title places it in the category of popular "secrets" literature, we have seen that the author has a clear notion of working within the discipline of natural philosophy, and that his discussion of astrology is reasonably complex. Having established that pseudo-Albert's treatise is in a class by itself with regard to thirteenth-century scientific literature, we are still left with the question of its place in contemporary intellectual life. Who read the *Secrets of Women*, and what significance did it have for them?

The existence of at least two commentaries on the *Secrets*, which are found in numerous manuscripts, demonstrates that some readers took it seriously. Since the commentary was the basis of teaching at the university, Lynn Thorndike has suggested that the *De secretis mulierum* served as a text for instruction, and that it may be included in the fourteenth-century bibliography of writings by Dominicans in Paris.[40] I have not found it mentioned in any of the published collections of university statutes or lists of *exemplaria* copied for the universities, and, if we consider the internal evidence, its origin in a religious community and references to confession render it unlikely that this writing was composed originally with university instruction in mind.[41] Further, the variant level of discourse and the philosophical limitations just described argue against a serious place for the *De secretis mulierum* in early-fourteenth-century university life.

Nevertheless, we cannot dismiss the possibility that the *Secrets* served as the basis of university lectures, and that the two commentaries excerpted here represent this tradition. Not every medieval university reached the high intellectual level of Paris, the leader in European academic life, and not every course was taught by masters like Albertus Magnus and Thomas Aquinas. In the undergraduate colleges (or the faculty of arts) a more elementary form of instruction was given, and certainly these courses varied in sophistication from school to school. Perhaps pseudo-

Albert's treatise made its way into some of the lesser European institutions and provided an introduction to one branch of natural philosophy.

It is interesting in this regard to consider the lectures on the pseudo-Boethian *De disciplina scolarium* composed in 1309 by William of Wheteley, the headmaster of the grammar school at Stamford in Lincolnshire, England. The *De disciplina* originated in Paris around 1230, perhaps to provide a pretext for teaching Aristotelian natural philosophy after it was banned from the university in 1215, and later, when Aristotle was reinstated, became incorporated into the curricula of the grammar schools. Michael Johnson, who is in the process of editing these lectures, has described the passages dealing with human sexuality in a recent article, and William's treatment of sperm and menses bears significant resemblance to pseudo-Albert's.[42] William even tells his pupils how menstruous women poison babies by their infected glance, a theme from the *De secretis mulierum* discussed in more detail in the section entitled "The Secrets of Women." From Johnson's account, William of Wheteley's lectures are considerably less sophisticated than those of Albert's commentators, and yet they made their way into medieval teaching, although on a more rudimentary intellectual level.

Of the two examples, Commentary B most resembles university material. Its author explicates pseudo-Albert's text in the same manner that lecturers normally used to treat an authoritative source, and the character of his discourse is decidedly scholastic. This means that he attempts to follow the rules of Aristotelian logic, that he aims for precise definition of terms, and that he habitually explores and refutes possible objections to each point made. Although Commentator A adopts this style as well, the author of the B version goes much further. He repeats pseudo-Albert's statements, and in analyzing them seeks constantly to make distinctions. For example, in answer to the question whether male or female has more pleasure in sexual intercourse, he distinguishes between pleasure understood intensively, extensively, principally, and executively. Commentator A is generally more straightforward in his exposition.

Nevertheless, whatever the eventual fate of the *Secrets of Women* may have been, from the internal evidence it does not seem that undergraduate instruction was pseudo-Albert's original intent. The references to "brothers" and "confession" that signal to us a clerical author, yet supposing for the treatise an origin in a religious community indicate that his purpose was narrower: he wanted to give instruction to his peers. Danielle Jacquart and Claude Thomasset have connected the *Secrets* with the expansion of political and economic importance of the clergy in the second half of the thirteenth century, due to the increased literacy of this group. With a new sense of power and expanded duties, pseudo-Albert and his contemporaries are nevertheless ignorant of the reality of human sexuality. They treat this topic clumsily, using their authority to create in men a fear of the dangers of union with women.[43]

The *De secretis mulierum*, then, was designed to be used within a religious community as a vehicle for instructing priests in natural philosophy, particularly as it pertains to human generation. Pseudo-Albert composed the treatise to present to his brothers a survey of this important subject, which would be useful to them in both their general education and their pastoral activities. A strong subtext of the *Secrets*, however, is the evil nature of women and the harm they can cause to their innocent victims: young children and their male consorts. Clearly, then, another purpose of this treatise is to malign the female sex, a tradition that extends back in Christianity to second-century misogynist writings.

SOURCES

Pseudo-Albert, like most authors of his time, relied heavily on other ancient and medieval writings in composing his treatise. Because the scholastic method included the premise that the works of authorities contain truth, he cites liberally from these texts throughout the *Secrets*. If we examine these citations carefully, however, we see that not all sources named are actually used by our author, and that indeed he sometimes misleads the reader as to the origin of a particular statement or passage. The same is true of the commentators, who are even more enthusiastic in buttressing their statements with the authority of famous names, even though this attribution may be a pure fiction.

Pseudo-Albert's and his commentators' use of authorities may be characterized as existing on three levels. The first of these is actual dependence upon the authoritative text for substantive ideas. In this category Aristotle is prominent, although real use of Aristotelian ideas is confined to specific topics of natural philosophy. We see Aristotelian doctrines emerge in relation to human generation considered in a large sense (in the introduction), the generation of imperfect animals without seed, the formation of compounds from the four elements (discussed in relation to deformities), and the function of heat and humidity in animal life (contained in the chapter on the formation of sperm).[44] Averroes' philosophical works form the basis for pseudo-Albert's metaphysical discussion of how celestial bodies influence the developing fetus. The Arab philosopher is invoked in treatment of the order of forms in prime matter and their presence in the first mover, and in treatment of the generation of the elements and their parts. Avicenna's *Metaphysics* is used to explain monstrosity as being caused by disobedience or insufficiency of matter.

In an effort to lend weight to his statements, pseudo-Albert sometimes inserts authentic quotations from authorities that are peripheral to his discussion. Aristotle, once again, is his favorite choice. Maxims such as "humid things naturally flow" and "nature does nothing in vain," for example, are interjected in a discussion of why menses flow in women and sperm does not flow in men. In the same vein, we see a commentator stretching the scope of a quotation. In treating the influence of the constellations on animal seed, Commentator B cites Albertus Magnus's *Physics* for the information that a cow gave birth to a calf that was half human. Although this is indeed found in the *Physics*, the rest of the story—that the villagers tried to burn the shepherd at the stake for having sexual intercourse with the cow—is not present in this text.[45]

Finally, the author and commentators on the *De secretis mulierum* present us with false attributions. Some of these may be the result of erroneous citations by authors from whom they are drawing; others may be due to errors in copying or other problems in the transmission of the text, and others, indeed, may perhaps turn out to be caused by a failure on my own part to find the correct passage. This phenomenon occurs frequently enough, however, so that we may consider it to be a definitive characteristic of the *Secrets*. An example of this false attribution is found in Commentator B's discussion of orgasm. The commentator raises the question as to whether the male or female experiences greater delectation in coitus. He responds that Aristotle discusses the question in his first book *On the Generation of Animals*, and that after dealing with the arguments on both sides, the philosopher replies that delectation can be understood intensively or extensively, and the answer will vary depending upon this interpretation. The passage is clearly scholastic in character; no one could possibly believe that Aristotle had answered the question in that manner. Similarly, when discussing the seven-chambered uterus Commentator B cites Aristotle's *Book on Sperm*, although he is clearly drawing here from the pseudo-Galenic *Liber de spermate*. We experience in these two instances almost a knee-jerk reaction: the commentator (or his source) wants to lend weight to his statements, so he attributes them to the philosopher.

An example of deliberate falsification in these texts, and one that has more serious implications, occurs in pseudo-Albert's discussion of planetary influences. He attributes to Avicenna and Albertus Magnus material that is clearly drawn from Arabic astrological writings. This is discussed in more detail in the section of this Introduction on "Astrology." The commentators choose antifemale statements for many of their false attributions. In order to support their denunciation of women with Aristotelian and medical authority, they claim to find in the revered authors affirmation of statements that condemn the female sex. Thus Commentator A tells us that Hippocrates stated in his book *On the Nature of Man* that a menstruating woman corrupts the air and fouls the insides of a man. Commentator B asserts that Avicenna held that the female womb is like a sewer situated in the middle of a town where all the waste materials run together and are sent forth. Finally, in a related passage, he declares that Aristotle believed the milk of a black woman was better than that of a white woman. I have found none of these references in the authoritative writings, thus I am assuming that these citations are pure fabrications, either on the part of the commentators themselves, or on the part of intermediary sources used by them.[46]

Although the commentators use the sources in the same way as pseudo-Albert, there are differences among the three. Commentator A is not prone to quote authorities, although he does mention Aristotle and Averroes on occasion. He also refers to the *Centiloquium* twice, and to Hippocrates once in the passages selected for this translation. Commentator B, on the other hand, appears to be more widely read or more eager to display his learning than the other two authors. In particular, he makes extensive use of Aristotle's writings on animals, which are germane to the topics discussed, especially in his treatment of physiological matters. He also uses Avicenna's *Canon*, Hippocrates' *Aphorisms*, Constantine's *Pantegni*, and Averroes' *Colliget* in the rather full treatment he gives to some medical matters. There is no significantly different pattern of citation in the passages that were not selected for translation in either of the two commentaries.

One problem that I have not been able to solve involves the citation of Avicenna's "Book on Floods" in discussion of spontaneous generation after a universal flood, where pseudo-Albert disagrees with the Muslim philosopher and uses Aristotle to disprove both the possibility of a universal flood as well as the generation of perfect animals without seed.[47] Pseudo-Albert goes on to relate that Avicenna said that if the hairs of a menstruating woman are placed in fertile earth under manure during the winter, in the spring or summer when they are heated by the sun a serpent will be generated, and it will produce another of the same species through seed. The Muslim claimed, according to pseudo-Albert, that a mouse was generated from putrefaction in his own time. In Book 8 of the *De animalibus*, Avicenna discusses the generation of animals, but all with seed, and the topic is not treated in the pseudo-Avicennan *De caelo et mundo*.[48] A number of Arabic alchemical treatises attributed to Avicenna touch on aspects mentioned in this passage: Pseudo-Avicenna gives an elixir to be made from hair, but says nothing about a menstruating woman; another treatise discusses putrefaction, but without bringing up spontaneous generation.[49] It is possible that the source is one of the many unpublished works of Avicenna listed by Marie Thérèse d'Alverny in various volumes of the *Archives d'histoire doctrinale et littéraire du moyen age*, or, indeed, pseudo-Albert may be using Avicenna's name simply to lend authority to his discussion.

A similar passage is found in the work of the twelfth-century abbess, mystic, and scientist Hildegard of Bingen, although pseudo-Albert presents no evidence of familiarity with Hildegard's writings, and therefore they may be drawing from a common source. In the preface to the eighth book of the *Subtleties*, Hildegard states that after the fall Abel's blood stained the soil and caused noxious humors to arise from which venomous and deadly reptiles were generated. These perished in the deluge, but others were generated from their putrefying carcasses.[50] The theme of spontaneous generation of lesser creatures was a favorite topic in the fourteenth century. Henry of Hesse, for example, outlined the process by which accidental qualities developed in the generation of a mouse from putrefaction.[51] None of the references I have seen, however, mentions Avicenna directly.

Finally, it is significant that the text provides more than one reference in the third person to the works of Albertus Magnus. Clearly statements such as "note that according to Albert in his treatise *On the State of the Sun and Moon* there are four phases of the moon" argue against Albertus Magnus's authorship of the *Secrets*. In the course of the *De secretis mulierum*, Albertus's *Meteorology*, *Commentary on the Metaphysics*, *On Generation*, and a treatise on menses are referred to specifically by the author.

HUMAN GENERATION

The topic of human generation holds a central place in the *De secretis mulierum*. Pseudo-Albert brings up the subject immediately: after a brief introduction he begins by citing Aristotle (fourth century B.C.), Averroes (twelfth century A.D.), and Boethius (fifth to sixth century A.D.) on the exalted nature of human reproduction and then proceeds to devote the first chapter to the generation of the embryo. Subsequent sections treat the development of the fetus and the influence of the planets and constellations upon it.

Although pseudo-Albert is clearly impressed by the importance of the generative process, he is extremely succinct in his treatment of how it comes about. Our author states simply that "every human being who is naturally conceived is generated from the seed of the father and the menses of the mother, according to all philosophers and medical authorities." He then devotes only two sentences to elaborating on a major controversy in scientific thought. "Aristotle," he tells us, "did not believe that the father's seed was part of the substance of the fetus, but rather that the fetus proceeded from the menses alone, and afterwards [the philosopher] states that the seed is a vapor that exudes from the menses. The doctors, in contrast, believe that the fetus is made up of male and female seed together."

Thus pseudo-Albert summarizes in a short paragraph a problem that occupied scientists for at least two thousand years, and one which Albertus Magnus treated at great length in his writings on animals. As pseudo-Albert implies, the main focus of the discussion was Aristotle's belief that "the female...provides the material, the male provides that which fashions the material into shape."[52] The material, according to the philosopher, was the "catamenia" or menstruum, containing no active principle but functioning solely as the "stuff" from which the animal, in this case the human being, was to be shaped. For Aristotle, "this...is the specific characteristic of each of the sexes; that is what it means to be male or female."[53]

Because he held that the male semen was not a true component of the embryo, the philosopher had to face the question of what did indeed happen to it. He took the position that the seed, or "soul-principle," was partly separable from physical matter, and partly inseparable. The fluid, watery part dissolves and evaporates, Aristotle states, and so we should not always be seeking to find it leaving the body externally. It is not a component of the embryo any more than we would find in curdled milk the fig juice that has served to coagulate it. Both sperm and fig juice undergo a change.[54]

The "doctors," represented by Galen (second century A.D.) and his medieval followers, adhered to a two-seed theory.[55] Both male and female have the same sexual organs; in the woman they are located in the interior of her body, and in the man they protrude on the outside. Because they have not been designed in vain, the female "testes" or ovaries produce sperm, just as the male's do. The two of these combine to form the fetus.

The ancient sources actually presented this topic in a far more complex fashion than pseudo-Albert reveals. In his *Generation of Animals*, Aristotle raised issues of efficient and final causes, pangenesis (the view that semen takes its origin from all parts of the body), the nature of semen, the function of menstrual blood, the forms of reproduction in different animals, among others.[56] Galen dealt at length with the vital faculties of the organism which produce genesis, growth, and nutrition, and described the stages of embryonic life and the anatomy of the placenta and membranes in general.[57] In order to explain human generation, these scientists brought up philosophical and biological concepts and related them to the events surrounding the beginning of the life cycle.

The original writings of Aristotle and Galen were of course not available to the Latin-speaking West. But ancient Greek science remained alive in the Arabic world, and during the twelfth and thirteenth centuries western scholars received Aristotelian and Galenic ideas along with their Arabic interpretations. In the thirteenth century, Michael Scot translated Aristotle's writings on animals from the Arabic, and these were incorporated into the arts curriculum at the medieval university.[58] Translations of Galen were carried out from the late eleventh century, although his Latin corpus was still incomplete in Albertus Magnus's time. The Persian physician and philosopher Avicenna included Galenic doctrines in his *Canon of Medicine*, translated during the twelfth century but not really used by scholars until the thirteenth when selections also became part of the university canon. Avicenna's treatise on animals, which gave fuller treatment to embryology, was translated between 1220 and 1232.[59] We can state, therefore, that these ideas were fairly new in the West and, as a result, we will see that medieval scientists were still struggling with them when pseudo-Albert set down his *Secrets*.

Although classical theories of human generation may have been new in pseudo-Albert's time and therefore posed some problems of interpretation, medieval schoolmen nevertheless dealt ably with Aristotelian and Galenic notions. Unlike pseudo-

Albert, they rose to the challenge presented by the more complicated philosophical and medical discussions and, also in contrast
to our author, they focused on a reinterpretation of Aristotle
which would leave room for the inclusion of some Galenic ideas.

Avicenna's *De animalibus* is a main source for thirteenth- and
fourteenth-century speculation on human generation. The Muslim physician couches this discussion in sophisticated terms: He
introduces concepts of spermatic humidity and generative and
maturative virtues, and he examines human digestion. Avicenna
addresses directly the dispute between Aristotle and Galen on the
male and female contributions to the embryo, and in the course
of this discussion attempts to reinterpret the philosopher and pass
himself off as an Aristotelian. The Persian physican states that
people believe that Aristotle thought that the male seed does not
become a material part of the fetus, but this was not his opinion.
Rather, he held that the sperm became absorbed into the matter
and served as an operator, drawing material to form the members
and becoming the stuff of the individual's spirit. Galen and his
followers, Avicenna tells us, oppose Aristotle, and the Persian
doctor dismisses the explanation, although he considers it to be
true. Indeed, he continues, they know nothing of the roots of science, but are familiar only with the branches.[60]

Avicenna directs more than one insult at Galen: He expresses
his wonder that the master claimed to know philosophy, accus-
ing him of false reasoning; he declares his doctrines lies, or
stupid statements.[61] Yet the Persian physician himself adopts a
position on human generation that is consonant with Galenic
teaching: He maintains that both male and female possess a seed,
but the female's has generative power only potentially, while the
male's puts it into action.[62] Avicenna also acknowledges the truth
of Galen's anatomical beliefs. Women do indeed have testicles
which hold the sperm, the physician states, for he has found
them himself, and he has also seen them eject copious seed when
treated for suffocation of the womb.[63] Further, he maintains that
Galen spoke well when he stated that bones and nerves are generated from sperm because of its viscosity.[64] Clearly the ancient
physician had some redeeming virtues.

The *De secretis mulierum* is based on the writings of Albertus
Magnus, the great medieval interpreter of Aristotle who devoted

almost one third of his work to the topic of embryology.[65] Like
Avicenna, one of his main sources, Albertus deals in a sophisticated manner with concepts of spermatic humidity and formative
virtue, and, also like the Persian physician, he adopts both Aristotelian and Galenic ideas. Luke Demaitre and Anthony Travill
have pointed out that Albertus's progressive move toward
Galenism caused some confusion in his thought; his formulation
of the idea that the menstruum has both a nourishing and a material component, they argue, "raises more questions than it
answers."[66] Nevertheless, his interpretation of the controversy
between Galen and Aristotle elaborates on Avicenna's, and
demonstrates a relatively complex level of discourse as well as
incorporation of Aristotelian and medical notions.

In Book 9 of his *De animalibus*, Albertus takes up the question of what happens to the male seed during generation. Since
the virtue by which the seed operates is in the spirit, he holds, it
is not improbable that the male seed is converted entirely or at
least in its major part into spirit because of its subtlety. The
scholastic philosopher then has this spirit enter into the female
humor; he specifically states that a skin forms surrounding the
seed, preventing it from flowing out, and guarding the spirit and
heat, lest they evaporate. "It is impossible for nature not to have
the greatest solicitude for this spirit and the place in which it is
kept, for otherwise if it were dissolved or weakened the entire
operation would be destroyed."[67] By emphasizing its transformation into spirit, which he discusses in the tradition of Costa ben
Luca as a materially existing entity, Albertus modifies Aristotle's
position on the fate of the male seed.

In contrast to Avicenna, Albertus Magnus, and, indeed, in
contrast to a contemporary like Peter of Abano who sets down
the opinions of Aristotle, Avicenna, and Averroes in his *Conciliator*, the author and commentators on the *De secretis mulierum*
underline the opposition between Aristotle and Galen, and treat
the controversy in an almost primitive sense.[68] Commentator A,
for example, tells us that the male seed passes through the womb
as a vapor because the womb is extremely porous, and after the
formation of the fetus the heat of the sun causes the male seed to
evaporate and leave the womb through the pores. Instead of a
discussion of potential and actual generative power, as we see in

Avicenna, or of the subtlety of spirit, which Albertus presents, pseudo-Albert's interpreter simply provides evidence for the porous nature of the womb. He states, for example, that the womb is porous because the child receives nourishment through the pores, and brings up and dismisses another reason offered, namely that it is a skin, and all animal skin has pores so sweat can escape (Chapter 1).

Along with this rudimentary treatment of the question of what becomes of the male seed, we find some confusion in the tradition of the text and its commentaries on the actual position of the author. The Lyons, 1580, edition, on which this translation is based, and other editions in this family make no comment as to the author's stance on the truth or falsity of either the Aristotelian or Galenic position on the generation of the embryo.[69] The Venice, 1508, edition, however, adds, "Having examined the opinion of Aristotle on one side, and of the doctors on the other, I make no determination on this question."[70] This purposefully noncommittal stance is found in a number of the manuscripts and editions, and so presumably existed in at least one version of the *Secrets*.[71] In the same Venice, 1508, edition, however, Commentator B intimates that pseudo-Albert may have been an Aristotelian: "Aristotle and other philosophers held that the father's seed does not become part of the substance of the fetus but rather disposes the mother's seed to the formation of the fetus, and afterwards he states that it exudes as a vapor, and this is the opinion of the author."[72]

Although an accurate interpretation of this passage is not possible until the textual questions are straightened out by a critical edition, it is clear from later chapters that pseudo-Albert adopts a Galenic two-seed theory when dealing with medical questions. In the chapter on suffocation of the womb, pseudo-Albert relates a story about one of his companions who noticed that his female partner had bled profusedly during sexual intercourse; pseudo-Albert offers his diagnosis that the flow "was not a flow of the menses, but rather a flow of seed during coitus because of an abundance of matter" (Chapter XI). Both Commentator A and Commentator B speak of female seed at different points in the text: with regard to impediments to conception (Chapter XII), nocturnal pollution in females (Chapter I), directions for sexual intercourse (Chapter VI), and suffocation of the womb (Chapter XI). It is likely that the Galenic view is adopted here because pseudo-Albert and his commentators are dealing with medical topics and relying on the standard sources; it is clear that the *De secretis mulierum* has no consistent or original position on this question and is more a compendium of information than a systematic treatise.

ASTROLOGY

Astrological theory and learning form a central part of the *De secretis mulierum*. Early in the treatise pseudo-Albert states clearly that a knowledge of astrological science contributes much to what he has set down in the book, and he will say something about the subject lest anyone think he is ignorant of it.

Astrology for pseudo-Albert and his contemporaries was intimately tied in with an Aristotelian approach to the cosmos. The philosopher's statement in the *Meteorologica* that motion in the lower world is a consequence of higher causation by the heavenly bodies served as a basis for a scientific outlook that endured until the sixteenth century, and was enthusiastically adopted by natural philosophers and physicians. Pseudo-Albert relies on this authoritative premise, which he expands by extensive use of Arab astrological writers.

Pseudo-Albert relies on two main sources in his astrological chapters. The first of these is the ninth-century Persian astrologer Albumasar, whose *Introductorium maius in astronomiam* was translated twice in the twelfth century. The second is Aḥmad ibn Yūsuf, the tenth-century author of the *Centiloquium*, attributed in the middle ages to Ptolemy and also translated in the twelfth century.[73] The *De secretis mulierum* is permeated through and through with quotations from these writers, yet, for the most part, our author does not name them. Although pseudo-Albert vaunts his own expertise in the science, and declares as well that his teacher was an astrologer, he remains silent about the exact nature of his astrological learning (Chapter III).

When pseudo-Albert refers to astrological sources, he is often purposefully vague or deliberately misleading. In the course of explaining how all the powers which the soul exercises in the body derive from the celestial spheres, our author attributes this to "the opinion of some who have spoken fittingly of nature" (Chapter II). Later on, pseudo-Albert tells us that the fact that the Sun impresses forms upon the fetus, creates the heart, and gives movement to the sensitive soul during the fourth month is in accordance with the statements of "certain astronomers" (Chapter II). Although one of the manuscripts does refer generally to the "Arabs [who] when referring to the constellations called them gods of nature," nowhere does pseudo-Albert name Albumasar or Aḥmad ibn Yūsuf, the true sources of many of his astrological statements.[74]

Other passages in the *De secretis mulierum* may demonstrate deliberate falsification of attribution, although this accusation cannot be tested until textual problems are cleared up by a critical edition. One example can be found in pseudo-Albert's discussion of accidents. Our author cites Avicenna to the effect that there are three kinds of accidents: one which is attributed to the matter, a second to the composite of matter and form, and the third to the soul, [which is a form] (Chapter II). Avicenna however, conceived of accidents in an entirely different manner. The Persian author held that there were two kinds. "The one is of such a nature that, in order to conceive it, it is not necessary for someone to regard anything other than its substance. In conceiving of the second kind, however, one has no choice but to regard something other than its substance." The first group is divided into quantity and quality, and the second has seven subdivisions (time, place, etc).[75] Clearly this text is not the source for pseudo-Albert's passage.

If we look at the *Introductorium maius in astronomiam* of Albumasar, we find accidents treated in terms that are closer to pseudo-Albert's presentation. There is no immediate textual parallel here, however, so we cannot assert that direct borrowing took place. At least two of the manuscripts give a specific citation of Avicenna (Book II of the *Sufficientie*) so it is unlikely that an "A." for Albumasar was interpreted as an "A." for Avicenna.[76] More probably, pseudo-Albert is drawing here from another source and using Avicenna's name because it has an authoritative ring, in accordance with his habit.[77]

Another case of false attribution, and one that is clearly deliberate, involves the phases of the moon. Here our author cites Albertus Magnus's treatise on the state of the sun and moon to the effect that there are four phases of the moon. In the first phase the moon is hot and humid until the half moon; after this, hot and dry until the full moon. The moon becomes cold as it wanes, and stays cold until it is joined to the sun. At this stage, it causes great humidity, rotting humid things.

Albertus Magnus's *De caelo et mundo* exists in a modern edition with a very complete and detailed index, and there is only one instance in which the author alludes to the humid state of the moon. Albertus tells us that the sun's rays, which are hot and dry, become cold and humid when they are transmitted by the moon.[78] If we look in the astrological sources, however, we find a close parallel with pseudo-Albert's discussion.

Albumasar's *Introductorium maius in astronomiam*, which was translated into Latin by John of Seville in 1133 and widely disseminated in the twelfth and thirteenth centuries, takes up the stages of the moon and their effects in Book III, Differentia 9, and in Book IV, Differentia 5.[79] In Book IV, the Arabic author tells us that the moon is hot and humid in the first quarter, hot and dry in the second, cold and dry in the third, and cold and humid in the fourth. In Book III he states that the bodies of animals have their heat and humidity increased as the moon waxes and thus they become stronger. As the moon wanes, they become weaker, and cold reigns in them. Humidities such as blood and phlegm are sent to the interior of the body and to the veins as the moon decreases.[80]

Albumasar's formulation is very close to pseudo-Albert's, and if we follow along in the *De secretis mulierum* we see further reliance on the astrological texts. Pseudo-Albert's next statement is "At the point when the moon increases humidity in all the members if you touch one of the members with a sword [or surgical instrument] you can be sure that you are gravely hurting it, because if you add humidity to humidity you are increasing the damage." Here, if we turn to the tenth-century *Centiloquium*, we find the statement, "To touch a member with iron with the moon in the sign of this member is harmful," with the explanation that the moon increases humidity in every member whose sign it has entered. To touch a member with iron is to wound it, and adding humidity to a wound multiplies the damage.[81]

After informing us how harlots use this principle to harm men in their genital members, pseudo-Albert continues his discussion of the fourth phase of the moon. If its rays enter a room at night, and fall on the head of a sleeping person, they cause headaches and a flow of rheuma. Albumasar says essentially the same thing: if a person should sit or sleep in the moonlight at night, a sluggishness will be generated in his body, and rheuma and a headache will develop.[82] It is clear that pseudo-Albert's discussion is steeped in Arabian astrology, yet he fails to make this known to his reader.

Pseudo-Albert's unwillingness to acknowledge his dependence upon Arabian astrologers is understandable given the intellectual climate of the late thirteenth century, when this treatise was composed. In 1277 the Bishop of Paris, Etienne Tempier, condemned 219 propositions, about one third of which were astrological in nature, insofar as they dealt with natural science or physics in relation to the action of the planets. This condemnation struck a significant blow at the relative freedom which had existed from the 1130s on, when Latin translations of Arabic astrological works became available to European scholars. Latin Christians in this period became increasingly concerned about the Arabian, "infidel" origin of these writings, as well as the deterministic position implied by their contents.[83] Western scholars, who were, of course, churchmen, had every reason to disguise their dependence on these texts, and pseudo-Albert, writing within a clerical context, is no exception.

Our author is obviously aware of the dangers inherent in these writings, and he faces them head-on in his treatise. Following his strong statement that celestial influences cannot be removed by terrestrial actions such as sacrifices to the gods, pseudo-Albert confronts the possibility that he might be accused of false statements. "First of all, judging merely from the surface meaning of my words, one might conclude that I am stating that all things come from necessity. Secondly, one might label me as a person who obscures the Christian faith" (Chapter III). Our author simply dismisses these possible criticisms, however, by maintaining that he has already given a full explanation.

If we look carefully at pseudo-Albert's discussion of this matter, we see that although he attempts to save orthodoxy by stating that planetary influence is ordained by God, he actually takes a strong deterministic stance. Basing his remarks, as is commonplace, on Aristotle's *Meteorology*, our author maintains that inferior things depend upon superiors both particularly and universally. The question of particular causation was under debate, and here pseudo-Albert takes a radical position. Although his source for this passage, *Centiloquium*, Verbum I Commentary, states clearly that the astrologer must not judge *specialiter*, but only *universaliter*, the author of the *De secretis mulierum* here takes exception to this axiom.[84] Buttressing his position by a citation from Averroes that individual animate beings are of determinate causes, he holds that the stars invariably determine terrestrial characteristics.[85]

Pseudo-Albert, therefore, exhibits somewhat of a devil-may-care attitude toward the condemnations of 1277, at least in terms of his philosophical positions. Yet we have seen him carefully conceal the sources used in formulating these positions—the Arabic astrological writings. Perhaps it was considered more serious after 1277 to quote the Arabs than it was to be a determinist, or perhaps direct citation was easier to pick up and therefore to censure. We know that Latin astrologers like Guido Bonatti, Leopold of Austria, and John of Eschenden were widely used in the West.[86] These men were Christians and so the ideas they expressed were not considered to represent the infidel Arabians, even though both said the same thing. We know as well that the Arab sources used by pseudo-Albert do not number among the forbidden books as listed in Albertus Magnus's *Speculum astronomie* which deal with magic, demons and invoking spirits from hell.[87] Pseudo-Albert, then, reacts to the climate of 1277 by relying on the most authoritative of the Arab astrologers, censoring all mention of them by name, and boldly expressing a fatalistic stance as his own.

The commentators on the *De secretis mulierum*, by contrast, are much more cautious in their approach. Commentator A openly identifies "Haly," the usual Latin name given to the author of the *Centiloquium* commentary, as the source for a description of how images of zodiacal signs carved in stone can cure illness. This acknowledgment of Arabian material is not due to boldness, however; the commentator is nervous about the entire subject of astrology, and perhaps wishes simply to be candid with his reader. He seizes the opportunity to remark on pseudo-Albert's statement that Saturn influences matter in a certain fashion because God ordained it thus from the beginning, by asserting that this proves that the author is a Catholic, for he takes a position contrary to the philosophers who believed the planets were disposed from eternity. When pseudo-Albert is somewhat less orthodox and declares that the effect of the planets cannot be removed through sacrifices, Commentator A is quick to point out the accepted point of view. "The theologian holds the opposite opinion," he tells us. "All things are in God's power; God acts freely, and he often listens to the prayers of the faithful." Commentator B is even more cautious about the matter: he warns the reader here that he is leaving nearly one full page out of the commentary, for pseudo-Albert expresses some doubts which are better handled by theologians, so he leaves them to theology.

Commentator B also relies on another astrological source not used by pseudo-Albert or Commentator A. The pseudo-Galenic *Liber de spermate* is a medical book dating from the eleventh or twelfth century containing material on how the conception of the child is altered by the stars, on the signs of the zodiac, and on the operation of the planets.[88] The treatise emphasizes the role of the four elements as intermediaries between the celestial bodies and the developing child, and counsels the physician to note the day and hour during which an illness began.[89] Commentator B cites the *Liber de spermate* in the chapter on the formation of the fetus to the effect that the diversity of the planets with different signs of the zodiac produces variations in the developing child (Chapter II). He cites the *Liber de spermate* again in the chapter on monsters for the information that a constellation of an animal can influence the seed in a mother's womb so that the child is generated with the head of a cow, pig, or other brute (Chapter VI).

The astrology handled here by pseudo-Albert and the commentators represents learned science: It has a theoretical basis in Aristotelian philosophy; it was clearly defined by Albertus Magnus as the "science of the stars;" its texts became prescribed reading for medical students in European universities in the mid fourteenth century.[90] This astrology is to be contrasted with popular astrology, which applied the principles of this science in a more or less haphazard manner to human events, formulating predictions and offering advice to clients.[91] We see an echo of this popular level in Commentary B, where astrology has obviously been conflated with folk magic: The commentator provides us with the information that when Jupiter is joined to the moon, powder made from a small bird will cause evil women to bark like dogs, and other similar tidbits.

Pseudo-Albert's treatise does not descend into such popular superstition, however neither does it provide a detailed account of the effects of the planets in circumstances other than fetal development. Although the *De secretis mulierum* contains a much more extensive theoretical discussion of astrological principles than it does of biological or medical precepts, essentially it is not a sophisticated text. The *Secrets* represents a compendium of astrological and medical learning, carrying the substance of the authoritative books in a relatively simple form for the purpose of transmitting them to a wider audience.

THE SECRETS OF WOMEN

Women's Secrets: A Definition

As its title indicates, an important concern of the author and commentators on the *De secretis mulierum* was women's "secrets." For Pseudo-Albert, this term clearly refers to matters pertaining to sexual and reproductive life. Indeed, it seems natural that women should want to keep their private parts secret. As the twelfth-century physician Trota put it, "Women, on account of the modesty and the fragility and delicacy of the state of these parts dare not reveal the difficulties of their sicknesses to a male doctor."[92]

Trota assumes that "sicknesses...abound in women around the organs involved in the work of nature," and seeks to address these illnesses and to provide relief for the victims.[93] In the collection of writings attributed to this physician, however, women's disorders are defined broadly: in addition to the usual gynecological material, the treatise includes a chapter on foul-smelling sweat, and others on spots of the eyes, lice, cancer of the nose, and toothache.[94] More typically, medical writings on women's diseases concentrate on the reproductive organs, dealing only with matters pertaining to the womb (its complexion and disorders), menstruation, sterility, conception, and birth.[95] Pseudo-Albert treats similar topics: Chapter headings in the *De secretis mulierum* include the generation of the embryo, the formation of the fetus, the exit of the fetus from the uterus, the signs of conception, the question of whether a male or female is in the uterus, the signs of corruption of virginity, the signs of chastity, a defect in the womb, and impediments to conception.

Physicians and natural philosophers used the same subject matter to different ends, as pointed out earlier. While the doctors wished to cure women, the *physici* intended simply to provide information about them. The historian in search of women's "secrets" approaches both types of writings with similar questions, however. By learning what we can about the patients who were the object of these cures, the methods used in their care, the practitioners who employed these methods, and the intended audience of each treatise, we can enter, to a certain degree, the world these writings reflect.[96]

How secret was this women's world? Even from the *De secretis mulierum* and its commentaries, we learn that it was a world populated by both sexes, and, despite societal taboos and female traditions, professional males came to know a good deal about it. Pseudo-Albert and his readers record for us medical precepts and cures that they have learned "from women": for example, the author of the *Secrets* tells us that many women have told him that when the fetus presents head first during birth the operation goes well, and the other members follow easily (Chapter V). Commentator B describes evil women who counsel young girls on how to induce an abortion. We learn as well about "folk" stories which reflect the world of popular culture and women's lore. Commentator B recounts the tale of a pregnant woman who wished to eat the testicles of her husband, and, when they were refused to her, she contacted the gravest malady (Chapter VII). Pseudo-Albert announces that he has "heard tell that a man who was lying sideways on top of the woman during sexual intercourse caused the woman to produce a child with a curved spine and a lame foot, and the deformity was attributed to the irregular position" (Chapter VI).

The *De secretis mulierum*, nevertheless, is written for men, unlike some gynecological treatises which were composed for female readers.[97] The intended audience is not as important for this context as the world the *Secrets* reflects, however; as Monica Green puts it, it was a "world of interface between male practitioners and female patients," a world in which women practitioners struggled to retain their role.[98] Certainly by the time the *Secrets of Women* was composed we have records of male physicians treating women in medieval Europe. Dr. Fauritius of Abingdon was present at the birth of Queen Matilda's first child in 1101, and in the late thirteenth century Taddeo Alderotti and his pupils treated ailments of the breast, womb, and vagina, and problems of sexual dysfunction and pregnancy.[99]

By the fifteenth century, evidence of male doctors attending to female patients becomes more abundant, and we also learn more about the details of practice. Physicians record their observations of childbirth: premature rupture of the amniotic membranes, walking about by the laboring mother, the use of forceps. Examinations of the abdomen and, occasionally, of the vaginal passage are noted, although, most commonly, women assistants are used for these intimate procedures.[100] Even though the female physician Jacoba Felicie maintained in her trial in 1322 that "a man should ever avoid and flee as much as he can the secrets of women and of her societies," male doctors became more and more involved in birth as the middle ages progressed, challenging women attendants, and relegating them to the role of assistants.[101]

Not only did men interact with female patients, but they, in turn, were influenced by women's culture and lore. Formal Latin medical treatises acknowledge the reality of malefice and curses, especially in the area of human reproduction. Male impotence and difficult childbirth are among the problems that can be caused by witches, and doctors warn against their powers and sometimes recommend participation in religious rituals to counteract the evil.[102] Although pseudo-Albert does not address directly the phenomenon of malefice (or evil sorcery), the discussion below will demonstrate that the *De secretis mulierum* became an important influence on the witchcraft persecution by serving as a direct source for the fifteenth-century inquisitorial treatise, *Malleus Maleficarum*.

Women's Secrets and Medieval Science

The "Secrets" which pseudo-Albert reveals are based on a theory about the composition of the female: She is an inferior creature, rendered base and impure by her menstrual essence which poses a constant danger to others. The age-old menstrual taboo is firmly embedded in pseudo-Albert's assumptions, and certainly he is not unique in condemning women for the poisonous character of their monthly flow. If we place the *Secrets of Women* in the context of earlier writings, however, we see that the author and commentators are representative of a fairly new trend in medieval science. Although condemnation of women's menses has existed since time immemorial, it is not until the thirteenth century that we see this idea regularly enshrined in learned scientific tracts.[103] As I shall demonstrate below, once the idea that women are evil because of their very nature becomes incorporated into natural philosophical treatises, theologians make use of these treatises in order to rationalize the persecution of women as witches.

Early Medieval Science.   Menstruation has, of course, always been an important topic to doctors; it is clear that a woman's health is connected with the state of her menstrual flow. This belief was particularly strong in the middle ages, when humoral balance and bodily evacuations were key medical concepts. Early medieval medical discourse on this topic was dominated by tension between the ideas of Hippocrates, Galen, and Soranus. As Monica Green has studied at length, these ancient writers differed on the questions of whether menstruation was necessary to retain health and whether amenorrhea could ever occur normally during the childbearing years outside of pregnancy and lactation.[104] According to Hippocrates, a woman who did not menstruate regularly would experience the accumulation of this blood in her body, causing diseases, and each successive month the situation would become graver. Galen, too, described the heaviness of the body, nausea, lack of appetite, chills, pains and fever that would result from menstrual retention. Of the three, only Soranus suggested the possibility that amenorrhea might occur in accordance with nature.[105]

These ideas were set down in the "core of the early gynecological corpus," the writings of Muscio, Theodorus Priscianus, and, to a lesser extent, the *Gynaecia Cleopatrae*.[106] These treatises reflected disagreement in their sources: Muscio, for example, held with Soranus that some healthy women do not menstruate during their reproductive years because they burn up all the blood of purgation through exercise.[107] What is significant here, however, is that even when it was clearly a disorder stemming from a physiological cause and inflicting upon its victim pain and suffering, menstrual retention was a problem for the sufferer and for no one else. Early gynecological writers address themselves to defining this disease and to providing remedies for the afflicted; they are not concerned with the effect of menstrual blood upon others, and they do not concentrate on its poisonous nature.

The *Secrets of Women*, as we have pointed out, is not a gynecological writing, although it certainly draws upon medical sources, and thus in tracing its antecedents we are bound to investigate the medical tradition. If we look for "natural science" in the early medieval period, our search is not as fruitful. "Natural science" is somewhat of an artificial concept before the twelfth century. One basic reason is that early medieval "scientific" writers drew no distinction between discussion of the natural and supernatural worlds: both were perceived in supernatural terms. God, the creator and ruler, was central to all thinking, and so the workings of nature were conceived of as the acts of the deity. The source of this science was the Bible and the Hexaemeral literature of the earlier Greek fathers: Gregory of Nyssa, Gregory of Nazianzene, and Basil of Caesarea. In the Western tradition, the important representatives of science in this period are Isidore, Bede, and Gregory the Great, and all three freely mix allegory and Biblical quotations into their scientific discussions.[108]

Because his chapter on menstruation was so influential for later medieval writers, and because similar ideas are found in the commentaries on the *De secretis mulierum* (e.g. Chapter I, Commentary B), let us look at what Isidore has to say about menses in his *Etymologies*. We are faced, of course, with an additional complication in considering this writing within the genre of natural science: Isidore conceived of his work linguistically (at least as far as we can tell from the title and the contents), and he supposedly aims to present here definitions of words. This is not merely a philological exercise for the Bishop of Seville, however; the Biblical "Word" is at the basis of his method. As Ernest Bréhaut has stated, Isidore elucidated words by reference to their origin, and he therefore used the dictionary method not as a matter of convenience, but on philosophic grounds.[109] Nevertheless, Isidore's ideas are widely cited by medieval scientific writers, and thus we can, in some sense, consider the *Etymologies* as an early example of natural science.

Isidore states that menses are superfluous blood in women, named for the lunar revolution, and that woman is the only menstrual animal. If crops come into contact with this flow they do not germinate; new wine becomes sour; grasses dry up; trees lose their fruit; iron rusts; metals tarnish. Dogs who ingest this matter become rabid, and asphalt glue, which is not dissolved by iron nor in water, is so polluted by this blood that it breaks up spontaneously.[110]

It is clear that for Isidore the menses are an impure substance, and that contact with this substance can have dire consequences. We will see, however, that despite almost omnipresent citation of the *Etymologies* in medieval writings, this neat, scientific codification of the menstrual taboo does not have much impact. It is not until the thirteenth century, with the recovery and assimilation of Aristotelian writings, that medieval scientific writers begin to show a similar enthusiasm for describing the polluted nature of woman's monthly flow. Until then, menstruation is treated fairly dispassionately in scientific literature.

The Twelfth Century. This chapter does not aim to present a complete survey of scientific ideas on menstruation from Hippocrates to pseudo-Albert, but rather to outline trends of thought on this subject in order to set the *De secretis mulierum* in historical perspective. Nevertheless, our discussion of twelfth-century medicine here will be somewhat detailed. Monica Green has studied the gynecological texts of this period thoroughly in her Princeton dissertation, and therefore we are able to profit from her research and her insights.

The most important center of twelfth-century Latin medicine was the school of Salerno, where doctors had access to the learning of Persian physicians. By translating the works of al-Majusi and Ibn al-Jazzar, Constantinus Africanus and his pupils provided a corpus of writings on gynecology that would become extremely influential in the Latin West. The ideas contained in these treatises were Galenic in nature; the tenets of Soranus were not taken up by the Arabs, and therefore were not passed on to the Latin West during the twelfth-century period of translations.[111]

Constantine's *Pantegni* (the Latin title given to his translation), in accordance with Galenic doctrines, states that menstruation is a normal bodily process. Because women are cold and wet, they cannot use up all their food, and unless it is utilized to nourish a child in the womb or converted to milk to nurse an infant, the waste material is eliminated by a special process of purgation. Retention results in numerous bodily ills, and therefore a number of remedies are set forth to cure this condition. Green comments that the *Pantegni*'s list of medicaments and description of how they are used "demonstrates how far Arabic physicians had surpassed the ancients in pharmacology."[112]

Constantine was an important influence on Salerno, and Salernitan texts on menstruation follow very much the same pattern. The *De aegritudinum curatione* (a general treatise on medicine), for example, cites a number of Salernitan masters who express the idea that menses purge the female body of superfluities, and thus maintain health. When the process of menstruation is disrupted, disease results. The Salernitan doctors address themselves to causes and cures of these diseases.[113]

Salernitan ideas were transmitted to later medieval writers not from the *De aegritudinum curatione*, however, but from the specialized works on gynecology attributed to Trota. Green has pointed out that this twelfth-century physician takes the topic of menstruation very seriously: in the *Cum auctor* he places the chapters on amenorrhea and hypermenorrhea in a prominent position at the beginning of the treatise and deals with the topics at great length."[114]

Trota tells us that "retention of menses occurs on account of excessive frigidity of the womb; or because its veins are too slender, as in extremely thin women; [or] because the humors, now thick and overabundant, do not have free passage by which they can erupt; [or] because the humors are gross, viscous and thick and because of this conglutination, their exit is blocked; or because the women eat [too many] rich things; or because they do not sweat much from any labor."[115] The *Cum auctor* provides extensive remedies for these conditions, for amenorrhea can lead to dysentery, pain in the heart, and other symptoms that are even worse.[116]

Although some of the causes of amenorrhea listed by Trota could theoretically be blamed on the victim (presumably a woman can control her intake of rich foods and the amount of physical exercise she engages in), the Salernitan physician does not choose to take this approach. Instead, he, too, is sympathetic to the patient: "Women," he states in accordance with standard medical doctrine, "are by nature weaker than men," and so "pitying their misfortunes" he began to study carefully their sicknesses. However, although weaker, females are not necessarily different. Just as women have menses, men experience *pollutio*, for "nature always, burdened by certain moistures, whether in man or in woman, strives to lay off its yoke and diminish its exertion."[117] For Trota, not only are women's menses discussed in relatively positive terms, but men, too, experience a parallel cleansing process.

If we turn from twelfth-century medicine to twelfth-century natural science, we must still deal with some ambiguity in our definition of the discipline. Although twelfth-century scientists knew the difference between the natural and supernatural worlds, the authors we shall consider here—Hildegard of Bingen and William of Conches—do treat religious questions within their "scientific" works. Another complication is that the first of these writings, Hildegard of Bingen's *Causae et Curae*, is often placed in the category of medicine, not only because of its title, but also because it does indeed contain a number of medicinal remedies.

Perhaps more important than genre here is geography; both Hildegard and William lived in northern Europe where the dissemination of Arabic writings and Arabic translations of Greek writings occurred much later than at Salerno, taking place only over the course of the twelfth century. Despite the medical pretensions in the title given to Hildegard's work, *Liber compositae medicinae* or *Causae et curae*, this author does not follow Constantine in her treatment of menstruation, and she has been characterized as "untouched by the influence of Arabic or even Salernitan theories current in her time."[118] Although William of Conches does cite the *Pantegni*, he, too, does not rely on Arabic medicine in this physiological discussion.[119]

The important sources for natural science are, of course, the Aristotelian writings, or Aristotelian ideas as they first appear in the West in Arabic astrological treatises. In the thirteenth century, natural philosophers would make use of these sources to produce systematic descriptions of natural phenomena divorced from theological speculation such as those we find in the writings of Albertus Magnus. Here, in the period of Hildegard and William, however, religion and philosophy do not find as rigorous a separation, and Aristotelian ideas are utilized only sporadically.[120] In examining twelfth-century science, then, we are looking at a world in flux, a discipline in the process of receiving new ideas and of re-forming itself in accordance with them.

Let us focus on Hildegard's *Causae et curae*, composed in the mid twelfth century. According to Joan Cadden's analysis of this work, Hildegard uses an account of divine creation and human procreation as a basis for understanding our common condition, and her conception of human generation does not include the basic Aristotelian idea that men are hot in nature and women cold.[121] If we examine specifically Hildegard's passages on menstrual retention we see themes very similar to those found in the Salernitan treatises, although they are treated in much less detail in this essentially nonmedical work. Retention of the menses can be caused by the superfluity of humors that is found in infirmity—the veins become constricted and the tempests of humor cause the blood in the veins to become alternately hot and cold, running back and forth, and causing the menstrual flow to dry up.[122] Emotions are also a factor; just as Trota maintained that excessive anger, grief, and excitement cause amenorrhea, Hildegard tells us here that sadness makes menses stop and happiness makes them appear.[123]

A woman who suffers from menstrual retention can be gravely affected by this condition. Some individuals have flesh that is weak and fat, and their wombs become fattened "so that more weakness and foulness grows than correct vigor."[124] Hildegard does not in any way allude to the effect this foulness might have on others, however; like her predecessors, she concentrates on the consequences for the victim of this disorder.

We see Hildegard introducing another theme that is also found in the Salernitan tradition: the parallel between male and female pollution. While Trota states that men and women both have to get rid of moistures, Hildegard asserts that when "the rivers of blood in the woman flow out inordinately in an improper time [a woman] is in pain, just like any man who is wounded by a sword and for a period of time takes very good care of himself lest he be harmed further, for even medical care is applied to him with caution for the same reason."[125] This comparison of the disabilities that a woman can suffer from her monthly purgation with the effects of a wound in a man is striking; it is the only medieval scientific discussion of this type that I have seen.

A final positive tone in Hildegard's discussion of menses is found in her account of their duration. According to our author, menses flow until the age of 50, except in women of great heat: once, a woman of this nature continued to menstruate and to bear children until she was 80.[126] This is quite a contrast to themes expressed by pseudo-Albert, for whom the notion of a vigorous, menstruating old woman would be inconceivable.[127]

Hildegard's view of menstruation is not entirely positive, however. In the end, menses are connected with the fall. Eve's veins opened when the flow of cupidity first entered her; if she had stayed in paradise her veins would have remained integral and healthy.[128] In balance, though, menstruation for Hildegard is a normal female bodily function which keeps the organism healthy, and although it may represent suffering that is somehow connected with Eve's expulsion from paradise, it is suffering for the woman which finds a parallel in pain experienced by the man.

William of Conches' discussion of menstruation is much more typical of what we would expect from a natural scientist, and, for that reason, much less interesting. The twelfth-century philosopher and scientist from the school of Chartres brings up menstruation in the context of his discussions of human reproduction. If we look at his last work, the *Dragmaticon*, composed between 1144 and 1149, we see that the menstrual flow is simply described and dismissed.

The *Dragmaticon* is written in the form of a dialogue between a duke and a philosopher, and, in response to the duke's question on how menses are made and why they cease after conception, the philosopher makes the simple statement that women, since they are naturally cold, are not able to digest their food perfectly, and so superfluities remain. Nature expels these every month, and so they are called "menses." Once conception takes place, the presence of the fetus increases the heat, with the result that the food is better digested and there is less superfluous matter. Whatever is left is used to nourish the fetus *in utero*.[129]

William does not address the disorders of amenorrhea and hypermenorrhea, and his treatment of this topic is quite unremarkable, except that the context of the discussion is somewhat striking. The dialogue introduces menstruation immediately after an interchange on sexual intercourse and conception. The duke allows that he dare not ask any more questions about coitus because it is not an entirely respectable topic, but the philosopher replies that "nothing that is natural is shameful, for it is a gift of the creator."[130] Presumably the same principle applies to menstruation, and, indeed, William's language in his description of monthly purgation is value free. Yet, throughout his discussion of human reproduction the Chartrian philosopher has felt perfectly free to point out that women are much more libidinous than men, and that a woman who is raped comes to enjoy the experience at the end because of the "fragility of the flesh."[131] William evidently does not have the appreciation for women that Hildegard exhibits, yet he does not consider their monthly purgations to be a source of evil.

Natural science in the twelfth century, then, still in its formative stages, remains similar in spirit to medicine in its attitude toward woman's menstrual cycle. A weaker nature may pose additional problems for women, but these problems do not include the possession of a poisonous nature. Menstrual disorders present a danger only to women themselves. Despite the theology that may creep into other areas of twelfth-century science, for the most part statements about women as the repository of filth do not become part of natural-philosophical treatments of menses and their retention.[132]

The High Middle Ages.   When we arrive at the high middle ages (for the purpose of this discussion, this encompasses the thirteenth through fifteenth centuries), we witness an explosion of source material in both medicine and natural philosophy. In the field of medicine, Avicenna's *Canon* is translated and quickly becomes the "single most consulted textbook in medical schools until the sixteenth century,"[133] and in the field of natural philosophy the translations of Aristotle, especially the works on animals, become significant for ideas about women.[134] Of course doctors (including Avicenna) read Aristotle, and natural philosophers (including pseudo-Albert) read Avicenna, or at least they learned about their ideas. It is in this period, however, with the rise of the university as the institutional framework of intellectual life, that each of these disciplines comes to maturity and develops its own identity. Although doctors and natural philosophers both have access to Aristotle and his antifemale ideas, it is only the *physici* who capitalize on the great philosopher's misogyny. Medical men remain concerned with their patients' welfare; the translations simply provide them with more information about the subject of their interest—the human body.

Avicenna's *Canon,* translated in 1187 but not used by Latins until the second quarter of the thirteenth century, presents us with a prime example of the medical approach. Not only does Avicenna abstain from negative value judgments about women, he regards the female purgative function in a positive moral light. For this physician, menstruation that is temperate in quantity and quality and that flows in the proper time not only contributes to the woman's health by cleansing her body, it also lessens her desire and makes her chaste.[135]

The converse, of course, is also true. Retention or paucity of menses causes a woman ill health: sicknesses of repletion, abscesses, pains of the head and of the other members, shadowy sight, and perturbation of the senses result from this disorder. A woman will, indeed, experience unchaste desire during amenorrhea, according to the great physician, but he does not go on to draw the conclusion that she will engage in immoral behavior.

Instead, Avicenna is much more concerned about how the victim of retention herself will be harmed—he specifies that the corruption of the womb and of its seed will prevent her from having a son.[136]

The *Canon* is particularly striking for its inclusion of the idea seen earlier in Soranus and virtually abandoned in Arabic gynecology that amenorrhea can be nonpathological.[137] There are certain women similar in nature to a man who share with the opposite sex power "over the last digestion and necessary distribution and expulsion of superfluities. They are fat, nervous and muscular, and among them are strong viragos whose hips are narrower than their chests, and whose extremities are heavier. They experience many evacuations through medicines, exercise, nosebleeds, hemorrhoids, wounds and other ways."[138] For Avicenna, then, some women who do not menstruate are strong like men; a woman without monthly purgation does not have to be a foul, poisonous creature, or even necessarily sick. Although he undoubtedly drew from Aristotle's writings on animals where viragos are mentioned, Avicenna, unlike his source, viewed menstruation positively.[139] Women who do suffer menstrual disorders are to be helped in the alleviation of their suffering, not guarded against for the evil they can cause.

As one example of thirteenth-century medicine, let us look at William of Saliceto, an eminent figure at the medical school of Bologna, who published in 1285 a treatise entitled *Summa conservationis et curationis*. William's *Summa* contains a thorough treatment of bodily organs and their disorders, and deals with the reproductive parts at some length. Although Avicenna is a major source for William's ideas on sexuality, the Bolognese physician does not follow the *Canon* as closely when he treats the topic of menstruation.[140] William's discussion is purely objective in tone; he does not include any of the value judgments about female purgation, direct or implied, that we find in his source.

When William brings up the topic of the menstrual period, he begins immediately with the retention of the menses. Surprisingly, this university doctor does not provide his reader here with any general information on the function of menstruation or the characteristics of normal menses; he begins instead with the statement that menses are retained either because there is too little blood and humidity in the entire body, or because the blood is thickened, or because of the provocation of milk, or because of abscess or other sicknesses which occur in the womb.[141]

Menses retained because of paucity of blood result in loss of weight, and yellow or leaden coloring. This occurs after illness, or it can also be caused by sadness, worry, obsessive thoughts about someone or something, vigils, afflictions of the soul and body, labor, or living in a climate that is excessively hot or dry. It is to be cured by fattening the body as effectively and speedily as possible. This involves rubbing the extremities, a special diet, baths, ointments, and pessaries or suppositories placed in the vagina. The opposite symptoms become manifest if retention is caused by grossness of the blood (e.g. fat and softness of the body), and a different diet is prescribed for this condition, along with phlebotomy.[142] William simply sets down here causes, symptoms and a regimen or cure; he does not tell his reader, as Avicenna does, that regular menses keep a woman chaste, and he nowhere mentions the healthy nonmenstruating virago. Menstruation is to be neither praised nor condemned in the *Summa conservationis*; it is a simple physiological fact.

A far more detailed account of menstruation is found in the *Lilium medicinae* of Bernard de Gordon (fl. 1283–1308), a professor of medicine at the University of Montpellier. Bernard's discussion of woman's monthly purgation is not only systematic and extensive; he also appends to his chapter on the menses some of the positive statements about this "cleansing" process that we saw in earlier writers.

Bernard begins his discussion of the diseases of women by speaking first of menstrual retention. Clearly for Bernard, as for other writers we have examined, menstruation is a function central to women's health and is therefore given primacy of treatment. The French physician introduces his chapter by stating that the normal ages for menstruation are between 14 and 50, but that these vary according to different circumstances.[143]

Retention of menses, Bernard tells us, can be natural because of these age limits or because of other particulars, such as conception. He makes no mention here of the amenstrual virago, although Avicenna is an important source in the *Lilium*. Menstrual flow, Bernard continues, is connected to the state of the moon—young girls bleed during the first quadrant, adolescents and middle-aged women during the middle two, and older women during the last. Similar statements are also found in the *De secretis mulierum* and one of its commentaries.[144]

The French physician then proceeds to rehearse all the possible reasons for unnatural retention that we have seen in earlier medical writers, both extrinsic causes (exercise, starvation, emotion, fat, etc.) and intrinsic ones (virtue, member, or humor). He introduces an interesting "lab test" for determining the cause of this disorder: Place a sample of the menses on a clean cloth, wash it, and then make a judgment from the color remaining.[145]

After extensive treatment of causes and cures of amenorrhea, Bernard sets down fourteen notable points about menses in general. These range from how to perform phlebotomy in order to treat retention to why animals do not experience a monthly flow. Of particular interest here are points seven, eight, and nine. "Seventh," Bernard states, we should "note that menses arrive naturally in a determined time because nature intends in a certain way to aid herself through the menstrual period, and thus it is not impure. Other superfluities are not as helpful, and they are dirtier and less pure, therefore they do not observe any order or cycle."[146] Bernard, then, makes a direct statement, presumably addressing himself to those who argue for menstrual impurity.

In points eight and nine, Bernard repeats Avicenna, although the Muslim physician is not mentioned here by name. "Eighth," he states, "understand that in the retention of the menses women have greater desire because of the tickling and itching menstrual blood induces, however these symptoms are not present during the flow or afterwards." "Ninth," he continues, "take notice that the retention of menses diminishes the appetite for food because it fills up the individual, and it provokes coitus because it stimulates her."[147] Like Avicenna, Bernard sets down the information that amenorrhea provokes sexual desire in a woman, but does not use this information to censure the sufferer. He proceeds directly to a discussion of menses in animals.

Bernard de Gordon is a particularly significant representative of late-thirteenth- and early-fourteenth-century medicine, because he not only considers the menstrual period so important and treats it in such detail, but he also provides us with evidence that he is choosing medical source material that is sympathetic to women

(Avicenna/Galen) over biological source material that is not (Aristotle). His fifth point in this section concerns the question of female seed and its relation to menstrual blood. Bernard outlines here a Galenic two-seed theory, arguing that women produce seed, for they have a third digestion, *didimos*, testicles, and other principal members. If Aristotle says women do not have sperm, he continues, he makes this statement by way of comparison to men, for female seed is undigested and watery. Avicenna, too, had tried to reinterpret Aristotle to agree with Galen, in his case, by stating that both male and female matter enter the fetus.[148]

The fact that Bernard, like Avicenna, adheres to the Galenic theory of generation over the Aristotelian does not in itself demonstrate that he is "profemale" while Aristotle is "antifemale." Both Galenic and Aristotelian approaches regard the woman as an inferior creature.[149] It is primarily through the Aristotelian tradition, however, that the development of scientific misogyny takes place in this period, and Bernard's stance against the philosopher's opinion on conception (maintaining all the while that Aristotle really believed that women produce a seed) helps to place him outside this growing movement to use the peripatetic tradition to censure women. He is not choosing Galen simply because he is a physician; Taddeo Alderotti and his school, as Nancy Siraisi has shown, adopted a decidedly Aristotelian stance.[150] I am not arguing here that Bernard adopted the Galenic point of view because he was a feminist, but rather that this position was consonant with his view of the human body in general and with his interpretation of the process of menstruation in particular. This entire complex of ideas would not have fit in with the thirteenth-century tradition (largely natural-philosophical) that used Aristotelian writings to develop the notion that women are evil because of their menstrual filth.

The major figure in the importation of Aristotelian scientific ideas into the Latin West was, of course, Albertus Magnus. It is in Albertus's writings that we see most clearly the shift toward censure of the female because of her impure biological nature. Albertus represents natural philosophy in its fruition—he has wide command of Aristotelian scientific material, and he raises his discussion of natural phenomena to a sophisticated, philosophical level.

For a clear illustration of how Albertus uses Aristotelian ideas to condemn women because of their menstrual impurity we need only turn to the *Questions on Animals*. Book 9, Question 9 asks "whether the flow causes infection in the eyes," and this point is particularly significant, as we shall see below in our discussion of the *Secrets of Women* and the *Malleus Maleficarum*. It would seem at first, Albertus tells us, that menstruation would not cause an eye infection, because the flow is cleansing in nature, but the philosopher says the opposite. Albertus maintains with Aristotle that the eye is very similar to the cerebrum, because it is cold and humid, and since menstrual flow and the emission of the seed weaken the cerebrum, in like manner they weaken sight. Indeed, a mark appears in the eyes of those who have a great deal of sexual intercourse. Similarly, the menstrual flow runs into the eyes and infects it. If the object of the eyes is clean, such as a polished mirror or the eye of another person, it is immediately infected by the menstruous eye, because this eye infects the air, and then this air infects the adjacent air, and the infection continues to travel until it reaches the looking glass. Albertus concludes from this, then, that although the flow of menses and its expulsion from the body cleanses the woman, while this substance is in the body it infects all members, and especially the eyes and their object.[151]

Albertus's *Questions* are filled with other negative statements about women and their menses. Because sperm and menses are emitted frequently, they cause individuals to burn with desire, and thus cloud the senses and the memory. Menstruation weakens the sensitive nerves, and brings on old age by consumption and evacuation of the radical humidity.[152] Retention of menses is retention of naturally corrupt matter, but it is not as grave as retention of seed in men, for the male sperm is naturally noble and thus its corruption by retention is against nature and more harmful.[153] Woman is less suited to morals than man, for the humidity in her complexion is easily mobile, and thus she is inconstant and always seeking something new. Thus if she were having sex with one man, if it were possible, she would want to be with another at the same time. Consequently, there is no faith in woman, and a sign of this is that wise men tell their wives as little as possible about their words and deeds. Woman is thus a failed man, with a defective nature.[154]

Albertus Magnus not only uses Aristotle to censure woman, but he goes as far as to connect her with the devil. In the ninth book of the *Ethics*, Albertus tells us, the philosopher provides us with evidence of women's lesser moral state. Indeed, it is commonly stated in proverb and in popular parlance that women are bigger liars, frailer, more distrusting, shameless, eloquent deceivers, and, briefly, woman is nothing other than a devil represented in human form. Albertus illustrates this with an example of a woman from Cologne whom he once saw who appeared to be holy, yet quickly ensnared all into loving her.[155] Later on in this question, he continues with the theme, maintaining that women acquire by means of lies and diabolical deception what they cannot get through their own power. "Thus," he concludes, "let me state briefly that one should beware of every woman as one would avoid a venomous serpent and a horned devil, for if it were right to say what I know about women, the whole world would be astounded."[156]

Along with the full development of natural philosophy based on Aristotle, then, Western scientific thought turns firmly to systematic censure of the female because of her physical nature. Menses are clearly an impure, corrupt matter that define a woman's being and produce moral turpitude. Although we see this idea worked out most clearly in Albertus Magnus, the master of thirteenth-century Aristotelian science, echoes are found throughout other contemporary scientific writings.[157] This theme of woman's essentially evil constitution is central to the *De secretis mulierum*. We will now look forward in time and examine how pseudo-Albert's rendering of this motif directly influenced the theologians who composed the fifteenth-century inquisitorial manual on witches, the *Malleus Maleficarum*.

The *Secrets of Women* and the *Malleus Maleficarum*

The preceding survey of medieval thought on menstruation has been designed to place pseudo-Albert's *Secrets* within the context of medieval science. The *De secretis mulierum* is very much a part of the tradition of Albertus Magnus; this is clear not only from the frequent attribution of this treatise to the master, but also from its content. The *Secrets*, indeed, takes one step further than Albertus (although, as we have seen, Albertus himself occasionally lapses into unrestrained censure) and slanders women with impunity. I will now argue that pseudo-Albert's accomplishment of exaggerating and popularizing the ideas about women developed by Albertus Magnus and other thirteenth-century natural philosophers directly influenced the fifteenth-century inquisitorial treatise on witches, *Malleus Maleficarum*, and that the authors of the *Malleus* used the *Secrets* and the tradition they represent as an ideological basis for concluding that women are prone to witchcraft, for which crime they deserve death.

By introducing the *Malleus* to this discussion, we are, of course, moving outside the field of science into the realm of theology, or perhaps a better term is "applied theology." A number of points need to be made here. The first is an intellectual, or disciplinary, one. Just as we have demonstrated in other chapters that the *De secretis mulierum* is not a high-level systematic scientific treatise, so, clearly, we shall see that the *Malleus* is hardly a sophisticated theological document. Both pseudo-Albert on the one hand and Kramer and Sprenger (the fifteenth-century inquisitors who composed the *Malleus*) on the other, take basic ideas from Aristotle and medieval natural philosophy, bandy them about, and come up with similar conclusions about women. We find like ideas in Thomas Aquinas, but in Thomas they form part of a systematic theological discussion—Thomas, of course, represents the height of medieval scholastic theology.[158]

The second point to be made is sociological in nature. As Joan Cadden has pointed out, science, medicine, and theology were intimately connected in the lives, careers, and studies of their practitioners. Many medical writers and natural philosophers were clerics (the Dominican friar and eventual bishop Albertus Magnus being a prominent example), and at the universities physicians and natural philosophers became versed in ethics, and theologians studied natural philosophy.[159] By comparing the treatise of a natural philosopher who was probably a monk with a manual by two Dominican church officials, then, we are not necessarily moving from one world to another. Indeed, Nancy Siraisi has commented that in medical, in natural philosophical, and in theological works written during the thirteenth to fifteenth centuries, "the same standard question topics;

the same scholastic apparatus of arguments, objections and solutions; and many of the same citations of authorities often crop up," and Mary Frances Wack has characterized physicians as "mediating...between the worlds—and worldviews—of clergy and laity."[160] Although the *De secretis mulierum* and the *Malleus Maleficarum* certainly belong to two different genres, their authors had similar intellectual training, shared the affiliation of a religious community, and absorbed only on an unsophisticated level the philosophical speculation of the time.

Both pseudo-Albert and the inquisitors build upon the misogyny, inherent in thirteenth-century scholasticism, that we saw already in Albertus Magnus. We can regard each of their treatises as moving progressively toward the ultimate consequence of such a mode of thinking—extermination of those who most embody the evil carnality that is so feared. Woman, the temptress, the follower of Eve, the "devil's gateway" had long been suspect to theologians.[161] Now, with medieval schoolmen's interpretation of Aristotelian natural philosophy, ecclesiastical statements on the evil nature of the lesser sex become buttressed by the weight of scientific authority. Pseudo-Albert fuses theological and scientific tenets and lays the groundwork for a new kind of misogynist document.[162] The Dominican authors then incorporate both the spirit and the letter of the *Secrets* into their virulent verbal attack on the female gender, which forms the basis for a much more serious assault on women by the inquisitorial procedure itself.

Ancient medical and natural-philosophical writers were unanimous in their opinion that woman, because of her cold, wet nature was inferior to hot, dry man. The *De secretis mulierum* adopts this position as well, but simple statements of biological infirmity are quickly seized upon by interpolators and commentators and developed into condemnations. In the expanded text of MS Paris B.N. lat. 7148, we read that woman has a greater desire for coitus than a man, for something foul is drawn to the good. A less damning argument on the other side presented here is that man seeks sexual union more than woman because he is naturally prior in generation, which is designed for the salvation of the species.[163] This passage may have been written by an interpolator, since it is not in the standard versions, but it demonstrates that sentiments of this sort became part of the textual tradition.

The commentators express similar opinions. Commentator B, for example, tells us that a hermaphrodite should always be referred to by the name of a man, for one should choose the worthier alternative (Chapter VI). Commentator A maintains that a woman is not suited for learning because of the coarseness of her brain, which is stopped up and deadened (Chapter I). Here, too, we see that woman's lesser worth is a basic premise of discourse in relation to this text.

None of these fairly mild statements comes near the vituperousness of the inquisitors Kramer and Sprenger, however. They, too, maintain that females are fragile and imperfect, and elaborate on women's intellectual infirmity. "As regards intellect...they seem to be of a different nature from men. [They] are intellectually like children." Women have weak memories, and it is a natural vice in them not to be disciplined, but to follow their own impulses without any sense of what is due." The inquisitors go on, however, to conclude that when a woman thinks alone, she thinks evil; that she has a slippery tongue, is more carnal than a man, quicker to waver in her faith, and immersed in vanities.[164]

The contribution of the *De secretis mulierum* to this mode of thought is based on its insistence on the venomous nature of the normal female process of menstruation and the horror provoked by the possibility of contact with menstrual fluid.[165] Pseudo-Albert's discussion of the matter appears initially to be merely factual. He defines menses as superfluous food which is expelled monthly from age fourteen or earlier. The author then poses and answers certain simple questions: what color is it (bloodlike); does it flow through the anus or vulva (the latter); why does it flow only in women (women are humid and men are hot and dry); what happens to the menses of a pregnant woman during coitus (they are expelled but women take in an abundance of superfluous matter so the fetus is not deprived) (Chapter I).

Even in this straightforward introduction, however, we find the basis for censuring women. Pseudo-Albert uses the principle that the heat in woman is weaker than the heat in man to conclude that all her food cannot be converted into flesh because of this. The residue, the menstrual blood, is a product of female inferiority. Pregnant women, he tells us, take in an abundance of superfluous matter which is not expelled by menstruation, and from the increasing quantity of this matter the vulva becomes hot, causing great desire. The logical conclusion of this is found in the famous statement of the *Malleus*: "All witchcraft comes from carnal lust, which is in women insatiable."[166]

Commentator B is more direct about the implications of undigested food. He takes here the opportunity to warn his readers how important it is for them to avoid menstruating women. The menses is poisonous and infects the body; if it touches the twig of a green tree the twig immediately dries up; a fetus generated from it becomes leprous; it will cause great harm to the male member (Chapter I). Later on in the text, both commentators are even more precise about this harm: like the fetus, the man will come down with leprosy, and the child might be epileptic as well (Chapter II, Commentary A; Chapter X, Commentary B). The *Malleus Maleficarum* devotes a full page to accounts of how witches cause leprosy and epilepsy; thus this danger has been incorporated into the inquisitors' concept of the evil nature of woman.[167]

Although pseudo-Albert was fairly objective in his initial discussion of the menstrual period, as the treatise develops he allows some of his deeper feelings to emerge. In the chapter on the generation of imperfect animals, he cites Avicenna to the effect that if the hairs of a menstruating woman are buried in the winter, when they are heated by the sun in the spring and summer, a long, stout serpent will be generated (Chapter IV).[168] The image of the serpent is also, of course, the image of the devil, and the *Malleus* clearly identifies serpents with witchcraft.[169] Commentator B explains the transformation of hair as follows: hairs are made from vapors that rise to the cerebrum, and in women these vapors are poisonous because of cold, undigested humors. Since her hair is venomous, a menstruating woman ought to hide it. A man need not do this because his humors are well digested, so his hair is not poisonous and does not rot (Chapter IV).

In the chapter on the signs of chastity we find more than similarity of thinking in the *Secrets* and the *Malleus*; here there is evidence of direct textual borrowing from the *De secretis mulierum*. By this point in the treatise, pseudo-Albert has warmed to his denunciation of women. He first warns men to beware of those who have their menstrual periods, and then proceeds to discourse on how the menstrual flow can poison children lying in their cradles by infecting the eyes of women, and transmitting this poison through the air to the child. We saw a milder version of this mode of poisoning earlier in the discussion of Albertus Magnus's *Questions on Animals*. Pseudo-Albert notes that old women, and poor women who consume coarse food, are particularly dangerous because of the abundance of evil humors in their bodies (Chapter X). The picture painted here of old, poor women who kill babies reminds us, of course, of the stereotype of the witch-midwife who, according to later inquisitors and their followers, put infants to death in the name of Satan.[170] The *De secretis mulierum* sets down the scientific justification for this persecution, which will be incorporated into the manual of witchcraft for inquisitors almost two centuries later.

In Part I, Question II of the *Malleus*, the authors adopt this material. The text states that "at the sight of some impurity, such as, for example, a woman during her monthly periods, the eyes will, as it were, contract a similar impurity."[171] Following the text of pseudo-Albert, the inquisitors cite in support of this argument Aristotle in his work *On Sleep and Waking*. The statement is not found in *On Sleep and Waking*, however, and Aristotle discusses infants and sleep in this treatise only cursorily. Pseudo-Albert, accustomed to using Aristotle to support his statements, and perhaps even of falsifying his sources when convenient, has brought in the philosopher here to lend authority to his argument. The authors of the *Malleus* have drawn on pseudo-Albert's text, including this citation from *The Secrets of Women*.

If we look at this point at Commentary A, by far the more popular of the two (at least with regard to the printed editions), we read next that the eye of a soothsayer once forced a camel into a ditch, for the evil within her generated evil humors, which exited through the eyes, and caused the camel to fall down in an attempt to flee (Chapter X).[172] Similarly, the *Malleus* introduces this point in the same order, stating that several universities, especially Paris, condemned this article: that an enchanter is able to cast a camel into a deep ditch by directing a gaze at it.[173] The Dominican authors are here concerned with orthodoxy and censure this statement which was condemned in 1277, explaining that a corporeal body would not obey a spiritual substance and undergo a transformation, for it is God alone who is absolutely obeyed.[174] The authors allow, however, that an angry and evil gaze, steadfastly directed on a child, may so impress itself on the child's imagination that actual results may follow, such as inability to take food, and illness.[175]

Commentator A continues with another example: A lizard, or basilisk is infected or killed when a mirror is place in front of him, for the poisonous humors that are emitted from his body are reflected back to him. Similarly, the *Malleus* discourses on the basilisk, elaborating on how it can kill a man, and how a man can destroy the basilisk by the use of mirrors.[176] The similarity of the two texts in this extended discussion provides a strong argument for direct borrowing on the part of Kramer and Sprenger.

Commentator B, although not the source of the *Malleus Maleficarum*, takes this section of the text as an opportunity to set down a series of "facts" about menstruating women: They cause men to become hoarse by getting near them; their color is poor; if they look in a mirror, a red mark appears on it. With respect to the part of the text dealing with old women, Commentator B concludes simply that they should not be able to play with children and kiss them (Chapter X). Once again, the stereotype of the old, evil woman which will be transformed into the image of the witch is depicted in this treatise.

Pseudo-Albert's final treatment of menses is in the chapter on the suffocation of the womb, a malady that occurs when the uterus is poisoned by retained menses. Women suffer difficulty of breathing, weakness of the heart, dizziness, and displacement of the womb from the cold that the corrupt menstrual matter produces. As a cure, they should have sexual intercourse so that this matter is ejected from the body, although pseudo-Albert states that this practice is not always acceptable in society (Chapter XI).

Since women are evil in their essence, which is clearly menstrual matter, pseudo-Albert and his commentators agree that they do evil as well. This, of course, is one of the main themes of the *Malleus*: the wickedness of woman. An important manifestation of her wickedness is her deceitfulness; the *Malleus* tells us that woman deceives because she is an imperfect animal, formed from a rib of the breast bent in a contrary direction to a man.[177]

Pseudo-Albert develops this theme by introducing a pregnancy
test that will foil the woman's attempt to state the opposite of
what is true; our author admits, nevertheless, that some women
are so clever and aware that they will succeed anyway in fooling
the questioner (Chapter VIII).

Pseudo-Albert's chapters on the corruption of virginity and
chastity are also designed to outwit deceitful females—he presents the signs of corruption and purity tests so that men can dis-
cover the truth. Pseudo-Albert and his commentators give an
account of the modest demeanor of a chaste woman and then
add a description of the urine of a virgin and nonvirgin because
"some women are so clever that they know how to resist detection by these signs, and so a man must turn to their urine." Similarly, they tell us how a virgin's vagina is always closed and a
woman's always open, but this is only true if the subject "did not
cause her vagina to contract by using an ointment or another
medicine so that she would be thought a virgin, as many women
are in the habit of doing" (Chapters IX and X).

Pseudo-Albert moves from female deceitfulness to deliberate
acts of aggression against the male, often aimed directly at his
sexual organs. In the *Malleus*, a main theme is how witches harm
men's private parts; entire chapters are devoted to "How
Witches Impede and Prevent the Power of Procreation," and
"How, As It Were, They Deprive Man of His Virile Member."
The inquisitors even tell us how witches collect penises in groups
of twenty or thirty, and keep them in nests, feeding them oats
and corn.[178] Pseudo-Albert's statements are not as dramatic, but
he does go out of his way to set down for us information on the
evil intent of women. In a discussion of the influence of the planets on the developing fetus, for example, our author tries to bolster his argument by describing the effect of the moon on the
body. Drawing from the *Centiloquium* he states that "at the
point when the moon increases humidity in all the members, if
you touch one of the members with a sword [or surgical instru-
ment] you can be sure that you are gravely hurting it" (Chapter
II). Although this passage has nothing whatever to do with
women, pseudo-Albert takes the opportunity here to bring up
the practice of evil women who place iron in the vulva in order
to hurt the male penis. Commentator B tells us that other com-

mentators explain that they do this "out of vindictiveness and malice," aiming to poison the man with menstrual blood which enters through the wound. He claims, however, that the true explanation of what is going on is that the women insert a cauterizing substance, which does not affect the vulva because it is less porous and they protect it with oil of roses (Chapter II).

An additional example of the fear of women's designs against the male organ is found in Commentator B's discussion of pica, the desire of pregnant women for unusual foods. The author explains that venomous humors from the retained menses act upon the stomach, causing an appetite for unusual foods, because similars seek out similars. He then chooses as an illustration the pregnant wife of a peasant who "so greatly desired to eat the testicles of her husband that if she could not have them she wanted to die, and because she could not, she contracted a very serious illness" (Chapter VII). Surely the selection of this example indicates once again the underlying assumption that women are driven by a desire to deprive men of their reproductive organs, and are thus to be greatly feared.

Another prominent focus of women's evil urges is their propensity to destroy babies. As witches, the *Malleus* tells us, they cause women to miscarry after they have conceived, by means of herbs such as savin and other emmenagogues, or, if they have failed to procure an abortion they kill the child, drink its blood and devour it as part of their ritual.[179] The inquisitors devote a full chapter to how witch-midwives in particular murder infants or offer them to the devil; clearly these poor women who assisted at so many stillbirths or were present in cases of infant death were blamed for these unfortunate occurrences.

Pseudo-Albert does not mention infanticide, although MS Paris B.N. lat. 7148 provides an account of how harlots perform various incantations with the amniotic membrane.[180] Abortion, however, is included in his "secrets," and in the chapter "On the Exit of the Fetus from the Uterus," he presents the reasons why a woman might give birth in the sixth month to something that is not "the nature of man but rather a certain fleshy and milky matter" (Chapter V).[181] Our author tells us that the matter of the menses might be corrupt, or the woman might move about too much, breaking the womb. Pseudo-Albert then makes it clear that this is a deliberate act by "harlots and women learned in the art of midwifery," who move from town to town leading dances, having sex, and wrestling with men in order to be freed from their pregnancy. Commentator B, like the authors of the *Malleus*, tells us that women sometimes produce an abortion by boiling down certain herbs. Both pseudo-Albert and the commentator assert that women suffer from this evil act—the commentator refers to physical pain, and pseudo-Albert maintains that women have a great desire for coitus because the pleasure they experience will help them blot out the grief they feel from the destruction of the fetus.

The *Secrets of Women*, then, lays the groundwork for the *Malleus Maleficarum* and the persecution of women it implies. Although pseudo-Albert's motives were not as evil as Kramer's and Sprenger's, for he purportedly aimed to provide information enabling men to avoid women instead of putting them to death, he sets down a rationale eventually used to justify torture and burning at the stake. A by-product of medieval scholasticism and its attempt to understand the natural world by rational means, the *De secretis mulierum* distorts nature in its presentation of women.

DE SECRETIS MULIERUM
(ON THE SECRETS OF WOMEN)

PREFACE

Text

To my dear companion and friend in Christ, may you be granted a long life filled with increasing wisdom.

Since you asked me to bring to light certain hidden, secret things about the nature of women, I have set myself to the task of composing this short and compendious treatise. I have done this despite the youthful frailty of my mind, which tends to be attracted to frivolous things. Its style is partly philosophical, partly medical, just as seems to fit the material. This is a serious work, therefore I beg you not to permit any child to peruse it, nor anyone of childlike disposition. If you keep this book to yourself, I promise to show you many things about different subjects as well as about the art of medicine which, God willing, I shall discuss at some length.

Commentary A

The subject of this present book is mobile being, applied specifically to the nature of the secrets of women. It is written so that we might be able to provide a remedy for their infirmities, and so that in confessing them we might know how to give suitable penances for their sins. And it is divided first into two parts, namely the introductory and the executive part. The executive part begins, "As Aristotle said," etc.

First the author salutes the person to whom he writes, saying, "I, Albert, staying in Paris, to my dear friend and companion in Christ." Then he brings up the efficient cause, the moving cause and the moved cause. The moving cause was a certain priest who asked Albert if he would write for him a book on the secrets of women. The reason for this is that women are so full of venom in the time of their menstruation that they poison animals by their glance; they infect children in the cradle; they spot the cleanest mirror; and whenever men have sexual intercourse with them they are made leprous and sometimes cancerous. And because an evil cannot be avoided unless it is known, those who wish to avoid it must abstain from this unclean coitus,[1] and from many other things which are taught in this book. Albert, seeing that the request was just, consented to it, and thus we have the efficient cause of this book....

Note that the author states that his petty, juvenile mind held him back, and so he avoids arrogance; his mind is called small because it is endowed with little intelligence. The intellect is not small in and of itself, nor through its accident, because it is not increased through expansion nor diminution.

Note that appetite is threefold, namely natural, animal and intellectual. The text refers to appetite in the sense of natural intellect. Therefore the priest desired through his natural appetite to know the nature of women, for men naturally desire to know, as is written in the first book of the *Metaphysics*.[2] He also experienced his intellectual appetite, for he perceived the utility of this knowledge.

Text

As Aristotle said in Book 2 of the *Generation of Animals*, generation is eternal and cyclical.[3] He gives the reason for this in the second book *On the Soul* where he says, "The most natural operation is for each thing to generate something similar to itself so as to participate in the divine and the immortal. That is the goal toward which all things strive so that each might endure" if not as an individual, then in species.[4] Thus we see Averroes state in his commentary on this passage that although God's care cannot cause individuals to live forever, nevertheless the Lord takes pity on man and grants the power for his species to continue. And the commentator adds, "And there is no doubt that it is better to have this power than not to have it, or indeed than not to exist at all.[5]

Commentary A

A question arises as to whether certain animals are sometimes entirely corrupted, for example certain worms, and flies in the winter. One can reply that if they are corrupted in one climate, then they are generated in another as Albert tells us, and as we read in the commentary on the first book of the *Posterior Analytics*.⁶ Or, one might say that the generation of animals which are of universal perfection is eternal; but taking into account the first reply one can question whether indeed these animals are of universal perfection, for it is better for many not to exist than to exist, for example serpents and other poisonous creatures. The answer is that it is good for them to exist, for they absorb the impurities of the earth, and if they did not do this, they would infect the air, and, as a consequence, they would poison man. Thus nothing exists without a rational cause.

Commentary B

We first address the part of the text that says it is the most natural operation [for each thing to generate something similar to itself]. Someone could say against this that a male generates a female and a woman generates a male therefore the text is false. The conclusion is apparent, and the assumption is demonstrated by experience.

The answer is that the statement that male and female are the same can be taken in two ways, referring either to specific nature or to the essence of life, and thus it is true. On the other hand, it can be understood to mean that they are the same according to corporal dispositions, and thus it is not true, as becomes apparent upon consideration. Against this, however, is the argument based on Avicenna that the principal members are the heart and the cerebrum, and the male and female have these the same so this is not a solution.

The answer is that the principal members are twofold. Some are principles of life which cause the existence of life. Others belong to the act of generating which makes the species continue, such as the genital members. I say that the woman and man certainly have similar members with respect to the existence of life, but not with respect to the act of generating. However according to the doctors, although the female does not have her genitals on the outside, she nevertheless has testicles inside attached to the womb towards the back, and a spermatic vessel just like the man has. Her seed runs out from these organs because of delectation just like saliva runs out of the mouth of a starving person.

Text

In the second book of *On Generation and Corruption* Aristotle gives us the reason why animals, and especially men, do not live forever in the same nature and matter and individual.[7] If the bodily substance of a being is corruptible, it cannot be replicated in number. The substance of individual man, however, is corruptible, and so human generation is limited.

Commentary B

Note that many things are required in order for generation to take place. First you must have a male and a female, and nature ordered that the male be of a hot, dry disposition, in relation to the female who is cold and wet. The second requirement for generation is that they possess genital members, one a male and the other a female organ. Thirdly, they should be properly disposed, that is, the male's penis should not be extremely short or long, and adjacent members should also be well put together.

Note on this point that there are three elements in coitus: appetite which derives from phantasms of thought, and from spirit and humor; appetite from the liver and heart and consequently from the cerebrum; for when these are set in motion during coitus, then all members of the body become heated and they are made erect by the heat. At this point the humor in the cerebrum is attracted through the veins and sent to the testicles and ejected through the male penis, for, as Hippocrates says, whoever has unusually small veins behind the ears will not be able to generate.[8] If he ejaculates anything at all during coitus, it is not semen, but watery humor, and no fetus can be produced from this. This happens as well to those who have the habit of performing the venereal act with excessive frequency so that they do not eject semen but watery humor. Sometimes this is diseased, and it is extremely dangerous.

Text

Yet even though human generation is not perpetual according to number, it is nevertheless most perfect. We can prove this proposition as follows: Man is the most noble creature, as Aristotle tells us in many places, especially in the second book *On the Soul*, because the more operations a thing has, the nobler it is.[9] Further, man is distinguished from other living things by his intellective reason. We have ample attestation of this statement in the writings of philosophers, especially Boethius in the second book of the *Consolation of Philosophy* where he says that men are similar to God in mind.[10] Aristotle, too, tells us in the second book of his philosophy that since motion takes its nature and species from its goal, the arrival of human nature in Socrates or Plato or in another particular man is motion which is called generation, and it will be the most perfect type of generation among all other animals.[11]

Again, generation is a motion from not being to being. However, being is most greatly desired, and especially by men because this among all motions is excellent in nobility.[12] And the motion under discussion is one that disposes differently what already exists, and this excludes first motion, which is the cause of the others.

CHAPTER I:
ON THE GENERATION OF THE EMBRYO

Text

Now that we have finished our introductory remarks, designed to prepare the reader's mind toward this subject matter, let us turn to the matter of the book, and first let us examine the generation of the embryo. Note therefore that every human being who is naturally conceived is generated from the seed of the father and the menses of the mother, according to all philosophers and medical authorities. And I say "medical authorities" because Aristotle did not believe that the father's seed was part of the substance of the fetus, but rather that the fetus proceeded from the menses alone, and afterwards he states that the seed exudes like vapor from the menses. The doctors, on the other hand, believe that the fetus is made up of male and female seed together.

Commentary A

Note[13] that there is a controversy between medical authorities and philosophers, for philosophers say that the male seed has the same relationship to the female menses as an artificer does to his work. For just as a carpenter alone is the efficient cause, and the house is the effect, in that he alters and disposes the matter of the house, so the male seed alters the female menses into the form of a human being. They say this because they see that even if the father is corrupt, the generation of a person and the transmutation of the woman's seed takes place, and for this reason it is an efficient cause. Because the end and the effect do not coincide, thus the male seed does not enter the matter.

The medical authorities say the opposite, however, because man is made from the most noble material, and thus the male seed must enter the fetus materially, because the female menses is a superfluity of the second digestion and the male seed is better cooked and digested. Therefore it is necessary that it enter into the matter and substance of the fetus, for it is seen that sometimes the fetus resembles the father in genitals and in other ways, and this would be impossible if sperm were not incorporated materially.

The doctors say further that in the male seed there is a certain generating spirit which penetrates the entire seminal mass, and this spirit has the power to form all members. Just as a smith fashions iron with a hammer, this spirit disposes and softens all the members, and it is this spirit that is the efficient principle. The philosophers, on the other hand, state that the male seed exudes as a vapor, for the womb is exceedingly porous and after the formation of the fetus the heat of the sun causes the male seed to evaporate and to leave the womb through the pores. It is evident that the womb is porous because the child receives nourishment through the pores. Another reason offered is that it is a skin, and every skin is porous in an animal because otherwise sweat would not be able to escape without pain, but this is false because pores are opened in the heat, sweat escapes, and hairs grow through the pores.

Note that the embryo is a certain fleshy mass formed from these two seeds, and this fleshy mass is altered to form a fetus.

Commentary B

Someone might say that it is possible for men to be generated naturally without seed, therefore the false conclusion of the text is clear. The assumption is proved by Avicenna in his *Book on Floods*.[14] To bolster further his argument, he states that after the Trojan war giants were generated from the many cadavers of the dead that were joined together. I say that Avicenna is making a false statement, as is proved by Averroes in the second book of the *Colliget* where he proves that human beings cannot be generated from putrefaction as other animals can.[15] To confirm this, it is stated that giants were not generated from these cadavers but from the seeds of their parents under the influence of the celestial constellation.

Text

Having set forth both opinions,[16] we must now see how that seed is received in woman. When a woman is having sexual intercourse with a man she releases her menses at the same time that the man releases sperm, and both seeds enter the *vulva* (vagina) simultaneously and are mixed together, and then the woman conceives. Conception is said to take place, therefore, when the two seeds are received in the womb in a place that nature has chosen. And after these seeds are received, the womb closes up like a purse on every side, so that nothing can fall out of it. After this happens, the woman no longer menstruates.

Commentary A

At this point the author takes up the formation of the fetus; he first discusses the topic and then brings in some relevant points. On this subject we should note that if the man ejaculates before the woman emits her menses conception does not take place. If both ejaculate at the same time but their seeds are not of the proper type or disposition, there is no conception. An example of this is if the male seed is not sufficiently hot. Those people who have sex rarely are quick to conceive because they are exceedingly hot.

And note that the vulva is named from the word *valva* [folding door] because it is the door of the womb, and the extreme part of the vulva is called the membrane because the "member" of the "anus" is the end of the vulva.

The womb closes up like a purse so that, as Avicenna says, not even a needle can enter, because it is so pleased by the heat that it has received that it does not wish to lose it.[17] The woman has more pleasure in coitus than the man because she both emits and receives seed.

A question arises as to whether a man who has had his testicles cut off can father children, and it appears that he cannot because he is lacking in the seminal vessels through which the seed must be borne. On the other side, experience shows us that a bull who has been castrated generates.

I say that the man will remain fertile if he was fertile beforehand, because he can emit spermatic material, although not as well as before. If his seed which is ejected to the ground were placed in the womb, there is a possibility that the woman would conceive. Thus, it often happens that a woman conceives if she is in a bath where a man has ejaculated because the vulva strongly attracts the sperm, and the sperm at this point is vigorous and has not evaporated, so that it can produce a fetus. This has been attested to by experience.

If a cat ejaculated on some sage, and a man ate some of this sage, then cats would be generated in his stomach and would have to be expelled by vomiting.

Commentary B

Averroes said in the passage above [II *Colliget*] that a girl from his neighborhood once confided to him, swearing that she was telling the truth, that she had never been impregnated by any man, and nevertheless she was pregnant; and she asked him to help her.[18] Averroes carefully examined the case to determine the cause, and he found that she had been bathing in tepid water in a bath[19] and suddenly was impregnated by attracting male semen, for a man had ejaculated in this bath and the female member on its own power extracted as much semen from the bath as it could. The commentator [i.e., Averroes] said that this was possible in the natural course of events, and the girl asked him to help her make it clear that she had not been corrupted by a man. But Averroes replied that she ought to engage in the venereal act, and have intercourse with men.

The question that arises is, was this girl a virgin or not? We reply briefly that there are two types of corruption. The first takes place through the emission of seed. The second occurs through a wound in the skin of virginity, that is, when the hymen is broken. Thus I would say that she was corrupted in the first way because she attracted and emitted seed, but in the second way she was not, for her skin was not broken.

We should note that many things are required to prevent seed that has not been spilled on the ground from being wasted. First, when the male and the female have sexual intercourse, they should not do it standing up, because then the seed is projected upwards and afterwards falls down, because what goes up must come down. Secondly, they should not have intercourse lying on their sides, because then the seed is poured in on one side of the womb and as a result is wasted and generation is prevented. Thirdly, it is required on the part of the woman that the womb not be corrupted and that the opening not be damaged, for, if it were, the seed would not be able to remain within; and further, the womb must not be exceedingly unclean or very slippery, because all these impede conception.

Fourthly, the womb must be able to open, because if it does not do so when sperm is ejaculated, then the sperm falls elsewhere and after some time a large mass of flesh is generated from this. This happens to many young women who are incapable of performing the venereal act because of the small opening of their womb. When they are in bed asleep at night lying on their backs the exceeding attraction and desire that they experience causes them to have an emission of their own seed. This pollution remains inside their body near the umbilicus and grows into a large mass of flesh, so that their abdomen begins to swell and they believe mistakenly that they are pregnant. This type of tumor, called by doctors the mole of the womb,[20] can be cured only by medical regimen.

A fifth cause for infertility is the length of the penis, because, as Galen says, it ought not to be longer than eleven inches at most, for if it were longer the seed would be dispersed in the womb and conception prevented.[21] The penis should be no shorter than one inch, because if it were any shorter it would not be able to touch the opening of the womb, and the seed would flow elsewhere preventing conception and causing the woman to suffer certain illnesses....

In order to understand the conclusion [that male and female seed enter the vulva at the same time and are mixed together, causing conception] you should know that the menses is of a double nature: one part is pure, and one part is impure. The pure menses is the proper seed of the woman, which is transformed into the substance of the fetus. The impure menses, however, is a certain superfluity and impurity caused by nondigestion of food. Because a woman is cold in nature, with insufficient heat to digest all food that is consumed, every day a certain unclean superfluity is left over, and this leaves the body every month, as will be shown.

A question arises as to whether the male or female experiences greater delectation in coitus. Aristotle discusses this question in his first book on the *Generation of Animals*.[22] After dealing with the arguments on both sides, he replies that the statement that one delectation is greater than the other in the venereal act can be taken two ways. We can understand it intensively, and in this sense the male's pleasure is greater, because his semen is hotter. We can also understand it extensively, and in this way the female would have greater enjoyment, because she has a double delight: one because she receives seed, and another because she emits it.[23]

A second question that comes up is whether during coitus delectation is experienced in the entire body, or only in certain parts, namely in the male penis and in the female member. The answer is that delectation can be understood in two ways, either principally, or executively. With reference to the question, I say that this delectation exists principally in the members pertaining to the act of coitus, but executively in all members, for all veins run together there.

Text

The menses in woman, just like the sperm in man, is nothing other than superfluous food which has not been transformed into the substance of the body. In woman it is called "menses" because it flows at least once every month when the woman reaches the proper age, that is, 12, 13, or, most frequently, 14.[24] This flow takes place every month in order to purge the body. In some women it begins at the new moon, in some afterwards, and thus all women do not have their pain at the same time. Some have more suffering, some less; some have a shorter flow than others, and this is all determined by the requirement and the complexion of the individual woman.

Commentary A

Here the author poses an important point, as is evident in the text. But one may ask why sperm does not flow in men the same way the menses flow in women. The answer to this is that sperm, or the male seed, is so well cooked and subtle that nature does not like to reject it, but rather it is saved for generation, or for nutrition if the fetus should need it. Another question is why urine, feces and sweat do not follow the motion of the moon the way the menstrual period does. The answer is that urine and feces are made every day from the superfluity of food because of the large bulk and greater quantity, and therefore they must be expelled daily.

Note that young women are very humid and therefore they normally have their menses in the beginning of the month, and older women in the end, because they are less humid. Black women have less menstrual flow than white ones, because although all women are of phlegmatic complexion, some have more of this characteristic than others. Further, the more women consume delicate and highly spiced foods, the subtler is their menstrual flow. And the opposite is true of poor women who eat coarse foods.

The author says that women begin to menstruate in their twelfth, thirteenth and fourteenth years. The reason for this is that at this point the heat of childhood begins to fail, and without this heat they cannot fully digest the humid nutriment.

Women are purged by means of their menstrual periods because the excess humidity is removed, and if it remained coarse humors would be formed from it. Therefore they are not suited for learning because of the coarseness of their spirits which stop up and deaden the brain. And note that coitus is beneficial for women because through it they lose their superfluous cold and receive heat, and this tempers their frigid natures; however the opposite is true in men. Thus women who have much sexual intercourse do not have their lives shortened as men do, and this is proved by the nature of the swallow who dies because he has sex too often.

Commentary B

All women suffer menstrual pain, however some have more than others. In relation to this we should note that the womb is a masculine kind of organ with a skin that is divided into many chambers suitable for the generation of a fetus.[25] It is located between the female member and the intestine, in the area above the bladder. Of its many chambers, two are situated in the hollow opening, where the veins carrying menstrual blood empty through the female member, and after these two chambers the female testicles are found. According to Averroes in the second book of the *Colliget* the mouth of the womb in a virgin is exceedingly veinous, and from this area veins arise which have a skin comprising two tissues, the smaller of which is arranged longitudinally, and the other latitudinally.[26] When these skins are broken by the male member the woman loses her virginity, and thus when a virgin is first corrupted in coitus the female semen flows in great quantity from her member, and this is the truest sign that she was a virgin.

If the sperm falls on the right side of the womb a male child is generated; if it falls on the left a female is conceived.

When in the text the author mentions the womb closing up like a purse, this is similar to someone having a friend and giving her as a gift something that she likes very much. If the friend were afraid to lose the gift, she would close her hand tightly, and in the same way the womb desires to retain the semen and for this reason closes up tight.

Note that the text says that the female menses is the superfluity of food, etc. In relation to this you should understand that digestion is manifold: the first takes place in the mouth and consists of chewing; the second is in the stomach and produces the superfluity of feces; the third is in the liver; the fourth is in the members, as medical authorities state, and sperm or semen is the superfluity of the fourth digestion. Someone might ask, if men have a third digestion, why do they not have menstrual periods? The answer is that the third digestion takes place in the liver, where the greatest heat burns in men and for this reason no impurity is left over. However, in women the heat is weak, and so superfluity remains.[27]

Note that according to some, menses is understood in three ways. The first way is natural menses, such as the menstrual periods of women. The second is supernatural, as the Jews experience. The third way is against nature, for example certain Christians of melancholy disposition bleed through the anus and not through the penis.

Someone might ask why menses do not flow in pregnant women. The answer is that they are converted into something, for as the text says two veins lead from the womb to the breasts, and thus the menses are transferred to the breasts, where they are cooked and receive the form of milk, and carried back through these veins to nourish the fetus in the mother's womb. For this reason nursing women, for example wet nurses, do not have as much menses as other women because it is changed into the matter of milk. Therefore we read in Averroes that some women, like wet nurses, cannot become pregnant, even though they have a great deal of sexual intercourse.[28]

Note that it is not impossible for the menses to flow for three months after conception, because the new fetus is not capable of receiving all the food, and many women are deceived because of this, because when they get their menstrual periods they believe that they are not pregnant, but the opposite is often true.

The proper place for the menses is in the womb, and it is transferred through certain veins running from the female member through the back, and the sign of this is that during their periods women often have great pain in the back.

Each phase of the moon has four quarters, and women suffer their periods in accordance with these phases. The first is when the new moon begins. This lasts about eight days and is characterized by blood because it is hot and humid and in this time women with a sanguine complexion suffer. The second is choleric, for it is hot and dry, and choleric women get their periods. The third quadrant is melancholic, that is cold and dry, and affects melancholic women, and the fourth is cold and wet, or phlegmatic, and touches these women. Despite this classification, almost all women frequently get their periods in the end of the month, for almost all have a cold, phlegmatic nature.

Someone might ask why brute animals do not have a menstrual flow. The answer is that [their superfluities] are transformed into hair, however some contend that animals have menses, but in small quantity.

Text

Many questions arise concerning the things I have just described. First, is that flow the color of blood or another color? And to this I reply that in all women except for corrupt ones the color of menses is bloodlike. When I speak of corruption, I refer to corruption by bad and viscous humours, for in women of this sort the menses is often livid, taking on the color of lead. I am not referring here to the corruption of virgins, because women have this flow when they reach the proper age whether they are chaste or not. The signs to that effect—namely, of menstrual flow—are many, and I shall speak about them later.

Commentary A

Here the author raises four questions in order, as we see in the text. As to the first, the menstrual flow is the color of blood. The cause of this is that menses is the superfluity of the second digestion, which takes place in the liver, and the liver is a red organ of the greatest heat, and therefore the menses takes on its color and form insofar as it is able. But one might reply that menses should really be white, because it is extremely cold, and cold is the mother of whiteness. I reply according to Albert that the menses would be white of its own nature, but since the liver which produces it is red, it takes on this color instead. Anent this, one might ask why the male sperm is not red, since it is hot and well digested. The answer is that the sperm is red of itself, because it is the blood of the third digestion, but it is whitened in the testicles because of their coldness. For this reason, a man cannot ejaculate unless he is made hot by the motion of the testicles.

Note that the red color is generated from the fact that in humid earthy substances, the humidity is consumed by burning, as appears in a red brick. The brick is not red before firing, but it is made red by the consumption of humidity by the heat, so that dry earthy substance predominates. Similarly the female menses is made somewhat red, even though in the liver the humid heat is not consumed in dry earthy substance. In extremely fat and earthy women, there is so much unconsumed humidity and so much earthy substance that their menses is livid, that is black. Earth is black, and because their menses is very earthy, it follows that it takes on the color of the earth.

Commentary B

Some women are corrupted carnally by the male penis, but others are said to be corrupt because they have a spoiled and sticky humor adhering to them. The text is not referring to the first type, but rather to the second. In this connection, note that maidens have greater menstrual pain than women who have experienced sexual intercourse because virgins do not have the same passage as corrupt women.

There is a similarity in nature between the female breasts and the male testicles, for just as milk flows through the breasts, so sperm is emitted through the testicles.

Text

The second question that arises is whether the menses flow out through the anus with solid waste, or through the vulva, with the voiding of urine. To this I reply briefly that the menses flow through the vulva in the form of crude, thin blood.

Commentary B

This second question is perfectly appropriate to ask because men who have dysentery experience a flow of blood from the abdomen which resembles the menstrual flow, and this dysenteric bleeding is suffered by both men and women. Melancholic males generate a good deal of black bile which is directed to the spleen, and then to the spine. From there it descends to other veins located around the last intestine which are called hemorrhoids. After these veins are filled they are purged of the bile by this flow, which, if it is moderate, is very beneficial. This is found in Jews more than in others, for their natures are more melancholic, although it is said that they have this flow because of a miracle of God, and there is no doubt that this is true.

Text

The third question is why menses, which are superfluous food, flow in women, and sperm does not flow in men, for this is also superfluous food. To this I reply that woman is cold and humid by nature, whereas man is hot and dry. Now humid things naturally flow, as we see in the fourth book of the *Meteorology*,[29] and this is especially true of that humid substance which is in women, for it is watery. In men, on the other hand, the humid substance resembles air, and, further, man has natural heat, and this heat acts upon the humid. Since nature never does anything in vain, as is noted in the first book *On Heaven and Earth*,[30] and because the heat in women is weaker than that in men, and all their food cannot be converted into flesh, nature takes the best course. She provides for what is necessary, and leaves the excess in the place where the menses are kept. Enough has been said on this subject, for to go into more detail would be to give more than the subject demands.

Commentary A

Here he raises the third question and solves it, as we see in the text. Note that the coldest man is hotter than the hottest woman if they live in the same area, have the same digestion, diet, etc.[31] A woman in Ethiopia who lives delicately would be hotter than a poor man in the West who always eats cold foods.

On the other hand, it seems that a woman is hotter than a man, because heat is founded in blood and there is more blood in a woman than there is in a man. Otherwise, blood would not flow continually every day in a woman, and this is not true in a man, therefore [woman would be hotter than man]. We reply to this argument that there is greater heat where there is more well digested and well-cooked blood, but this is not the case in women, therefore [women do not have more heat].

Note that the text says that nature does what is best. The reason for this is that nature, being ruled by an infallible intelligence, expels the gross humidity of the woman by means of this flow. We see from experience that when any gross humor exists in an animal that is harmful to the body, nature turns it into one of the limbs of the body, causing a scaly foot and hand, lest that humor consume the principal members, such as the heart, liver and others.

Commentary B

It is logical to raise this third question because just as the menses are a superfluity in the woman, so is sperm in the man. Note in connection with the answer that male sperm does not flow monthly the way female menses do, and the text tells us that the reason for this is that the humidity in women is watery. From this it follows that the menses of women is extremely poisonous and infects the body, so that Albert tells us that if menses touch the twig of a green tree it immediately dries up, therefore nature makes a great effort to expel this matter. From this we see why male sperm is not as abundant as female menses, although nature does expel it sometimes when the man is sleeping.

Nocturnal pollution happens for many reasons. Sometimes it is caused by exceeding drunkenness and too much food or drink which is then digested, and the emission often occurs after digestion. Secondly, it happens at night after too much concentration on shameful things, or too much talk. Thirdly, it sometimes occurs through demonic illusion and deception. Fourthly, an excess of humors leads to emission, for when an individual is filled with many humors and much blood, this natural purgation takes place. Fifthly, it is caused by excessive fasting which excites the natural heat and acts on the humid, and in this case the emission is harmful. Sixthly, too much labor which dries out a man leads to natural pollution that is the emission of seed while sleeping. Because of this, theologians say that the first two ways should be considered sins, but the others should not.

Text

The fourth question is as follows. If, as I said before, the menses are retained when the woman conceives, how can they flow out when she is having sexual intercourse with a man. To this I reply that when the woman conceives, the menses are retained so that the fetus which is in the uterus can be nourished. However, when a woman is having sex with a man she experiences such great pleasure from the male member rubbing back and forth on the nerves and veins in the vagina that the vagina dilates and ejects the menses. This ejection is natural during coitus because coitus is a natural act, but it is violent [or unnatural] with respect to the natural flow of menses. Further, every day food is taken in which is suitable for ejection during coitus. And this provides an answer to the question why pregnant women so greatly desire sexual intercourse. They take in an abundance of superfluous matter which is not expelled by menstruation, and from the increasing quantity of this matter the vulva becomes hot, causing great desire.

Commentary A

Here he raises the fourth question and resolves it. However this brings up a related query, namely, from what bodily members are the male seed and the female menses drawn, taking the term *menses* for the seed which is emitted during sexual intercourse. It would appear that it comes from all members, for the fetus resembles its parents in all members. However, if this were true, it would follow that a person imperfect in his members would generate another imperfect individual, which is false. The falsity is apparent through experience, for if the father is blind, lame, or mutilated in his finger, he does not always generate a child similar to himself. Thus the answer is apparent. The seeds in coitus are drawn from the four principal members, namely the cerebrum, heart, liver, and female womb or male testicles, and as a consequence it is in these members and not in other parts of the body that the fetus is said to resemble the parents. I say, therefore, that the principal members suffice, as these influence other members, and they are especially drawn and distinguished by the cerebrum. Therefore we see that people who have a great deal of sexual intercourse have pain in the head and have their members dry out exceedingly, and their sight is especially weakened.

Commentary B

The text is referring to impure menses, which was discussed above, and this is unsuitable for the generation of the fetus. If a fetus were generated from this type of menses it would be leprous and fragile, and therefore it is forbidden for men to have intercourse with women during this time of month, and it is also very harmful to the male member.

In reference to sperm, note that it is defined by some as male seed composed from the pure substance of all members.

In response to the question of when an individual first becomes capable of performing the sexual act, some say that coitus begins in the fourteenth year. However others argue against this, stating that coitus flourishes in childhood to a greater degree than afterwards, and that therefore those who say it begins in the fourteenth year are wrong. They prove this by stating that childhood is hot and humid, and therefore it would follow that a child would have much seed. I say that this opinion is wrong, and as proof I state that there is another factor that prevents children from having sexual intercourse. In childhood the passages through which the sperm must leave the body are closed, however they are open during other stages of life.[32] In old age coitus rarely takes place because of the cold.

It is not good to have sexual intercourse after eating because the natural heat is diminished and the food cannot be properly digested, however the best time is after sleeping because digestion is then completed.

Some herbs and foods help coitus and others hinder it. The following are helpful: pepper, pennyroyal, fresh meat, egg yolk, the testicles of a fox, eastern saffron. The following diminish libido: cold foods, anise, rue, lettuce, melons, bitter grapes and similar substances.[33] Flax seed cooked with camel's milk when eaten acts as an aphrodisiac. According to Macer, if you boil together lentils and lettuce seed and drink this potion, it will kill all desire.[34]

Aristotle says in his book *On the Generation of Animals* that all animals except for the human female spurn coitus when they are pregnant.[35] The reason for this is that the woman has a memory of the past, and because of the exceeding pleasure she experienced she wants it again. Other animals do not remember and therefore they do not desire coitus. Another reason for the desire of pregnant women is explained in the text. According to some people, the mare desires coitus when she is pregnant because this animal eats a great deal and digests well. Therefore she has much seed, causing her to want sexual intercourse more than other animals do.

CHAPTER II:
ON THE FORMATION OF THE FETUS

Text

Now that we have examined the preceding questions, let us turn to the formation of the fetus in the womb. The first matter received in the womb has the nature of milk for the first six days, for the natural heat in the male sperm and in the womb causes it to become white as milk. Then that matter is changed to the nature or color of blood that is thickened, as if it were well cooked, and this lasts nine days. During the next twelve days the members of the fetus begin to be formed.

Commentary A

A question arises as to which members are first formed and generated in the fetus. On this point some say that it is the liver, because the first nourishment is in the liver, as is the quickening of spirits. Also, because the seed is drawn from the liver before the heart, it seems that the liver is first to be generated. However we say with Aristotle that the heart is generated first because it is the first to live and the last to die, and next comes the liver, and then the cerebrum, then the testicles, and the others follow.

Text

We note here that according to the philosopher each living thing is composed from the four elements, such that terrestrial matter is used for the composition of bones and watery matter for the watery parts of the body, and thus with the others. During the following eighteen days the face is formed by nature, and the body is disposed according to three dimensions, namely length, width, and depth. After this, nature begins to strengthen the fetus until its exit. This can all be summed up in the following verse:

> Its first six days are white and warmed
> Then bloody red for nine days' course
> In twelve its members almost formed
> Eighteen complete, then it gains force.[36]

Commentary B

Note that the fetus in a woman is in a similar position to a fruit on a tree, for when the fruit first forms from the flower it is fragile, and afterwards it hardens and adheres firmly to the tree, and does not fall easily. In the same way, the fetus, when it is first produced from the fertilized seed is attached by ligaments that are not firm, and it is easily expelled by a certain medicine or purgation. This is true during the first three months. When ensoulment occurs, then it adheres more firmly. Thus Hippocrates said that a pregnant woman ought not to have her blood let or be purged before the fourth month lest the fetus be destroyed.[37] Because of this, evil women instructed in this art draw blood as soon as they are impregnated, or take certain herbal decoctions in an attempt to corrupt the fetus, as we shall explain in more detail later on.

When the text talks about the four elements you should keep in mind that these elements have different natures, for one is gross and hard, like earth, and others soft and subtle. Air is an element ten times as gross as fire, and water [is grosser] than air, etc.

Note that with respect to the formation of the fetus the face comes first, that is of the extrinsic members, because the face of a human being is the noblest of these members.

After 33 days the form of a male or female appears, and after forty days the human nature is complete and the infant grows and opens his mouth, and his bones begin to enlarge from his natural heat. As the philosopher says in the 16th book on animals, the fetus first exercises vegetative operations because it is nourished and grows from the superfluity of the woman's food;

then it exercises operations of the sensitive soul because it perceives with its senses.[38] Thus Aristotle says that the embryo lives the life of a plant, then the life of an animal, and afterwards the life of a human being. After the fetus in the womb is fully mature, the child moves about forcefully and is sent to the point of exit, for nature begins to render the members apt for the task of leaving.

Text

There are some people who hold that during any specific period of time a certain planet is ruling. And because a knowledge of their science contributes much to what I have written in this book, and lest anyone think I am ignorant of it, I shall say something about this subject.

Note first that according to Avicenna there are three kinds of accidents.[39] The first group follows the matter in a composite, and forms [or accidents] are attributed to this matter.* The second follows from the composite of matter and form, and since this composite is a natural object made of matter and form, there are three bases for predicating accidents of it [nature, matter and form]. The third type consists of accidents ascribed to the soul [which is a form], for example the power of existing and moving. Since, according to the opinion of some who have spoken fittingly of nature, all the powers which the soul exercises in the body derive from the superior and celestial bodies (for from the highest orb, which encloses in its daily motion all the inferior spheres, the powers of existing and moving are communicated principally and radically to matter), the sphere of the fixed stars gives to the fetus a power varying in its form [or accident] according to different configurations and happenings of the heavens; and this power is suited to the fetus in virtue of the fetus having a form. But the fetus receives another power in addition to the power of existing and moving from that orb which gives it being, and this other virtue varies according to the diverse characteristics of this orb.

---

* Phrases in square brackets are not in the Latin text, but are added here in an attempt to make the argument clearer.

After the sphere of the fixed stars, Saturn comes next according-
ing to the astronomers, and it confers upon the soul the powers of
discerning and reasoning.[40] Following Saturn is the sphere of Jove
from which the soul receives generosity and many other passions.
Mars is next in line, and grants animosity, anger, and other
desires. Following their order, from the sun the soul receives the
power of knowing and remembering; from Venus concupiscence
and desire; from Mercury joy and delight; and finally from the
moon, the root of all virtues in lower nature, the ability to grow.[41]
Although these virtues and many other accidents stem from the
soul, and together with it follow from various influences of the
celestial bodies, we nevertheless attribute them to the soul,
although not to the naked soul, but to the entire composite, for a
simple substance cannot support an accident.

Now we must discuss the body and first we shall treat the
creation and formation of the body which is created from the
embryo and formed through the effects and operations of the
stars which are called planets.[42] First, the matter of the embryo,
or of the person who is being generated, is compressed and coag-
ulated through the coldness and dryness of Saturn. Thus the
power of growth and natural motion is transmitted by Saturn to
the matter of the embryo insofar as this matter is capable of
receiving it. Medical authorities tell us, therefore, that for a
period of a month or more after conception, depending upon the
nature of the seed, Saturn reigns, because by its cold and dryness
this planet constricts and consolidates the seed.

A question immediately arises from the preceding: does Saturn reign in the conception of every single embryo? For if it does
not, this would contradict what has been said above.

In response to this it should be noted that prime matter is
subject to the supercelestial bodies and their motions. And this is
what the philosopher says in the first book on *Meteorology*, that
all inferior things are caused by superiors, and governed by their
motions.[43] Thus it is necessary that these inferior things both particularly and universally depend upon superior things, understanding by universality the entire supercelestial body. First, inferior things depend in a universal way upon the superior bodies
because nothing is made from elemental matter unless by virtue
of the superior bodies. The commentator testifies to this in the

second book of the *Metaphysics* when he says that nature does not act unless it is governed by the supercelestial bodies, that is, by the intelligences.[44] Secondly, there is particular causation by superiors in the inferior realm when one part of the heaven has the property of introducing a certain determinate and special form, and another part, another form. This agrees with the statement of the commentator in the first book *On Generation and Corruption* that the generation of the elements and their parts is ordered and conserved through the motion of the supercelestial bodies, and through the motion of the elements which cooperate in a general way in the production of mixtures. The commentator adds, however, that individual animate beings and planets are of determinate causes and determinate as to existence.[45] And thus universally as well as particularly, inferiors are governed by superiors.

Since first matter is subject to the supercelestial bodies, it must take on the form of a certain species which has been determined by a particular part of the heaven. It cannot receive this form from the entire celestial body in common, because the whole celestial body is related to this matter or to that form indifferently [i.e., has no preference for one or the other]. Thus the same reason that would cause it to give form to one would also cause it to give others form, since all forms which are potentially in prime matter are in act in the first mover, as the commentator says in the twelfth book of the *Metaphysics*.[46] Therefore when matter is properly disposed there must be a certain determined part in the first mover, specially and primarily influencing the matter actually prepared for such a reception. Hence a particular physical cause does not suffice, even with the common influence and movement of heavenly bodies. This is evident because the seed which has been fully formed and hence detached from the man retains in itself the power of the one who produced it, and this power is not governed uniformly by the supercelestial bodies, such that one part of the heaven has no greater influence than another in the governance of this seed [because it would then be deprived of its own action, and, hence, of its own end]. And this is the reasoning of Aristotle in the second book *On Generation and Corruption* where he says when the sun ascends [the ecliptic in the spring] the animals revive, and when the sun descends [the ecliptic in the fall] the animals come to a stand-still.[47] This is also evident in the remarks of the commentator on the second book of the *Metaphysics* where he states that prime matter does not receive directly all forms indifferently, but first forms of elements, and, by means of these, forms of the composite.[48] But this order of forms that Averroes describes could not exist unless it were derived from a certain force governing matter and its reception of forms.

Commentary A

The text says that the seed which has been detached retains the force of the individual from whom it derived. This might cause someone to ask whether that detached seed is animated, and the answer would seem to be yes, for insofar as the seed is in the father, it is alive, possessing the life of the father, and if it has the same nature in the womb, it will be alive there. I reply that the seed which is poured into the womb is not alive formally, for it is neither a plant nor an animal, but it is alive naturally for when it receives a spirit it is brought to life.

You might ask, since it is inanimate, how does it produce a soul? The answer is through the mediation of the womb, which is animate, and through the mediating powers of the soul, in the possession of the stars and planets. According to Albert, these represent the spiritual influence and cause the images of men to be diversified, and thus it sometimes happens that a human being is generated with the head of a pig, because at that moment a certain star dominated which influenced such a disposition. Thus it was demonstrated that the image of a scorpion or a serpent was made on a certain stone because a particular star or constellation influenced it and impressed itself upon that figure. From this it happens that the images of certain signs carved in stones bring about the cure of some infirmities, as Haly tells us in the *Centiloquium* of Ptolemy, and he saw that the sculpted image of a scorpion cured a lesion made on a squire by a living scorpion,[49] and thus we see that whenever the dead entombed bodies of men lie for a hundred years or more without incineration this is brought about by the nature of the stars respecting that cadaver which is conserved without combustion. In addition, we can see from this that whenever best friends become enemies by one particular causal agent, this happens through the influence of the opposing planets to which they are subject.

Text

Thus we have made clear the proposition about Saturn, that is that it causes matter to be disposed, and introduces a certain form. When Saturn is said to reign in the conception of the embryo, it is meant that it communicates a particular disposition that another part of the heaven could not bestow. If Saturn is said not to reign in certain hours of the day or night, this means that its power ceases, and another planet or star influences matter in a way that Saturn could not, because active causes [or agents] act only on a subject that has been well prepared. And if anyone should ask why all things follow such a course, I reply that God has thus ordained them, who disposed all things in the beginning, and he has granted them a suitable power according to the requirement of their nature.

Commentary A

Note that in the text the author demonstrates that he is a Catholic, since he states that God disposed all things from the beginning. The philosophers, speaking from the point of view of nature, state that God disposed the planets and stars from eternity, and not anew each time.

Text

The next planet is Jupiter, which by its power disposes matter to receive the form of members. By its virtual and causal heat it reinforces the matter of the fetus, and by its humidity it fills those places which Saturn has caused to dry out during the first month. Thus the second month of fetal development is controlled by Jove.

   Third comes Mars, which by its heat and dryness forms the matter, dividing the arms from the sides and the neck from the arms, and forming the head. The third month is allotted for this operation.

Commentary A

Note that we read in the text that the head is formed from Mars before the heart is formed from the sun. According to medical authorities, the reason for this is that all principles of life are in the head, and therefore it is formed first. However Aristotle says that the heart is formed first, because the heart influences all the members.

Text

In the fourth month the sun exercises its power, impresses forms, creates the heart, and gives movement to the sensitive soul. This is in accordance with the statements of medical authorities and of certain astronomers, but, if we believe Aristotle, the heart is the first part of the body to be generated, and all other members derive from it.[50] Some go even further in this opinion, saying that the sun is the root of all vital power.[51]

Commentary B

Note that on this point there is a disagreement between the medical authorities and the philosophers, for the doctors say that the head is generated first, and the philosophers that the heart is. In the interest of finding an agreement between the two, you should know that each of them speaks correctly in different respects. With respect to perfect formation the head is formed first, for then the fetus is perfect. However with regard to imperfect formation the heart is generated principally. Thus, each opinion is saved.

In addition, note that the heart resembles the sun, for the sun holds the same position in the order of planets in the heaven as the heart holds in regard to the other principal members of the body.

Text

In the fifth month Venus by its power perfects certain of the exterior members and forms certain others: the ears, the nose, the mouth, the penis in males, and the pudenda, that is the vulva, breasts, and other members in females. It also causes the separation of the hands and feet and fingers.

In the sixth month the influence and reign of Mercury form the instrument of the voice, compose the eyebrows and eyes, and make hair and nails grow. From this operation of the sixth month arises the verse:

> Nine instruments to every child belong
> Two lips, four teeth, one palate, throat and tongue.[52]

In the seventh month, the moon brings the operation to an end, for it fills the spaces of the flesh with its humidity, and it completes the surface skin, for Venus and Mercury, bearing humidity to the entire body, give it nourishment.

Afterwards comes the influence of Saturn, who controls the eighth month. Saturn makes the fetus very cold and dries it out, and as a consequence compresses it, and for this reason some astronomers say that the child who is born in the eighth month is moribund or dead, as we will explain later.

Then in the ninth month Jupiter dominates, and delights the fetus by its heat and humidity. Thus the baby who is born in this month is strong and healthy and of long life, and his strength is caused by the heat, and his long life by the humidity.

It must be noted at this point that the members of the organic body are attributed to the twelve signs of the Zodiac. First of all, therefore, the sign of the entire celestial sphere is Aries. When the sun is enclosed in this sign and when its heat is moderate, it becomes hot and humid and causes generation. Therefore the motion of the sun in Aries is called the principle of life and the root of vital power. Because of this, man's head and his conditions are ascribed to Aries, for Aries is the most digni- fied part of the heaven because it is the first of the division of the sphere through twelve signs, just as man's head is called the wor- thiest part of the body. Thus it is fitting that the head is assigned to Aries. Another reason for this is that the sun as it courses through Aries causes it to become hot and humid, and the head in man is called the principle of the vital spirit.

The neck is attributed to Taurus, the shoulders and shoulder blades to Gemini, the hand and arm to Cancer, the chest and heart and diaphragm to Leo, the stomach, intestines, ribs and upper arms to Virgo. And these signs, which make up half the heaven, that is the northern part, rule over half the body. Libra begins the other half of the body, controlling the kidneys, and is therefore the principle of the other members. Scorpio rules over the place of desire, both in male and female; Sagittarius is responsible for the nose, the excretory organs, and the posterior; and Capricorn influences the knees and other lower parts. The shin bones are attributed to Aquarius, and, lastly, the formation of the feet and of the sole to Pisces. Thus I have briefly given the judgment from the twelve signs.[53]

Commentary B

The word zodiac comes from the Greek *zodion*[54] which is *vita* (life) in Latin and from *cos*, which means guardian, for it is the guardian of life. Under this circle and these twelve signs all planets move which influence the destruction and the salvation of things in the inferior realm. And you should know that these signs and grades of signs have different natures. Thus the fetus is disposed in different manners when it is generated under their influence....

Galen stated in the *Book on Sperm* that the diversity of planets with the difference of signs in the zodiac produces variations in the fetus.[55] This is apparent from the fact that sometimes a child is born who resembles neither father, nor mother, nor any other relative. Galen stated on this point that every animate corporeal substance is joined to the planets and the signs of the zodiac in that it receives their influence.[56]

Text

Let no one think that what I have described is fiction, for it can be proved by many experiments. Everyone knows that it is dangerous to wound any bodily member when the moon is in the sign that dominates this member, and the reason for this is that the moon by its nature increases humidity.[57] This is evident by the fact that if fresh meat is placed at night in the rays of the moon worms will be generated there. However, this does not always happen in the same way, but takes place especially in a particular state of the moon.

In order to understand this more clearly, note that according to Albert in his treatise *On the State of the Sun and Moon* there are four phases of the moon.[58] In the first phase the moon is hot and humid until the half moon, after this, hot and dry until the full moon. It becomes cold as it decreases to the half moon, and stays cold until it is joined to the sun. In this stage it causes great humidity, rotting humid things. At the point when the moon increases humidity in all the members if you touch one of the members with a sword [or surgical instrument] you can be sure that you are gravely hurting it, because if you add humidity to humidity you increase the damage.[59]

O my companions you should be aware that although certain women do not know the secret cause of what I shall describe, many women are familiar with the effect, and many evils result from this. For when men have sexual intercourse with these women it sometimes happens that they suffer a large wound and a serious infection of the penis because of iron that has been placed in the vagina, for some women or harlots are instructed in this and other ill deeds. And if it were right to talk about this, I would say something about them, but because I fear my creator I shall say nothing more about these secrets at present.

Commentary A

Here the author discusses some noteworthy points. Some women are so wary and cunning that they take iron and place it in the vagina. This iron wounds the penis, but the man does not perceive it at first because of the exceeding pleasure and sweetness of the vulva. Afterwards, however, he feels it.

A man should be especially careful not to have sexual intercourse with women who have their periods, because by doing so he can contract leprosy, and become seriously ill.[60] The veins from individual bodily members come together in the testicles, and therefore when the testicles are wounded the whole body is quickly affected. Thus, as Diasidus says, "If you knowingly go with a menstruous woman your whole body will be infected and greatly weakened, so that you will not regain your true color and strength for at least a month, and like a liquid adhering to clothes, this stink will corrupt a man's entire insides."[61] The venerable Hippocrates said in his book *On the Nature of Man*, "Do not go near a menstruating woman, because from this foulness the air is corrupted, and the insides of a man are brought to disorder."[62] Note that the author fears God, and he does not fully write down all the secrets, for he is afraid that someone might be able to make use of them for evil ends.

Commentary B

The menstrual flow varies with the different quarters of the moon, and thus women can tell the state of the moon by their menses. Some evil women know how subtly to inflict a wound on men when having sexual intercourse with them in the last state of the moon, and from this wound many incurable illnesses arise if remedies are not taken immediately. In the male penis all sensitive veins run together, and therefore when it is wounded the entire body is affected.

Note that in the text the author refers to iron, and some who are expounding on the text say that the iron of which Albert speaks is sharp and subtle. When women have their menstrual periods, the commentators claim, out of vindictiveness and malice they wish to injure the penis of the men who have sexual intercourse with them. Since there is menstrual blood in the vagina it enters the wound on the penis and infects it with its venom, because the penis is a porous and thin member which quickly absorbs this matter; and because all veins come together there, it is quickly dispersed through the body.

Although this explanation seems to go well with the text, nevertheless experience indicates the opposite, for the man is capable of feeling such an injury. Therefore this "iron" should be understood rather as a cauterizing substance, either of a potential or a virtual type, for according to medical authorities these are the two kinds of cauterizers. The first type consists of corrosive medicines such as alum or lime that cauterize the flesh or another member which they are designed to treat. The second type is actual, such as an iron instrument with which an incision is made in a bodily member to extract the humors from it. In reference to this text, I say that Albert means to discuss the first type of iron and not the second. And an example of this is that certain women who are knowledgeable about this matter place these corrosive substances in their lower members when they have sexual intercourse, and since the male member is extremely porous, it is immediately corroded and harmed by them.

Someone might perhaps wonder why the woman does not harm herself. One possible answer is that the vagina is not as porous as the penis, but a better guess is that before the woman uses the corrosive substances she anoints her member with oil of roses to protect it. If such a wound is inflicted when the moon is in its last quadrant in Scorpio, and there is a conjunction of the moon and Venus, it is incurable.[63] The reason for this is that Scorpio and Venus dominate over the penis, and therefore the humors cannot escape from the wound, and healing cannot take place.

Text

We can further demonstrate the effect of the moon in the fourth phase by another experiment. When the rays of the moon enter a room at night and fall on the head of a person asleep, they cause headaches and a flow of rheuma [a cold].[64] And we stated earlier the cause of this.

Commentary B

Someone might ask why this humidity causes pain in the head. The answer is that it brings about an obstruction of the pores in the cerebrum so that vapors and heavy fumes cannot escape. When nature begins to labor in order to dissolve this humidity that has flowed into the cerebrum, a flow of rheuma to the nose and chest results. This flow of rheuma is caused by the crude phlegmatic matter. Individuals who suffer this malady ought to eat, drink and sleep little so that a multitude of vapors from the superfluity of food, drink, and sleep does not end up directed toward the cerebrum, humidifying it, and augmenting the flow of rheuma. Thus the verse says: "You should hunger, thirst and keep vigil; thus you cure a cold."

This malady is the greatest when the moon is in the last quadrant, and during this period it is recommended that everyone take care lest the rays of the moon enter at night through a narrow opening when he is asleep and touch the head, bearing this infirmity, for according to medical authorities this is the mother of all sickness in the human body.

CHAPTER III:
CONCERNING THE INFLUENCE OF THE PLANETS

Text

Now we shall return to the influence of the planets, which the ancients call the gods of nature, over the bodies and souls of men.

Saturn, which is higher, thicker, heavier, and slower than the other celestial planets, causes the child who is born under its domination to be dark in color with flat, black hair, a tormented face, a thick beard, a small chest, clefts in his heel, and this is how his outward appearance is disposed. Insofar as his character is concerned, he is evil, greatly distrusting, malicious, irate, sad, and of wicked life. He likes foul-smelling things, and is always dressed in dirty clothes. He is not sensual, having little interest in Venus, whom, indeed, he abhors. Thus I briefly note that according to my teacher, who was learned in that science, whoever is born under Saturn has all the bad dispositions of the body.

Commentary B

Note that ancient philosophers called the planets the gods of nature because they say that through the influence of the planets corruption and generation occurred in the inferior realm. Further, before the time of Aristotle, they did not know anything about the first cause and the intelligences, but only about the celestial bodies and thus they said that these were the gods. On this point, Empedocles states that the sun is the god of gods. Another reason why the planets are called the gods in nature is because nature is ruled by them together with the intelligences, thus the commentator says in the twelfth book of the *Metaphysics* that the work of nature is the work of the intelligences.[65] However the intelligences do not direct nature immediately, but rather they do this with the planets and celestial bodies mediating, as Aristotle said that this inferior world is subject to the celestial bodies so that all its virtue is governed by them. Thus Aristotle said in the first book *On the Heaven* and in the eighth book of the *Physics* if motion did not exist in the realm of supercelestial bodies, then there would not be motion in the inferior realm, and thus there would be neither generation nor corruption.

Text

Jupiter is the regal star, dutiful, sweet, light, temperate, and prosperous. The child born under its domination is of the finest nature because he has been endowed with a beautiful face, clear eyes, and a round beard. It causes the two upper teeth to be large and evenly divided; it colors the face white mixed with red; and it makes the hair grow long. The temperament of the child born under Jupiter is good, honest, and modest. He will live a long time, desiring honor, appreciating beautiful and ornate clothing, and delectable flavors and odors. He will be merciful, generous, joyful, virtuous, and true in his word, with a proper gait and his eyes often cast down to the earth.

Commentary B

If someone is born in the hour of Jove he is sanguine, benevolent, likeable, delightful, wise, praiseworthy, and he has one friend and one enemy. His friend is the moon, and his enemy is the sun, for when he is joined to his friend the moon he rejoices and reigns, and this is a good time for him to begin a task because it comes to a good end. It is also the right time for him to speak with women, for he has plenty of blood. Experimentors say that if anyone should take a small bird which is called "quivering tail" and dry it into powder or burn it and place this dust in a crucible, if any evil woman is around she will bark like a dog.

When Jove is joined to the sun, he loses his powers. Thus it is said that if anyone should take the tongue of a dog and reduce it to powder and give it to a small bird in its food, the bird would die immediately. If you should take the head, the bird would avoid water.

Jupiter has death and life, for its death sign is Libra and its life sign Gemini. When it is in Gemini the individual is in his honor and lordship. At this time if anyone should take the hair and nails of a woman and pulverize them and eat them he would sleep a long time, and if someone should wish to wake him up, he should place vinegar in his right ear.

When Jupiter is in Pisces, if someone should take a salamander and reduce it to powder and place it in the ear of any animal, that animal would die immediately.

Text

Mars, since it is intemperate in heat and dryness, causes the new-born to have red, burned skin, appearing as if he has been out in the sun. He has short hair and small eyes, and a curvy body that is somewhat fat. In his character he is false, inconstant, shameless, irascible, arrogant, and a traitor, sowing discord and wars.

Commentary B

Note that when Mars reigns there is discord especially between kings and princes because their radical humidity is extremely subtle. Because Mars is very irascible, since it is of a choleric complexion, all choleric people are incited to anger, as appears in the *Book on Complexions.*[66] If an individual travelled straight upwards for ten miles a day, he would reach Mars in 43 years and 12 weeks and 10 days.

Text

The sun is a regal star, the light and eye of the world. The child born under its domination is plump, has a beautiful face, large eyes, pink and white complexion, full beard, and long hair. Some say that he will have an evil disposition and be a hypocrite; others that he will know a great deal. I have found still another opinion about the character of the child born under the sun—that he will be a monk, profoundly devout, wise, rich, cleaving to the good and avoiding evil.

    Venus is a benevolent star, and causes the newborn to be beautiful, with much flesh around the eyes and eyebrows, and of medium height. Insofar as his character is concerned, he is fawning, elegant, eloquent, and voluptuous. He likes music, joy and dancing; he is careful about the adornment of his body; and he walks dandily.

    Mercury, who the astronomers say follows the sun, is always limited by the sun's rays. It makes the child graceful in body, of just the right height, with a handsome, thin beard. In his spirit he will be wise and subtle, a lover of philosophy and study. His comportment and his speech will be flawless. Although he will have many friends, he will not be very wealthy. He will give good advice, and be sincere and faithful. He will shun infidelity, and never act as an accomplice in an evil deed.

Since the moon's motion is faster than that of the other planets, it makes the newborn a wanderer, true in his word, but not good for much. He will be gay, of medium height, with one eye bigger than the other.

It should be known that all stars and other parts of the supercelestial body carry out these influences through divine providence, and they do so unfailingly, and they cannot be dismissed as far as their own influence or action is concerned. Therefore it is just to say that all inferior things are governed by superiors. Terrestrial actions such as sacrifice to the gods and sacrifice of beasts cannot remove the power of granting life and death which is ascribed to the supercelestial bodies.

Commentary A

Someone might ask in what manner, how, and by whom are the stars thus ordered. The answer is that they are disposed in this way by divine nature, for God arranged the rule of the planets, and this is made apparent in the twelfth book of the *Metaphysics.*[67] The author holds that the course of the planets cannot be removed through fast and sacrifice of beasts. The proof of this is that the motion of the heaven is always uniform and regular, as we see in the seventh book of the *Physics*, and always invariable.[68] Therefore whatever God established from eternity will remain for eternity. It can be argued against this that Ptolemy and the theologians hold that a wise man has dominion over the stars, and this would not be true unless the course and effect of the planets could be altered. The answer is that a wise man dominates the stars when he sees a certain necessary effect of Saturn, such as cold, and then is able to beware of its harm, but he cannot simply impede their effect when they always act in a certain manner.[69] The author speaks in a natural sense, since he states that the effect of the planets cannot be removed through sacrifices, for the theologian holds the opposite opinion, that all things are in God's power, and God acts freely, and often listens to the prayers of the faithful.

Text

From these statements one might believe that I fall into a double sin. First of all, judging merely from the surface meaning of my words, one might conclude that I am stating that all things come from necessity. Secondly, one might label me as a person who obscures the Christian faith, however because I have fully explained about this, I shall leave it out here. I have spoken so clearly about the planets and other celestial bodies which influence inferior things that enough has been said on this subject.

Commentary B

Let the reader be warned that I leave out nearly one full page of this commentary, for Albert exposes some doubts which are better handled by the discipline of theology, and so I leave them out here.

CHAPTER IV:
ON THE GENERATION OF IMPERFECT ANIMALS

Text

In order to help the reader to understand better what I have said about the formation of many fetuses in the womb and about multiple births, I shall digress somewhat from the generation of man and take a look at the generation of imperfect animals, that is, generation not by seed but by putrefaction. These imperfect animals, for example flies, are not always generated in the same way as perfect animals are, for they are not formed by seed but from things that have rotted, as appears in the fourth book of the *Meteorology*.[70]

Many people wonder whether the same animals can be generated either from seed or without seed. For the opinion of Avicenna in the book *On Floods* is that the same animals can be generated both with and without seed, and the reason he gives is that another universal flood could take place in which all living things would be corrupted.[71] After this corruption celestial influences would work on the rotten cadavers of the dead and this heavenly power would cause the same type of being to be generated again. Thus the same species would have been born both from seed and without seed.

Avicenna demonstrates this possibility by an example from his experience. Take the hairs of a menstruating woman and place them in the fertile earth under the manure during the winter, then in spring or summer when they are heated by the sun a long, stout serpent will be generated, and he will generate another of the same species through seed. The same thing is true of a mouse which in Avicenna's own time was made from putrefaction and created offspring through seed. Many other explanations can be given, however what has been said suffices because it would be too long to tell about all that is relevant to this subject.

Commentary A

Note that a mouse which is generated from the rotting earth is fatter than one made from seed, and it has a longer tail, and is extremely venomous, for the matter from which it was produced was exceedingly putrid.

Commentary B

Note that when the text states that a serpent can be generated from the hairs of a menstruating woman, this type of generation cannot be accomplished in any time whatever, but must take place under a specific constellation, namely when the moon is in Scorpio or Aries, or when Venus is in Virgo. It is in this particular time that if you take the hairs of a woman and place them under the manure during the warm period of the winter, then when the sun comes out a serpent will be generated from the heated matter. The reason for this is that hairs are made from vapors that have risen to the cerebrum, and these humors are undigested in women, and they are poisonous because of the cold that remains in them. Therefore, from this type of rotting a serpent is generated.

A woman who has her menstrual period ought to hide her hair, because in this time her hair is venomous. It is naturally cold and humid because during the menses the defect of natural heat tends to move to the rear of the body. Serpents cannot be generated from the hairs of males because the humors in men are well digested so their hair is not poisonous nor does it rot as fast as a woman's does.

Text

Briefly let me state that Avicenna's opinion is not true. I give as a reason for this the statement of the philosopher in the eighth book of the *Physics* that just as each thing has its proper matter, so it has its particular agent, because each matter has its own form, and the act of the matter and the act of the form are distinct, as is stated in the eighth book of the *Metaphysics*.[72] Since these animals have different forms, they therefore have different matters, and as a consequence they will have different agents and generators. For the philosopher said in the seventh book of the *Metaphysics*[73] that the same animals, at least according to species, can be made from seed and without seed, just as health is sometimes brought about by art and sometimes by nature. But in this he differs from Avicenna, because Aristotle said that perfect animals were never made without seed; Avicenna, however, held that the opposite was true. They disagree because Aristotle says in the first book on *Meteorology*[74] that a universal flood would be impossible in nature either by fire or by water. Albert gives this reason for Aristotle's view: that a flood is caused by a humidifying constellation, therefore if such a constellation were to control one part of the earth, then another constellation, that is, one that dries things out, would have power over another part of the earth. Thus while one would be inundating one region, the other would dry out the other region, and therefore Avicenna's statement is impossible.[75]

Commentary A

Note that it is impossible for a universal flood to take place because the planets are not able to converge in that manner, but a particular flood is indeed possible. If it were to happen that all cold planets were to come together in the cold sign of Pisces, a flood might be generated in one region that respects that sign, for Pisces is of the greatest cold, but this universal flood could only take place miraculously. We read that a universal flood took place because of the evil of men, however this has nothing to do with our subject because we are speaking in a natural manner.

Text

Let us reply to this and state that some things are generated without seed, and the evidence for this generation is provided by the philosopher in the fourth book *On Meteorology* when he says: Heat disintegrating a body that has been composed causes the extraction of what is subtle and leaves behind what is heavy.[76] But this is not heat absolutely; rather it is the power of the celestial constellation. The philosopher's opinion is that the matter which makes up the animal who is born without seed is a certain subtle humidity on which the natural heat of the constellation acts. When this natural heat comes into contact with the matter that is destined to receive the form of a particular animal, it separates this humidity from the heavier terrestrial parts. Further, in the seventh book of the *Metaphysics*,[77] the philosopher states that this generation is univocal, virtually if not formally. This solves the objection that certain people raise when they say that everything which is generated univocally is generated from something of the same species. It is true, either virtually or formally, as has been demonstrated. Note in connection with this that many types of imperfect animals arise from the same matter, for example from horse manure there arise flies, wasps, beetles, and many others of different colors and shapes.

Commentary A

Note that according to Albert animals are generated from rotting matter as follows: When the heat of the sun extends to the rotting matter, it extracts the subtle humidity from that matter, and certain membranes are formed which prevent the interior heat from escaping. However, the power of the sun causes the heat that is in the rotten matter to seek an exit, which it is unable to find. From this motion up and down a certain pulsating spirit is generated, and by means of this spirit life is produced in the matter.

Text

Differences among animals are caused by the division of seed in the womb, and this is true principally in perfect animals. There are many cells in the mother's womb, and whenever the seed which has been emitted by the father collects in these cells so that each one gets a part of the seed, multiple generation has its beginning. Likewise, the start of generation in imperfect animals must be understood in similar fashion. In this case there is something in place of the womb and something else in place of the seed from which the above-mentioned humidity originates. This humidity is then divided according to the places from which it is extracted from among the rotting matter, and hence such animals as are produced become numerous and varied. The reason why these animals are similar is that a similar humidity is brought forth from the body in homogeneous parts. The differences in species among these animals are caused by the opposite, that is by humidity that comes forth in heterogeneous parts [presumably from various places].

Commentary A

Here the author states the reason for multiple births, and there are many causes of this. The first reason offered is that the seed is divided among the cells of the womb, but this is not sufficient, because midwives have observed that once a woman gave birth to a mass of flesh with seventy human faces, and it is certain that there are not seventy chambers in the womb.[78] The second explanation is that there is too much seed which is divided and scattered and creates many fetuses. The third cause is excessive motion on the part of the woman during coitus, for then the seed is dispersed all around and many fetuses are made.

Commentary B

Note that according to some people a woman has only two cells in her womb, one on the right and the other on the left, and it is designed this way because she has only two breasts, and thus can nurse only two babies. Others say that she has three individual cells, that is, one on each side and the third in the middle and they claim that because of this women are sometimes seen to bear triplets. Still others claim that there are nine cells, of which three are the principal ones and are located on the right, the left, and the middle, and each of these principal cells has two subsidiary ones. They claim that because of this a woman is sometimes seen to give birth to nine children. But you should be aware that there are only seven chambers in the female womb where the sperm is received, as Aristotle says in the *Book on*

Sperm, and therefore a woman can conceive seven children at once if the seed runs into all the cells during coitus.[79]

Text

Certain animals are created long and straight, and certain others short, and this is caused by the diversity of the humid complexion. From the hot and dry choleric complexion the body is made long, straight, and graceful because of the heat which is dispersed through it. From the phlegmatic, which is cold and humid, the animal becomes short and wide because the watery humor spreads out while the cold does not extend itself. The sanguine hot and humid yields an animal halfway between long and short, on account of the temperate heat and humidity. But from the melancholic there arises a straight and short animal, because cold does not permit itself to be extended and dryness does not permit itself to be dilated. Because of the burning nature of the choleric an animal is born that is long and exceedingly graceful because the fervor of its heat is greatly spread out, and the moderate dryness tempers it. And note that most frequently choleric is of a saffron color, sanguine is red, melancholy black, and phlegmatic white. And if something were of a mixed nature, its quality and color would necessarily be mixed.

Therefore we have shown in this chapter the manner of generation of imperfect animals in comparison with that of the perfect, and in what manner many fetuses are made at the same time both in imperfect as well as in perfect animals, and why one animal is long, and another is short, and why they are of a particular color most of the time.

CHAPTER V:
ON THE EXIT OF THE FETUS FROM THE UTERUS

Text

Now let us turn back to the subject of the generation and formation of the embryo in the uterus, and say something about the manner in which it leaves the uterus. First we must see how the three powers of the soul, namely the vegetative, sensitive, and intellective are conferred on the matter of the fetus, and in what order. This is really off the present subject, because it refers to the material in the book about animals, nevertheless let us briefly touch upon it.

The sperm collected in the womb immediately begins to grow when it has entered and the womb is well closed. Its nourishment or growth is caused by the vegetative power of the soul, and this vegetative power is derived from the father or from the one who engendered by means of sperm. This is evident in the second book *On the Soul*, where it is said that there are two operations of the vegetative power, namely to generate and to use food, because a plant generates a plant, and an animal generates an animal.[80] Thus it is seen that a generative power flows from the soul which helps and agrees with the generation of the embryo. Following this, in accordance with the requirement of nature, the sensible soul is added to the matter, and afterwards the soul of a particular species. The vegetative and sensitive powers are distinguished through their operations, and differ further through their objects, however they are not dissimilar in their essence to the point of forming two essentially distinct powers, for there is one and the same vegetable essence [from which they both stem], although in different respects, as the philosopher says in the *Book on Animals*, Chapter 16.[81]

The embryo first lives the life of a plant, secondly the life of an animal, and third the life of a particular species. Men have as well an intellective power, which derives not from matter but from the heaven. It is infused by the celestial forms, and from these celestial forms the end and perfection of all forms existing in the inferior realm derive. Now it is the custom among medical authorities to say that the first life is hidden and secret, the middle apparent and manifest, and the last indeed excellent and glorious. Natural sense derives from the first; animal sense from the second, which gives the man sense, sight, hearing, and voluntary motion; and from the third life comes the spiritual sense, which grants discernment, action, and other abilities.

The fetus leaves the uterus most frequently in the ninth month, but sometimes is born in the eighth, and sometimes in the tenth or eleventh month, but not later than this. Some women habitually give birth in the sixth month, and abortively, for they do not produce something with the nature of a man but rather a certain fleshy and milky matter. This can happen for a variety of reasons: either because the matter of the menses is corrupt, or because of too much motion on the part of the woman which breaks the womb, or on account of other evils that befall her. For this reason harlots, and women learned in the art of midwifery, engage in a good deal of activity when they are pregnant. They move from place to place, from town to town: they lead dances and take part in many other evil deeds. Even more frequently they have a great deal of sex, and they wrestle with men. They do all these things so that they might be freed from their pregnancy by the excessive motion.[81] The reason for their great desire for coitus is that the pleasure that they experience will help them blot out the grief that they feel from the destruction of the fetus.

Commentary A

A fetus that leaves the uterus in the ninth month usually lives because it is fully mature and strong enough, for the ninth month corresponds to Jove. Jupiter is the benevolent planet; it has a hot and humid nature and therefore it is the servant and messenger of life, for life consists in the hot and the humid.

The author states that sometimes birth takes place in the eleventh month, however this is not true, for women are mistaken in their calculations. Sometimes they conceive a mass of seed and then are impregnated again after a fortnight. They believed, however, that they were pregnant from the beginning, and at the second conception the first mass of seed is ejected.

When a child first leaves the womb he places his finger in his mouth because his nature requires him to. The reason for this is that when the baby leaves the womb it is like leaving a warm bath, and when he comes into the air he feels cold, so he places his finger in his mouth to warm it up. He also cries when he is born, because he suffers from the cold air. If he makes noise while in the womb this is a sign that he will not be born alive because the only cause for a child to cry in the womb is a certain lesion or pressure on him.

Commentary B

Note that the ninth month is the time specified by nature for the exit of the fetus, and the baby who is born in the ninth month is usually healthy and of long life, for in the ninth month he is mature. The astronomical cause, however, is that Jupiter disposes the fetus as was said above. But when the child is born in the eighth month he is sickly, and there are two reasons for this: first, because he is not yet mature, and second, because Saturn reigns over him.

When someone says that a woman gave birth in the tenth month, this is not to be understood absolutely, but only according to the estimation of certain women. Sometimes they think they are pregnant and they are not, although it is possible that they can bear a child in the beginning of the tenth month....

Whenever the fetus leaves the womb before the seventh month, this is referred to as a miscarriage. In the first month the fetus is not strongly fastened to the womb, and therefore is easily aborted, just like the fruit on a tree which in the beginning falls down for the slightest reason. There are many causes for this. First, if the matter of the embryo is corrupt and imperfect, a human being cannot be formed from it. Further, frequent motion and hard work on the part of the woman can loosen and corrupt the ligaments in the womb so that the fetus cannot be retained. It is for this reason that pregnant women are advised that they should not work or walk around too much. There are some evil women who are aware of this and counsel young girls who have become pregnant and wish to hide their sin that they should jump around, run, walk, and briskly move about in order to corrupt the fetus. Sometimes they produce an abortion by boiling down certain herbs which they know well. You should be aware, however, that corruption of this type causes extreme pain to the woman.

Text

It should be noted that young women are often affected by the fear which they experience from a thunderbolt in such a manner that the fetus, if it is alive, dies. If it did not yet have life, the lightning can cause the seed to lose its human form. The reason why fear would affect the fetus in this way is that it causes the woman's body to be changed and disposed to sickness, and thus the fetus is harmed and dies. Lightning, however, penetrates the interior part of the body, and destroys it by burning, without leaving any trace of this destruction on the outside because of the subtlety of the vapor. This vapor is sometimes so strong that it kills a man by penetrating to the vital inner members, yet the subtlety prevents it from leaving any trace of burning, so that it harms more by its blow than by its heat. The fetus is killed in this way because its natural interior disposition is affected and its radical humidity is consumed, thus causing its death.[83]

You should be aware that these things are not fictitious because Albert, in his passage on the operation and effect of lighting, tells us that a blow of lightning caused a shoe to be burned, leaving the foot unharmed, and the reverse.[84] It happened another time that a thunderbolt burned the pubic hairs, because a thunderbolt can penetrate the interior parts in the manner I have just described. Another proof that this can happen is that a venomous serpent that has been hit by lightning in a few days becomes wormy and rots, and the venom is taken away from this serpent by means of this celestial influence. A final demonstration is that a winecask hit by a thunderbolt will retain the wine for some time before it pours out. However to go into the reasons for these things is beyond the present topic.

Commentary B

The text especially speaks of young women because their bodies are thinner and more porous than those of older women, and so they are penetrated more easily. For this reason, they are advised to go to a hidden, confined place during a thunderstorm.

Someone dies from extreme fear for natural reasons, just as sometimes a person dies from great joy, which impresses itself on the natural heat surrounding the heart and extinguishes it. The same thing happens from exceeding fear, which often causes an abortion because the woman's body is greatly altered by the thunder, and the fetus in her womb is weak and therefore easily corrupted.

Many questions arise in connection with the present subject, and I leave to you the solution of these problems. The first is as follows: if, when a man and woman are having sexual intercourse, a thunderbolt strikes, can the seed receive a new impression at the moment of ejaculation which would dispose it to be something other than its particular nature intends?

Although the author does not answer these questions, we will. Lightning can affect the seed in two ways. The first way is that it can have a deadly effect on the power existing in the seed, causing the fetus to be entirely destroyed and thus aborted. The second way is that the seminal matter can be merely weakened by the blow, and in this case it is possible that some alien characteristics would result which the particular agent did not intend. A blow of lightning can render seminal matter incapable of generation, and the reason for this is that the blow causes the seed to become extremely dried out. This can be confirmed by what Albert says in the second book on *Physics* in the chapter on monsters where he relates that a woman once gave birth to a toad, and the cause of this was simply that at the moment of ejaculation the seed was infected and badly disposed by the lightning, because the vapor of lightning is sometimes poisonous.[85]

Text

Secondly, if the lightning strikes at the moment of ejaculation, can the influences of the planets be prevented, and are the male and female seeds equally affected?

Commentary B

To the second question we reply that it is possible for seed to be so altered and disposed by lightning that the newborn child would not receive the influence of the planets that it was due to receive at first. The reason for this is that the acts of active agents require a subject that is prepared for them. The answer to this question sufficiently follows the answer to the first one.

Text

Thirdly, if the lightning should strike both male and female matter alike, can it influence the power within the seed that causes a masculine form in what was first destined to be a female form and disposition, and vice versa?

Commentary B

To the third question we reply affirmatively, that it is indeed possible that by a bolt of lightning the disposition of a fetus to a male would be taken away and a feminine disposition introduced, and vice versa, for lightning is variously disposed and conditioned. Thus, according to Aristotle in the 16th book *On Animals*, woman is a failed male, that is, the matter that forms a human being will not result in a girl except when nature is impeded in her actions because of the disposition of the matter and of natural heat, for a particular nature always intends to produce a male and not a female.[86] If a female results, this is because of certain factors hindering the disposition of the matter, and thus it has been said that woman is not human, but a monster in nature.[87]

Text

During the seventh month, the fetus is frequently in good form, and motion is natural to it. If, however, it remains in the womb until the eighth month it is naturally disposed toward its birth, and begins to labor to leave the womb. Therefore, although it was healthy in the seventh month, and very active, if it leaves in the eighth month it will suddenly die, because of its great labor in the seventh month which weakened it. If, however, it is born in the ninth month, it is healthy, because it rested through the eighth month from the labors it experienced in the seventh.

Commentary B

Note that the child born in the seventh month can certainly live and the reason is that at this point all the planets have completed all their operations. It is better if he leaves the womb in the beginning of the month than at the end, because he is weaker at the end, after laboring all month toward his exit. But the baby who is born in the eighth month is moribund and poorly structured, for the reason noted above.

After the sixth month, the fetus is said to work toward its exit. The ligaments with which it is joined become weakened from the fact that they are greatly stretched out because of their great size and because they lack nutriment, for the fetus attracts all the food, and thus the ligaments are easily dissolved.

If a woman dies from an illness before giving birth, the infant in the uterus can live for some time if he can get air. Thus doctors say that the mouth of the woman should be held open with a certain instrument so that air can enter, and if the body is then opened the child will live. In this manner, the first person to be called "Caesar" was born. *Caesar* means "cut" (*caesus*) from his mother's womb.

When a child is born he immediately begins to cry. According to philosophers, this is because the baby finds birth painful because of the narrow openings, and also because of the cold air that he feels when he leaves the womb. If a child is male he naturally has a coarser voice than a female. Women say that a male cries "Ah! Ah! Ah!" because "A" makes a coarser sound than "E," and the opposite seems to be true of girls, for they have a thinner voice and cry "Ay! Ay!"[88]

Text

Certain women have more pain in childbirth than others, because sometimes the fetus presents its hand and sometimes its feet, and these are dangerous situations. In these cases the midwives carefully thrust back the hand or feet, and this causes great pain, weakening many women and causing death except to the very strong.

Sometimes in childbirth there is a rupture of the vulva up to the anus, so that these two openings become one. In this case experienced midwives use a certain unguent, rubbing it on the vulva, and skillfully push back the womb because the womb is often harmed and injured in the vulva. Therefore it is necessary that the women who assist in childbed be skillful, and expert in their work. I have heard from many women that when the fetus presents the head during birth, then the operation goes well, and the other members follow easily.

Commentary A

Note that when the fetus presents a foot or a hand, it cannot successfully leave the uterus, because then it is lying on one side, and it causes great torment. At this point women push it back, and the pushing causes the greatest pain. When the woman's vulva is narrow and the fetus is large, a rupture can occur up to the anus, and this happens especially in fat women because their fat causes a small and narrow passage.

Commentary B

The exit of the fetus from the womb can be hindered by many causes. Sometimes the reason is extreme cold or heat; sometimes the midwife is uninstructed, or the womb was wounded before conception. Other reasons are that the fetus leaves before its natural time, or the passages are narrow. This last occurs when the mother was a virgin before conception, because then she is not accustomed to bearing children, and she has greater pain than other women. Also, women who are extremely fat have difficulty giving birth because the mouth of the womb is coated with much fatty tissue. Difficult births are also caused by a fetus who is too fat or too large, or a fetus with a big head, or one with two heads (which actually happened), or if there are twins. As the text says, in case of problems with childbirth, it is helpful to apply aromatics to the woman's nose, for these aromatics attract the womb upwards and the child can exit easily.

Women know when they are going to give birth because some time beforehand a liquid flows from them and the reason for this is that certain membranes are ruptured. Women and doctors know well how to take care of this, however.

One might ask in what season of the year childbirth is easiest. The answer is that it is best in spring because then heat and humidity prevail and cause greater vigor in the woman. Some people say that summer is the easiest time because bodies are more refined in summer. However, I disagree with this because in my opinion the loose texture of the body does not make up for the decline in vigor that takes place in summer because of the evaporation of natural heat.

Note that according to Constantine there is a certain skin in the womb in which the fetus is enveloped and this is called the secundine[89] and it is generated with other skins from the seeds of generation.[90] Both in natural and unnatural birth it leaves the woman's body, but sometimes it is retained after birth either around the woman's member or in the womb. If this happens, it brings on many harmful effects because humors and smoke enter and produce pain, sometimes in the heart, sometimes in the head, and occasionally in the entire body.

Text

In connection with this subject the most curious question of all arises: how does the baby lying in the womb receive food, since the womb is closed up everywhere? The child is enclosed in the womb by a natural power which is hidden in the complexion of the fetus. The first thing that develops is a certain vein or nerve which perforates the womb and proceeds from the womb up to the breasts. When the fetus is in the uterus of the mother her breasts are hardened, because the womb closes and the menstrual substance flows to the breast. Then this substance is cooked to a white heat, and it is called the flower of woman; because it is white like milk it is also called the milk of woman. After being cooked in this way, it is sent through the vein to the womb, and there the fetus is nourished with its proper and natural food. This vein is the umbilical cord which is cut off by the midwives at birth, and thus we see newborn babies with their cord tied with a piece of iron. This is to prevent anything from leaving the baby's body from this vein, which is called the umbilicus, and which is suspended in the mother's womb with the amniotic sac.

Commentary A

Here the author raises a question, as appears in the text. Note that according to Aristotle in the fifth book of the *Metaphysics* that vein and the umbilicus ought to arise one after the other or at the same time, because the mother's womb and the child's umbilicus are joined by the mediation of that vein, so that the food travels through it from the mother's breasts to the umbilicus.[91] Note that in individuals who are well formed the umbilicus is directly in the center of the body so that through its mediation food is equally distributed to all members from the mother's breasts. And the word "umbilicus" is derived from "*umbo, -onis*" which is the middle part of a shield,[92] and "*ycos*" (guardian), for it is the guardian of the *umbo* in the middle of the body.

Another question is why the breasts are up high in women, and down below in other animals. The answer is that there are two reasons. First of all, if women's breasts were low on her body they would impede her walking, and thus wise nature ordered them in this manner. The cow, goat, and other animals have four feet, and thus their breasts do not hinder their passage. The second reason is that heat in women is dependent upon the heart, and this heat extends itself to the breasts which are situated in the chest next to the heart. In brute animals, on the other hand, heat depends upon the liver which transmits it to the breasts, and so they are underneath. In this way they are better milked by the fetus.

Someone might ask why men do not have breasts. The reason for this is that men do not have menstrual periods and they do not nurse babies, and therefore breasts are not necessary. They do have extremely small ones, just as women have very small testicles.

You might wonder whether small breasts are better than big ones. The answer is that medium-sized ones are the most beneficial. Large ones are not useful because the heat in them is diffused all over, and since they do not have much heat their digestion is poor. Small ones are not good because they have little nourishment.

The disposition of the fetus in the uterus depends upon the nourishment it receives, and for this reason pregnant women are told to stay away from strong drink, such as strong wine. This is hard to digest and does not agree with the fetus, since it is still very tender and weak.

Commentary B

Note that in natural as well as unnatural birth the fetus is wrapped in a certain membrane in which the superfluity of the second digestion, that is urine, is taken care of, and there is another skin in which the superfluity of the third digestion is received. However it is not necessary for there to be a third membrane to receive the superfluity of the first digestion, namely feces, because the first digestion precedes the second and third. And the reason for this is that the fetus does not receive its nutriment through the mouth and the stomach in which the first digestion takes place. Instead, the umbilicus receives the food, as is stated in the text. From the liver, pure blood in the form of

milk is transmitted to the liver of the fetus by way of the umbilicus and because pure blood does not have gross fecal superfluities, therefore the fetus enclosed in the uterus does not receive
feces, and as a consequence does not require a third membrane.

When girls are of marriageable age they grow breasts. Someone might wonder why women have breasts on the front part of
their body and other animals have them toward the rear. The
reason for this is that women are hotter in the superior parts,
namely around the breast bones, because of the heart and the
liver, so their breasts are placed there because the conversion of
menstrual matter into milk requires great heat. However, brute
animals that nurse their young have greater heat in the posterior
parts, so the answer is obvious.

Since some women are white and others black, the question
might be raised as to whether the milk of a white woman or a
black woman is more beneficial to infants. Aristotle replies to
this in the third chapter of the *Book on Animals* where he states
that the milk of a black woman is better.[93] The reason for this is
that black women have much heat, and the strength of this heat
causes the menstrual substance to be well cooked into milk. In
white women, who have less heat, it is not as well cooked.
Therefore, doctors state that the milk of black goats is better
than that of white goats.

Another question is, when the child is born, what happens to
the vein that joined the child to the mother at the umbilicus. The
answer is that nature and the heat of the mother consume it, and
when she becomes pregnant again the vein is generated again.
This vein is found not only in humans but also in brute animals
that nurse their young, although it is not as apparent in these
animals as it is in a newborn child who is tied with a thread
around the umbilical cord.

CHAPTER VI:
CONCERNING MONSTERS IN NATURE

Text

As Aristotle says in the second book of the *Physics*, just as there
are errors in nature, so there are in art.[94] This statement is very

pertinent to the present work and sheds light on our subject. Note therefore that monsters or errors in nature are those individuals of a certain species which in a certain part of their body are outside the bounds of the common course of the nature of the species, just as can be seen in men having only one foot or only one hand, etc. The miracle that philosophers are accustomed to call a monster of nature happens in many ways, either from too little matter, or from too much matter.

A monster can be caused by too little matter in different ways. The first way is caused by the matter itself. When the principal members of the child are to be formed and ordered, nature, who is wise and ingenious, does all she can to make them complete. She first forms the principal ones, and then applies herself to fashioning the others from the matter that is left. If there is too little, this will result in one part being smaller, and this is when the error occurs. Thus it happens sometimes that the head is sometimes bigger or smaller than the nature of that particular individual requires. If the quantity of matter had been sufficient, the head formed from it would have been in proportion to the nature of the individual, and to the other members. The same thing can be concluded about the other principal members, for there is a certain order in the production of these members, as natural philosophers and medical authorities testify.

Commentary A

Note that nature is twofold: nature of intent, and nature of production. Nature of intent does not err, because she always aims for the best. But nature of production sometimes errs, either because of an abundance or a deficiency of matter, with the result that monsters are produced because of this defect of matter. This happens in two ways, either because of a discrete quantity, for example sometimes a person is generated with one foot, or with four fingers in one hand. The other reason is because of continuous quantity, as when someone is produced with an extremely large head, or a very big hand. If this should happen through abundance, there are two methods: The first is according to discrete quantity, and in this way people are born with two heads or six fingers in one hand or similar things; and the second is through continuous quantity, as when someone is generated with a very large head, outside the common course of the species. Monsters are intended by nature through accident, and not through themselves, for if nature cannot produce five fingers in a hand, she produces four or three according to the requirement of the matter.

You might ask why monsters are brought into being. Philosophers answer to this that they are created for the adornment of the universe. For if different colors on a wall decorate that wall, so different monsters embellish the whole world. Monsters are caused especially by celestial influences, for whenever a special constellation reigns, different forms are influenced by it. Thus two twins have been formed who were joined in the back, having different heads or members, and distinct hands, but not feet, etc.

Text

In another way, insufficiency of matter can be seen to affect a special part [as opposed to a principal part]. For in the opinion of the philosopher every compound is made up of four elements, and the element of fiery nature is used to make up something with a fiery substance, and the element of earthy nature is used in something with an earthy quality, and thus with the others.[95] Someone might think that I mean by this that the elements exist formally in mixed substances. But this would contradict what the philosopher says in the second book *On Generation and Corruption*, where he claims that they are present there only virtually.[96] From this we can see that it is sometimes possible to have too little seed because of a particular impediment. If this impediment were caused by the earth, there would be a diminution in the bones which are formed radically from the earth, and thus with the other elements. For it sometimes happens that an individual is born with one foot, or with small arms, or with one finger, and other things of this nature.

If the opposite were true, that is, if there were too much matter in a mixed substance, another type of monstrosity would appear. For example, some people have eight fingers on a hand, or eight toes on a foot, or two heads, or something else.

Monstrosity is caused not only by too little matter, but also by a poor disposition of the womb. If the womb is slippery, defective, or harmful, it does not retain all the semen. Instead, it scatters it before the moment when the seed is all collected in a mass and the womb closes by force. Thus too little semen is received from which the fetus ought to be formed. This happens in many ways, however to go into them in detail would take too long, so I shall leave them out here, and say only that in this case the scarcity of matter is caused by the womb.

Some monstrosity is caused by an irregular form of coitus. For if a man lies in an unusual manner when he is having sex with a woman, he creates a monster in nature. I have heard tell that a man who was lying sideways on top of the woman during sexual intercourse caused the woman to produce a child with a curved spine and a lame foot, and the deformity was attributed to the irregular position.

Commentary A

Irregular and extremely violent coitus is to be avoided in order for the fetus to be produced in the proper manner, and to avoid having the seed be received in the wrong way in the womb. Coitus that is performed standing up is irregular in nature (although the unlearned do not care about this) because the seed cannot be received as it ought to be. From this it appears that there are many sins that are sins not only according to law but also according to nature, because nature intends to perform in a regular manner as it ought to.

Commentary B

Since so many imperfections result from irregular coitus, this act should be performed only for the purpose of having children. Further, medical authorities tell us that it is good to know the proper manner of having sexual intercourse, which is as follows. The man and the woman should be of compatible complexions, temperate in their qualities, and moderate in food and drink and in the other six nonnatural things, that is, motion, quiet, sleep, waking, and the rest.[97] Their food should be digested and its superfluities should be expelled; then after the middle of the night or before daybreak the male should begin to excite the woman to coitus. He should speak to her in a jesting manner, kiss and embrace her, and rub her lower parts with his fingers.

All this should be done to arouse the woman's appetitite for coitus so the male and the female seed will run together in the womb at the same time, for, absolutely speaking, women emit their seed later than men because of their coldness, and this often prevents conception. Then, when the woman begins to speak as if she were babbling the male ought to become erect and mix with her. At this time, the woman must remain absolutely still lest the seed be divided and a monster be generated. The man should copulate gradually; he should not raise himself up very much but rather should remain touching the woman's chest so that air cannot enter the lower members and prevent conception by corrupting the seed. After ejaculation the man ought to lie on top of the woman without moving for about an hour, so that the seminal matter does not scatter and form a monster, and he ought not to get up until the seed arrives in its proper place. After this, the woman should extend her legs so that the seminal matter can spread itself out, and her member should not remain open, because if the cold air enters, this can impede conception. Then she should lie quietly and sleep. If she lies on her right side after coitus this helps to conceive a male, and if she lies on her left side this will help to conceive a female.

Text

An error in nature sometimes happens from a superabundance of matter, which is the opposite of a scarcity of matter, and this occurs in many ways. Sometimes there is too much matter for every part, according to the requirement of both nature and form, and in this case many tortuosities and tumors appear in the members. The reason for this is that if nature has too much of the seed designated for the body or the head, she does what she is naturally capable of. Sometimes this results in two heads, and sometimes two feet, with one much larger than the other, or, most commonly she will create a lump on the breast, or sometimes on the back.

Commentary B

Sometimes a monster is created because of a universal efficient cause, for example from the celestial power of the first constellation. Galen tells us in his *Book on Sperm* that sometimes a constellation of an animal influences the human seed that has been placed in the mother's womb and causes a man to be generated with the head of a cow, a pig, or another brute animal.[98] The opposite can also occur; a human constellation influences the seed of an animal, and as a result an animal with a man's head is generated. Albert tells us about such a case in the second book of his *Physics*, "On Monsters," where he relates that once in a village he observed a cow give birth to a calf that was half human.[99] When the villagers learned of this, they assumed that the shepherd had had sexual intercourse with the cow and therefore they wanted to burn him at the stake. However Albert observed the planets and concluded that the monster had been generated by a special constellation so the shepherd was freed.

A monster of this type can also be caused by a special action of the imaginative power of a woman who is having coitus. It is possible that when such a figure springs to mind the fetus will be disposed in accordance with it. Thus Galen did not allow such figures to be painted in places where men and women usually have sexual intercourse, such as bedrooms, etc.

Text

The most surprising of all the cases which Albert told of was that of a child born with two sets of sex organs, one male and one female, so that he could either lie underneath a sex partner or participate actively from the top. This was caused by a super-abundance of matter because there was enough to generate both members. Avicenna and Albert tell us about the case of too much semen designated for the formation of such members as we shall show below.

Commentary A

Here he takes up the extraordinary phenomenon of hermaphrodites, and Albert says that a hermaphrodite has two members and can take the active and passive roles, not with respect to himself but with respect to another. This arises from the fact that there is too much matter for a single male member. The male member is always superior and the female inferior. You might ask why nature does not produce two male members and two female members. The reason is that nature, when acting on contingents, does what is best, and it is best to order them in this manner. Otherwise, one would always be superfluous, for if nature made two male members each could do whatever the other could.

In another vein, it often happens that a hen is generated with a member that is indisposed to coitus and as small as that of a cock. This happens from a defect of matter. If it happens that a female is produced without the appearance of a female member a skin is superimposed which must be removed.

Note that if a hermaphrodite appears to be closer to a male, he will live as a male, and if closer to a woman, he will live the life of a woman. He will not be able to participate in both sexes because it is against the law.

Commentary B

Nature always intends to produce a male, however when it happens that all the principal members of the fetus are generated from the seed and the matter is not properly disposed to form only a single male member, then a female member is generated afterwards. The hermaphrodite is always incapable of generation with respect to the male member.

The question arises whether a hermaphrodite ought to be called a man or a woman. One might answer that he can be called by either name because he has either sex, but this is incorrect; he should be called by the name of a man alone. The reason for this is that when a determination must be made about something, the worthier alternative should be chosen.

Text

Note that according to Avicenna if the semen falls in the left side of the womb a female is generated, and if it falls in the right side the child will be a male.[100] If it should land in the middle, however, a hermaphrodite, participating in both the nature of male as well as female, is conceived. The hermaphrodite is given the masculine species, for the male is the worthier, although he really has both natures.

Albert tells us that just as monstrous bodies are created, so are monstrous spirits. He gives the example of twins, one of whom had the power in his right side that no matter where he was carried, he opened all bars and closings. And the other had the power in his left side of closing all the locks that had been opened. (I am referring to the opening and closing of bars in the doors of houses.) The cause of this does not come from the matter, but from a special constellation of the heaven. But it does not derive from the constellation alone, but also from a special disposition of the matter to receive the impression, because active agents act only on matter that has been well prepared, as is said in the second book *On the Soul*.[101]

Commentary A

Note that there is greater heat in the right side than in the left, because the heart lies in the left and sends heat to the right. Therefore males are generated in the right side because of the heat, and the right side of the body is stronger and more vigorous than the left. Thus motion derives from the right as we see in the second book *On the Heaven*.[102] Because of this the right foot is slightly larger than the left, and similarly with the right hand, etc.

We have an explanation for the generation of Siamese twins joined at the back. Sometimes it happens that the seed is received in two cells of the womb, and the membrane that divides the cells is corrupted and the two seeds are joined at the back but they have distinct heads and distinct hands and distinct souls, and they ought to be baptized as two human beings.

Note that the celestial power operates in a wondrous manner, that is hidden in the inferior realm. Thus it is possible in two twins that the celestial power respects one twin in the right side, conferring such power that it endows him with the power of opening bars on doors without contact, because the affected part of the right side strongly alters the air, and the air alters the bar to the point of opening. People who have this power are often thieves, because they can open doors. Note that this is the cause of the difference, because the celestial power operates in matter as it finds it disposed.

Commentary B

Note that on a certain night Albert saw one special constellation and afterwards told the people who were present that if a child were born that night, he would be a master in the art of thievery. The group of people noted this, and wishing to prove it because they placed great faith in Albert's words, they conducted an investigation and found a certain infant born that night whose nature allowed him to open all bars that he touched as if they had been opened with a key.

Text

Let no one think that these things are false, because similar things can be seen in certain stones in which a particular constellation impresses the figure and form of a man or of another species, which is visible when they are divided.[103] Thus it is not strange that constellations affect twins, because, as can be seen, they influence other things as well.

All types of monsters can be reduced to two categories: those caused by disobedience of matter and those caused by insufficiency of matter. This is the opinion of Avicenna in the second book of the *Metaphysics*.[104] By disobedience I mean indisposition, which takes place when the matter is not well prepared and therefore does not obey the agent. By insufficiency I mean scarcity or impediment caused by the womb.

Commentary A

Note that the celestial power is multiplied in stones, for Albert tells that in Cologne he spied in a window a stone with the image of a king in it, and then a great king had to be born.[105] A human face is carved on many stones, and different medicines are made from those stones. If someone should sculpt the image of a fish on a stone when the sun is departing from Pisces, he can gather together all the fish in the water, that is in a specific time. Haly tells about different signs and miracles in the *Centiloquium* of Ptolemy related to the inscription or sculpting of stones.[106]

Text

Someone might argue that if monsters can be created, it would follow that nature, which is supposed to act with perfect regularity, would be deprived of an end. But I would reply with Avicenna that it is not always possible for a particular nature to bring all matter to its end, nor can it be conceded that privations of actions have ends.[107] Indeed sickness and death cannot be used as an argument, because they do not come from a particular nature, but rather from what rules that nature, that is, what philosophers who have fittingly spoken of nature call the intelligence. And we have said enough on this subject.

CHAPTER VII:
ON THE SIGNS OF CONCEPTION

Text

We have sufficiently treated the generation and formation of the fetus, and how this is accomplished, and many other incidental matters. In order to complete our topic we must note the signs of conception in a woman, which are many. The first sign is evident by the sexual act. If a woman feels cold and has pain in her legs immediately after coitus with a man, this is a sign that she has conceived.

Commentary B

Albert gives us many signs of conception here, but he does not give us the reasons for them. We can provide the reason for the first sign, however. At the moment of conception the natural heat in a woman travels from the rest of the body to the womb in order to warm and preserve the fetus that has been conceived. Since the kidneys are located next to the womb, the natural heat crosses from the kidney to the womb immediately after coitus. When the kidneys are deprived of heat, they become cold and painful.

Text

The second sign that she has conceived is if she emits little seed, or none.

Commentary B

The reason for the second sign is that after conception the womb is closed on every side, as we saw earlier, so that it can emit seed in only very small quantity. However, the opposite sometimes happens in some young women who have such great pleasure in sexual intercourse that their wombs open and emit a large quantity of seed.

Text

Another sign of conception is if the man feels his penis drawn and sucked into the closure of the vulva.

Commentary B

The reason for this is that when the woman conceives, her womb attracts the male sperm with all its power, just like a lodestone attracts iron, as we see in Constantine's third book of the collection.[108] The womb sucks in the penis, for it is attracting the sperm because of the great desire it has, and as a result the sperm does not flow out of the womb during coitus. Therefore if the penis is dry when it leaves the female member, this is a true sign that the woman conceived.

Text

Another sign is if the woman after coitus continually wants to have more. However this sign is valid only in certain women, because others desire to have more even when they have not conceived, as was seen above in one question.

Commentary A

After conception, the desire for coitus is caused by the menses. Another reason for this desire is the memory of the great pleasure that the woman experienced previously during sexual intercourse.

Text

The woman also knows that she has conceived if after coitus the menstrual period does not arrive in its accustomed way and there is a titillation in the mouth of the womb.

Commentary B

The reason for this sign has already been given, because when the womb is closed on every side the menses cannot flow, but rather they move upwards towards the breasts. The woman feels a titillation because the menses are retained in pregnant women, and they cause the womb to become warm. Thus, hot matter continually runs around the cervix, which is tightly closed. The woman desires to have sexual intercourse, but sometimes she cannot do so because her womb is closed. Since the opening has become extremely venomous, there is a titillation, and this sensation causes her to want sexual intercourse immediately. This is the reason why some women have a greater desire for sex after coitus than beforehand.

Text

Another sign is if the color of the face is changed from its usual appearance, for women are normally flushed after conception on account of the heat. Also, if unusual foods are desired, for example, if the woman asks first for earth, then for charcoal, then apples, then mulberries, then cherries; this is a sign that she has conceived.

Commentary B

The reason why the color in the face is changed is that during conception the entire complexion of the body is altered. This means that the blood is changed as well, and the woman's color becomes different as a result.

The reason for the last sign is that during pregnancy the stomach is greatly affected by venomous humors because the menses are retained. They act upon the stomach, causing an appetite for unusual foods, because similars seek out similars. Thus the story is told of the pregnant wife of a peasant who so greatly desired to eat the testicles of her husband that if she could not have them she wanted to die; and because she could not, she contracted a very serious illness. Therefore unusual foods ought not to be mentioned in front of a pregnant woman.

CHAPTER VIII:
ON THE SIGNS OF WHETHER A MALE OR FEMALE IS IN THE UTERUS

Text

Now we shall treat the signs of whether a male or female is in the uterus, and these are as follows. If a male is conceived, the woman's face is of a reddish color, and her movement is light.[109]

Commentary A

The reason for this first sign is that a red color is the sign of great heat, and if there is great heat in the womb then there is sufficient power to produce a male, and the woman moves lightly because heat is the beginning of motion.

Commentary B

The first sign is caused by the nature of the male, which is exceedingly hot and causes the woman to become hot. The heat causes good digestion, and this leads to good blood and then a reddish color. The reason for the second sign, that is, the light movement, is that this is to be understood with respect to women who are pregnant for the first time.

Text

Another sign of a male is if the abdomen protrudes on the right, and if it is rounded.

Commentary A

The reason for this sign is that a male child is carried on the right side because it is the stronger and hotter side, and thus the abdomen is rounded because it has been stretched and filled up.

Text

A further sign of a male is when the milk that flows from the woman's breasts is thick and well digested, such that, if placed on a surface that has been well cleaned it does not separate, but rather the parts adhere to one another instead of spreading apart.

Commentary B

Digestion of milk is caused by heat, therefore it is well digested and thick, and the parts remain congealed.

Text

Another sign of a male is if the milk of a pregnant woman, or a drop of her blood extracted from the right side, is placed either in a clear fountain or in her urine, and it goes straight down to the bottom. If it floats on the top, this is the sign of a female.

Commentary B

The reason for this sign is that the milk is well digested and the parts cohere and are not divided. Because it is so compact, it sinks to the bottom.

Text

If the right breast is bigger, the child is male; if the left breast is bigger the child is female. If salt is placed on the nipples and does not liquefy, this is the sign of a male.

Commentary A

When a woman conceives a male, her nipples are extremely hot, and heat tends to harden salt rather than liquefy it. This sign is especially true of the right breast.

Text

Another sign of the child's sex is if the woman moves her right foot first; then she is carrying a male.

Commentary B

The reason for this is that one always places the heavier foot first. We see the same thing happen in a person who has pain in a foot; that foot will be placed first. Thus the movement of the right foot first is a sign that the fetus is being carried on the right side. And, for the same reason, if a woman gets up from her seat and places her right hand first on her knee, this is a sign of a male; if she places her left hand first, this is the sign of a female.

Text

Other signs of a female child are: the woman is heavy and pale; her abdomen is of an oblong shape; it is round in the left side; the breast on the left side grows black; the milk it produces is black, undigested, bluish and watery; if it is poured on a stationary body it clearly divides into parts; if placed on a fountain or on urine it remains on the top, etc.

Another test is: if there is pain on the left side the child is always female; if it is on the right side the child is a male.

Another test that I know to be tried and true is as follows. If someone should wish to know whether a woman is pregnant, he should give her hydromel to drink. If she has cramps around the umbilicus, she has conceived; and if she does not, she has not conceived.

Hydromel is a drink which is made from water and honey. To prepare it take two spoonsful of water and one of honey and mix them together. The woman should drink this when she is going to bed or immediately afterwards. Since women who are aware of what is happening might tell you the opposite of what is true, the experimentor should say nothing about impregnation. He should rather wait until the woman complains of pain in the head or somewhere else, as women are accustomed to do, and then give her the drink as a remedy against it. In the morning he should ask if she has pain anywhere, and if she says she feels discomfort around the umbilicus, then a judgment of conception is indicated. If she replies otherwise, then she has not conceived. Some women, however, are so clever and so aware of the trick that they refuse to tell the truth, but rather say something else instead.

Commentary A

Here the author sets down a good sign of simple conception, and he describes a true experiment, as appears in the text. Note that the reason behind this experiment is that the honey obstructs the nerves and veins, and this obstruction generates pain around the umbilicus.

A sweet substance is not healthy, because all sweet fat is harmful, and the fat of fish is the worst because of its viscosity. Thus sweet substance floats in the stomach, and because the heat of the stomach is weakened on account of the fetus, the woman feels pain around the umbilicus after taking hydromel.

Commentary B

Hydromel is a sweet drink and therefore it cannot be easily digested because sweet things float around the opening of the stomach and this makes them hard to digest. There is one digestion that takes place in the bottom of the stomach where it is fleshy and hot, but in the opening the tissue is sinewy and it is cold. Therefore, a moderate walk is good after a meal to transfer the food from the opening of the stomach to the bottom.

The experiment described above comes from Hippocrates' Fifth *Aphorism*.[110]

The reason why women have less natural heat after they become pregnant than they did beforehand is that in the time of conception the heat flows from the stomach to the womb to help preserve the fetus, and finally it runs to the breasts, converting the menstruum into milk. Therefore, if a pregnant woman takes hydromel in the evening and drinks it this will cause cramps around the umbilicus and cause pain.

CHAPTER IX:
ON THE SIGNS OF CORRUPTION OF VIRGINITY

Text

Now let us take note of the signs of corruption of chastity.

Sometimes virgins are gravely corrupted so that their vagina is greatly enlarged because the male member is exceedingly large and inept. When this happens the woman's vagina becomes so widened that the man can enter there without any pain to his member, and this is a sign that the woman was first corrupted.

This is the reason why when young women first lose their virginity they have pain in the vagina for a time, because it is being enlarged and disposed for coitus. Another reason for this pain is that there is a certain skin in the vagina and the bladder which is broken. But the more they have sex, the more they become accustomed to it.

Commentary A

Another sign that is not noted in the text is that the vagina of a virgin is always closed, but a woman's is always open, therefore a virgin voids her urine higher up than a woman does. If you want to determine if a virgin has been corrupted, grind up the flowers of a lily and the yellow particles that are in between the flowers, and give her this substance to eat. If she is corrupt, she will urinate immediately. Another way to tell is to have her urinate on a certain kind of grass which is commonly known as "papel de mane";[111] if it becomes dry she is corrupt. You can also take the fruit of a lettuce and place it in front of her nose, and she will urinate immediately.

Commentary B

Note that in the text there are mentioned two causes relating to corruption in women, one of which is particular and the other common. The particular is that some young women suffer extreme pain when they are first corrupted because of the ineptitude of the male penis, and this is referred to as particular because it is not found in all women, and is rather a sign than a cause. The second cause is universal, because all virgins, when they first consort with men, have a certain membrane broken, called the hymen, and this is the guardian of virginity. It is located near the bladder and the opening of the womb above the vulva. This is a universal cause because it is found in all women when they are first corrupted.

The more women have sexual intercourse, the stronger they become, because they are made hot by the motion that the man makes during coitus. Further, male sperm is hot because it is of the same nature as air and when it is received by the woman it warms her entire body, so women are strengthened by this heat. On the other hand, men who have sex frequently are weakened by this act because they become exceedingly dried out.

CHAPTER X:
ON THE SIGNS OF CHASTITY

Text

The signs of chastity are as follows: shame, modesty, fear, a faultless gait and speech, casting eyes down before men and the acts of men. Some women are so clever, however, that they know how to resist detection by these signs, and in this case a man should turn to their urine. The urine of virgins is clear and lucid, sometimes white, sometimes sparkling. If the urine is of a golden color, clear and heavy, this is the sign of a temperament with an appetite for pleasure, however this is found in women who are not corrupted. Corrupted women have a muddy urine because of the rupture of the aforementioned skin, and male sperm appear at the bottom of this urine.

In menstruating women the urine is bloody, and when a woman suffers menstrual pain she has watery eyes, the color of her face is changed, and she has no taste for food. A man should beware of having sex with women in this condition, and prudent women know how to keep themselves apart, and remain separated from men during their monthly flow.

Commentary A

Note that the urine of virgins is clear, because they are hot and digest well, and urine takes on its color while crossing through the place of digestion, so it is colored in the kidneys. The experimentor should take the urine after the first sleep because then digestion has been accomplished, and he should take care that it is not variegated, that is with disease and thick nutriment.

There are three regions in the urine, the first of which is the upper, which we examine for the superior members, such as the cerebrum and the head. The second is the middle region, where the central members such as the kidneys and heart are considered. In the third, or lower region, the testicles, loins and womb are inspected. Thus the text says that the seed always appears on the bottom because of its heaviness.

Note that when a woman has her menstrual period, humors ascend to the eyes, because the eye is a porous part of the body, and experiences things immediately. At this time the woman becomes pale in the face and loses her appetite because her cerebrum and sense of smell are affected. It is harmful to have sexual intercourse with these women, because children who are conceived tend to have epilepsy and leprosy because menstrual matter is extremely venomous.

Commentary B

There are still other ways to tell if a virgin has been corrupted. If a girl's breasts point downwards, this is a sign that she has been corrupted, because at the moment of impregnation the menses move upwards to the breasts and the added weight causes them to sag. If a man has sexual intercourse with a woman and experiences no sore on his penis and no difficulty of entry, this is a sign that she was first corrupted. However, a true sign of the woman's virginity is if it is difficult to perform the act and it causes a sore on his member. This is only true, however, if she did not cause her vulva to contract by using an ointment or another medicine so that she would be thought a virgin, as many women are in the habit of doing. Another true sign of virginity is if the man feels the woman's seed flow abundantly. And there are many other signs that make use of herbs and stones which are known to those who perform these experiments.

Text

It should be noted that old women who still have their monthly flow, and some who do not menstruate, poison the eyes of children lying in their cradles by their glance, as Albert says in his book *On Menses*.[112] This is caused in menstruating women by the flow itself, for the humors first infect the eyes, then the eyes infect the air, which infects the child. This is the opinion of the philosopher in the book *On Sleep and Waking*.[113] What happens in women who do not menstruate is that the retention of the menses results in an abundance of evil humors, and old women no longer have enough natural heat to digest such matter. This is especially true of poor women who are nourished by coarse food, which contributes to the poisonous matter. Therefore non-menstruating women are even more seriously infected, because the menstrual flow has a purgative function.

Commentary A

Evil humors leave the body through the eyes rather than through another member because the eye is watery, as is written in Aristotle's second book *On Animals*.[114] This is evident because if the eye is pressed it begins to tear, and women cry a great deal because they have much humidity that their body must expel.

The eye of a soothsayer once forced a camel into a ditch. The evil woman knew so many bad things that evil humors were generated in her spirits, and they left her body through the eyes. The camel fell into a ditch in an attempt to flee these humors. In the same way, a lizard is infected by seeing himself, because he emits poison. If you take a looking glass which will reflect the humors back to the place where the lizard is he will be killed or infected by them.

Someone might ask why women do not poison themselves if they are poisonous. The answer to this is that venom does not act in itself but rather in its object. Therefore, since women are naturally poisoned they do not poison themselves. Another reason is that they are used to poison, for, as Averroes tells us in the prologue of his third book on *Physics*, some people were so accustomed to eat poison that it became their food.[115]

Commentary B

You can tell when women have their menstrual periods because they normally wear many veils on their heads at this time. The reason for this is that they have headaches and so therefore they try to protect their heads from the cold by covering them. Another reason for this is that women know that their color is not good in this time therefore they cover their faces so that no one can see them.

Menstruating women are also somewhat sluggish and do not enjoy sexual intercourse and similar things. When men go near these women they are made hoarse, so that they cannot speak well. This is because the venomous humors from the woman's body infect the air by her breath, and the infected air travels to the man's vocal cords and arteries causing him to become hoarse. It is harmful for men to have sexual intercourse with menstruating women because should conception take place the fetus would be leprous. This also frequently causes cancer in the male member.

Another sign that a woman has her menstrual period is if she looks at a new mirror a red mark like a vein will appear in it....

Note that old women ought not to be permitted to play with children and kiss them, because they poison them to such a degree that sometimes they die. The reason for this is that in these women the natural heat is so deficient that the menses collected in them cannot be expelled. Since these menses are venomous, they are continually borne to the eyes. Because of the porosity of the eyes, they infect the air, which reaches the child, for he is easily infected because of his tenderness. This infection is caused especially by old women and poor women, because old women do not work and poor women consume gross foods, and therefore their humors are more venomous.

Someone might ask, why do they kill infants more than adults? The answer is that the bodies of infants are more porous. But the question might arise, why do menses kill children and not the women themselves? The answer is that women of a certain age are accustomed to them, and so they are not harmed by menses, for illness is not caused by what you are used to. Thus Avicenna, in the fourth book of the *Canon*, tells of a certain young woman who was so accustomed to eat poison that she was entirely venomous, and she later killed many kings and lords who had intercourse with her.[116] One natural cause could be that nature always does what is best, and that she ordered the bodies of these women to be filled with menses for some time, so she saw to it that they could tolerate this. That this is possible naturally appears from poisonous animals, such as spiders and snakes.

CHAPTER XI:
CONCERNING A DEFECT OF THE WOMB

Text

Now that we have treated the menses, let us proceed to talk about the place where these menses are kept, because the womb suffers accidents. For example, it often suffers suffocation. Suffocation, according to medical authorities, is a compression of the vital spirits which have departed [from the body] because of a defect of the womb, resulting in a difficulty of breathing. This happens when the womb is taken from its proper place; then the resulting coldness of the heart causes the woman to suffer a syncope, that is, a weakness of the heart, and this is sometimes accompanied by dizziness in the head. The great doctor Galen tells about a certain woman who was suffering a suffocation of the womb so serious that it prevented her from talking, and she fell down as if she were dead, with no sign of life.[117] Many doctors were called who looked at her and, not knowing the cause of these symptoms, pronounced her dead. Galen then came on the scene, considered the cause, and freed the woman from this illness. This sickness happens in women because they are full of corrupt and poisonous menses, and therefore it is good that these women, whether young or old, often use men, so that this matter might be expelled. This is especially helpful in young women, because they are full of humidity. This is why young women, when they begin to have sex, become very fat before they conceive and have to take care of children. It is care or worry that makes one age [and therefore lose this humidity], as the philosopher says in the *Secret of Secrets*, and these women do not experience it.[118] Rather, they greatly desire coitus because of the abundance of matter that they have. Therefore it is a sin against nature to prevent this, and to keep them from having sex with the man they choose. This practice, of course, goes against custom, but that is off the present topic.

Commentary A

Note that suffocation of the womb is caused by the womb being displaced against the heart, and thus great cold is extended to the heart, so that the heart suffers a syncope. And "syncope" comes from *syn*, which means "with," and *copos*, which means "incision," because it is like an incision or a weakening of the heart. Another name for this is "ecstasy." This affliction happens most often to widows, women whose husbands are no longer with them, and so their menses become corrupted in the womb and thick humors are generated, which in turn produce weakness in the heart. Coitus is exceedingly beneficial to these women.

Commentary B

Suffocation of the womb, according to doctors, is the name for a compression of the respiratory members arising from a defect of the womb, for the woman's breath is compressed and impeded. This derives from the fact that the womb is separated and removed from its proper place. These women suffer a weakness of the heart from the cold that accompanies this malady. Sometimes they even suffer vertigo in the head.

Note that suffocation of the womb is a displacement of this organ toward the diaphragm which compresses the heart and the respiratory members, and according to the judgment of witnesses to this affliction the woman's breath is taken away. This is caused when corrupt and venomous vapors emanate from the womb and are raised upward and draw the womb up with them. These vapors arise from two causes. The first is from seed that is retained in the womb, and thus this illness is especially common in widows who were accustomed to have sexual intercourse, and no longer have it. It also happens to adult young women who have not experienced the venereal act. In this second case, it is caused by corrupt humors existing in the womb and then rising upwards.

From this infirmity, two others arise. The first of these is called syncope, and this is an illness which derives from a weakness of the heart when it is greatly debilitated from the suffocation of the natural heat and of the respiratory members. The other infirmity is called vertigo, and this is caused by corrupt vapors raised up toward the head and eyes and moving in a circular manner, giving the patient the impression that her head is being turned around in a circle.

You might say, since this happens in men, how do they contract it? The answer is that it is different in men and women, for in women it happens most often from a menstrual defect, whereas in men the reason is the stomach. A man's stomach is sometimes filled with bad humors, and these humors or corrupt vapors ascend toward the head, where this infirmity is generated. Sometimes women have this problem as well, so they can experience vertigo either because of their stomach or because of their womb. As Avicenna said, the womb of a female is like a sewer situated in the middle of a town where all the waste materials run together and are sent forth;[119] similarly all superfluities in the woman's body run together at the womb and and are purged from that place.

Women who suffer this illness lie down as if they were dead. Old women who have recovered from it say that it was caused by an ecstasy during which they were snatched out of their bodies and borne to heaven or to hell, but this is ridiculous. The illness happens from natural causes, however they think that they have been snatched out of their bodies because vapors rise to the brain. If these vapors are very thick and cloudy, it appears to them that they are in hell and that they see black demons; if the vapors are light, it seems to them that they are in heaven and that they see God and his angels shining brightly.

Doctors say that when this happens the woman's feet ought to be rubbed with salt, and she ought to be tickled under her arms and cleaned with a new linen cloth. Then one should tie her tightly at her thighs and place some foul-smelling substance at her nose, such as manure or even the smoke from human hair or from the soles of brute animals.[120]

This affliction sometimes happens to pregnant women, and then it is more difficult to cure. Note that young women consume more food than old women because they are hotter, but more food means more superfluities.

The matter specific to this illness is temperate in itself, but it becomes corrupted and transformed into the nature of poison. This happens when a woman who is accustomed to sexual intercourse no longer has it, and the matter which she had regularly expelled is retained in the womb and corrupted, and thus either the womb is suffocated or a mole is generated. This suffocation is caused more often by corrupt seed than it is by menstrual matter. The reason for this is that although there is a larger quantity of menses than of seed, the corruption of the seed is more effective than that of the menses, and so when it is corrupted larger quantities are affected and because of this they are poisonous.

The doctors say that closing up the nose for a short period of time is especially helpful in this disease because when the breath is held the downward expulsion becomes stronger. Although the body is generally affected by fetid substances, nevertheless they are very helpful here in the cure, because they cause the womb to descend. Thus you should prepare a suffumigation with good drugs, as the text spells out.

Text

During confession one of my comrades asked me why, when he slept with his beloved young girl, he found his abdomen covered with blood up to the umbilicus after the sex act was finished. He did not know the cause for this, and he did not dare to leave his beloved because of the great love between the two. Therefore, sometimes the flow of menses is beneficial to the woman, and sometimes it is harmful, depending upon whether the matter is more or less abundant. And that flow of which my comrade was speaking was not a flow of the menses, but rather a flow of seed during coitus because of an abundance of matter.

Commentary B

Note that when the text reads that it is very helpful to women to have a great deal of sexual intercourse when they have their menstrual periods, and yet it states as well that it sometimes harms them, this is owing to the difference in quantity of the menstrual material. Sometimes women have a great deal of menses, and coitus helps them greatly, but when they have only a little it is harmful. The reason for the first is that coitus aids greatly the menstrual flow, but if the menses are in small quantity, then this hurts the woman, for she loses too much blood, and is weakened.

CHAPTER XII:
CONCERNING IMPEDIMENTS TO CONCEPTION

Text

Now let us say something about the impediments to conception, which are many. An impediment sometimes happens from exceeding humidity of the womb, sometimes from great cold, and sometimes from dryness. Sometimes it is caused by excessive fatness of the body because fat surrounding the opening of the womb constricts it and does not allow the male semen to enter.

This can be seen in a woman whose kidneys are hidden and buried in fat on every side. If a woman of this sort receives semen during coitus, it cannot enter the womb, and so she ejects it with her urine. Thus if you examine her urine after coitus you will be able to tell whether or not the semen is collected in the womb. If it is, her urine will be clean and thin. If it is not, the urine will be thick, and of a different color from normal because of her intercourse with the man, for afterwards the semen is ejected with the urine. Sometimes it happens that the seed is not totally expelled in the urine, for if women are very hot they consume it by their own heat. Certain other women have wombs that are so delicate and well lubricated that they cannot retain the seed. There are many other causes of this, which I will not go into at present.

Commentary A

If the male and female seeds are not well proportioned in the qualities of heat and humidity, conception is impeded principally. The reason for this is that an agent and patient ought to be proportioned according to a certain harmony, that is, they ought to be in a fixed and determined combination, as Aristotle wrote in the second book *On the Soul*.[121] Substances cannot act upon one another indiscriminately, nor can they be made from one another indiscriminately.[122]

Commentary B

With regard to the text, a question arises whether a woman who is having sexual intercourse in a natural manner, that is with delectation, can be prevented from conception. The answer to this is no. In the production of any effect whatever, an instrument is necessarily required. If it is ordered and disposed in the proper manner, the production of this effect cannot be impeded, and this is the case with a woman who is with a man.

About this subject, you should know that conception in a woman can be prevented in one way because of superiority in the first qualities, that is, exceeding heat and dryness in the woman. The sign of women like this is that they have lips that are copper-colored, hard, round, and creased. Conception can be impeded in another way by exceeding cold and humidity in a woman, and these women are fat, somnolent, with flowing eyes. All women who have large veins above their eyebrows on the face are good companions, and thus with regard to the argument, I concede the major premise. To the minor premise I say, that although such women are well proportioned in their members, this is not sufficient, for a proper disposition of the womb and a temperate character to the seed in first qualities are necessary. The reason is that for conception it is required that the womb and the woman at the same time be in proper relation with the seminal matter from which the conceptus will be made. If they are improperly proportioned, conception will not take place.

Conception is impeded when the womb is exceedingly fat, and the reason for this is that then the male seed cannot enter the womb through its opening which is surrounded by a great deal of fat.

Note with regard to what Albert says Hippocrates stated in the second *Aphorism* that women who have cold, wet wombs cannot conceive because of the cold and wetness.[123] Women who have humid wombs cannot conceive either, because the seed escapes. Women who have burning wombs do not conceive because the seed is burned up in them.[124]

Uncleanness of the womb also greatly impedes conception for two reasons, one internal and one external. Internal impediment is found in some women whose wombs are fouled by exceeding superfluity so that they are not able to retain the male sperm. External impediment is often found in harlots, who continuously receive a great deal of seed from men, so that the sperm of one man corrupts the womb when it meets the seed of another man. It suffocates and extinguishes it, and as a result generation ceases.

Text

Note that the male is often the cause of infertility because his semen is as thin as water, and when it is poured into the womb it escapes because of its liquidity. This sometimes happens because of cold or dryness of the testicles, and according to medical authorities this semen is not fit for generation.

If you wish to know whether the man or the woman is the cause of infertility, take two pots and place the man's urine in one and the woman's in the other. Add wheat bran to each of them, and carefully close up the pots for nine days or longer. If the defect is in the man, there will be worms in his pot; or if you put a cooking pot on top of the container of urine you will find a fetid tree frog or fetid bran. If the fault is the woman's, menses will be found in her pot. If both are to blame, something of the aforementioned is found in each pot.

Commentary A

Women who have frequent sexual intercourse because of the pleasure that they experience from it produce weak fetuses. They should abstain from coitus and then they will have strong children who will become strong men, because then their seed will have enough vigor. For this reason, we see that one brother can be stronger than another.

The reason for the experiment [about infertility] is as follows: if the male's seed is extremely thin, it is quickly transformed into worms because it does not have the power of resisting the action of the celestial body. Since the humidity in the bottom is not dense and well hardened, it is soon altered.

Note that if the woman drinks sage that has been cooked for three days she will not conceive for a year because sage is cold. Let a woman eat a bee and she will never conceive.

I conclude from these that women as well as men often have sexual intercourse because of the great mutual pleasure that they experience, because the vulva in itself possesses an exceeding sweetness for the male, but I am saying nothing more about these matters at present.

Commentary B

Sometimes infertility is caused by a defect in the man's penis. For example, if it is too short the semen cannot reach the place it is supposed to. On the other hand, it can be too long, for, as Albert says in his commentary on the first book of *On the Generation of Animals* a penis that is too long prevents conception for two reasons.[125] First of all, it projects the seed beyond the proper place. Secondly, since it is a sinewy member it is cold in nature. Therefore the sperm becomes cold because of the long time that it must stay in this member, and conception is impeded. We can add a third cause, because after a penis of this sort ejects its seed to its natural place, because of its extreme length it divides part of the seed from the rest while it is moving and thus prevents conception....

Note that this experiment of Albert proves true when the individuals are made sterile by reason of bad complexion, for then the man's urine is corrupted and is deficient in natural powers. Thus, it easily putrefies and worms are generated. The same thing is true of the female menses.

If sterility were caused by another reason, namely the indisposition of the male penis, or if the woman had exceeding fat in the womb, then this experiment would not prove true.

Note that according to Averroes in the second book *On the Soul* in order for a person to conceive and generate three things are required.[126] First, she must reach the proper age. Second, her nature must not be deprived with respect to natural complexion and disposition, so that she is not extremely hot or cold and has no defect in any of the genital members. Third, she must generate by settlement of seed and not by putrefaction. If you want to know what is the proper age, the answer is found in Aristotle's fourteenth book *On Animals* where he says that males do not generate before fifteen years have passed, but a female is sexually mature when her menses begin to flow.[127]

Text

If someone should wish to help a woman so that she might become pregnant and conceive a male, let him take the womb and intestines of a hare, dry them out and pulverize them, and then let the woman drink this mixed with wine. Let him then perform the same processes with the testicles of the hare and give this to her at the end of her menstrual period, and then when she has sexual intercourse with her husband she will conceive a male. Then let her place a goat's hair in the milk of a female donkey and let her tie this around her at the navel while she has sex with her husband, and she will conceive. And I say this provided there are no other unknown causes or impediments. If someone should wish to know what these impediments might be, he has only to look at what we have just said on this subject.

Again, let someone take the liver and testicles of a small pig and dry them out and pulverize them and give them in a drink to both the man and the woman. If the man was first incapable of generation he will now generate, and the woman who could not conceive will become pregnant.

Commentary A

Note that if the womb and intestine of a hare are dried and pulverized they become very hot, and similarly a pig's liver is hot in itself, and these will generate heat sufficient for conception. This should be administered in the end of the menstrual period, because the womb is dry in this time, and somewhat hotter than usual because of the retreat of menstrual cold.

There are also other experiments. Let a woman take the herb camphor in a pulverized form and drink it with wine and she will conceive. If the urine of a man is drunk, it will impede conception. If she takes powder made from the vulva of a hare mixed with liquid honey, and adds a bull's heart, slowly bringing this to a boil, and consumes this during one week at a particular time of day, then she will conceive. The woman ought to eat good, hot foods, and she should become a little inebriated and should be well massaged,[128] and she should take care that her elevated legs do not cause the semen to spill out, so that she immediately exerts effort to retain it, and sleeps right afterward; in this case without doubt she will conceive.

Commentary B

The reason for the first experiment is that the drink can alter the temperament of the woman's seed, if it [this seed] contains too much cold, gross matter, by making it hot. This potion can also be interpreted as something that aids the entire process of conception, and therefore it would benefit any sterile women of the proper age.

One might ask how long one should wait after taking this drink before engaging in coitus. The answer is that the woman ought to drink the mixture of this powder and hot wine when she goes to bed, and then the man should have sexual intercourse with her the following morning at daybreak in the manner described above.

Note that there is a second experiment. Take wool that has been newly cut, [place it in the milk of a female donkey, and tie it around her navel during the sex act] and this helps in conception. The reason for this is unknown to us, however it is known to nature.

Thirdly, take some powder made from testicles [and give it in a drink to the man and woman], and the reason for this is that this substance greatly tempers the seed of the man as well as the woman, rendering it subtle and suitable for conception. Therefore, it benefits both sexes.

You should know that whoever wishes diligently to help a man or a woman in this matter ought carefully to consider the complexion of each. If the complexion is extremely hot, he ought to temper it with cold, and vice versa, and he ought to proceed similarly with other qualities and their opposites.

Text

If someone is in the presence of a pregnant woman he should take this precaution: He should never name in her hearing any food which might whet her appetite unless he can present her with it. Should he do so, this could cause a miscarriage, because the resistance given to her appetite would weaken and eventually kill the fetus. Therefore it is advisable that when a pregnant woman requests charcoal or something similar it should be given to her.

Commentary B

Pregnant women often desire unusual and foul smelling foods. The reason for this is that their stomachs are infected with evil humors, because the menses that have been retained flow to the stomach and cause them to desire foods that are similar to these humors. A woman sometimes craves something to such an extent that if it is not given to her the fetus dies because she is so weakened by the desire, or else the ligaments that hold it are dissolved and a miscarriage takes place.

Text

I know of the case of one pregnant woman who asked for a fresh apple, and, when she could not have it, took to her bed, and neither ate nor drank anything for a day and a night. She was surrounded by young women and maids who had not had children and did not know about these things, so, when they were presented with the request, replied that they could not find what she asked for. They told her this because, speaking among themselves, they decided that it was harmful to give her apples, since the same symptoms are observed in those who have a fever. However, they were mistaken about this. The pregnant woman was so weakened from the lack of apples that she gave birth to a stillborn child before term, having labored three days and three nights. Before the birth she had had nosebleeds for two days and one night, and the blood she shed was really menstrual blood, which is the sign of the sickness of a fetus. For, according to Hippocrates, it is impossible for the fetus to be healthy if there is a menstrual flow.[129] Therefore in order to avoid these dangers, one should keep watch over a pregnant woman, and see that she moves about only moderately, that soft, light foods be offered to her, and that she be given everything her appetite desires.

Commentary B

The reason for this is that when a woman is pregnant, as we have said, the menses move towards the breasts and are transformed into milk that nourishes the fetus in the uterus. Since in this case the fetus was dead, it did not require nourishment, and so the menses moved upwards and were expelled through the nostrils. If a pregnant woman had a great deal of blood then a nosebleed would not harm her, but rather it would benefit her because it would relieve her. This occurs often in young women who have much blood, and especially in the beginning of the pregnancy when the fetus does not yet need a large amount of nourishment.

Text

Before we turn to another topic, we must note one further sign that a pregnant woman is carrying a male. Take clean water from a clear, pure fountain, and place in this water a drop of blood or of milk taken from the right side of the woman. If the drop sinks to the bottom, this is the sign of a male; if it remains on the top, the child is a female. Again, if the right breast is larger than the left, she is pregnant with a male; if the left is larger, she is carrying a female.

Commentary B

Now it is time to bring up the topic of how to assist a mother in childbirth, but this topic is a medical one, and so is omitted here.

The reason for the first experiment is that the blood and the milk of a woman who is pregnant with a boy are well digested. As a result of this, they are thickened so that their parts adhere together and fall down to the bottom of the water. But this milk must be taken from the right breast because it is better digested there, for there is greater heat near this breast. Someone might object that the left breast is hotter than the right because the heart is on the left. Since the heart is hotter than the liver which is on the right, this experiment cannot be valid. However the reply to this objection is that even though the heart is located more towards the left side, it has greater influence over the right side. Therefore, all members on the right side are nobler than those on the left side.

Another question is how can men who are refined and well put together father unattractive, clumsy children and vice versa. The answer is that when a man has sexual intercourse immediately after eating and drinking heavily the child who is generated is gross in both body and soul. However, when coitus takes place after the food has been digested, the offspring is refined and capable.

Another question is why do some men always father girls even though their seed and the female seed are both sufficiently well disposed to generate boys. One possible answer is that this is caused by the fleshy construction of the penis, so that in some men their seed tends to be projected to the left side of the womb.

LAST CHAPTER [CHAPTER XIII]:
ON THE GENERATION OF THE SPERM

Text

Before we bring this work to a close, so that our teaching might be more complete, let us say something about the matter of sperm in man, since we have already treated menstrual matter. We shall have much to say on the subject of sperm, which can be defined as excess food which has not been transformed into the substance of the body.

The first thing we should note about the production of sperm is that according to medical authorities there are four digestions in man: one in the mouth, another in the stomach, the third in the liver, and the fourth in individual bodily members which must be nourished and must grow.[130] Natural philosophers disagree with the doctors on this subject because they believe that the primary—that is the last digestion—which is best and most perfect, takes place in the heart.

The first digestion, which takes place in the mouth, is nothing other than a thorough chewing of the food. According to medical authorities, the reason why nature has given teeth to man and other animals is so that they might use them to chew their food. To animals lacking teeth, nature has provided two stomachs on their upper jaw, one to contain the food, and the other to collect the nourishment that must be ruminated, so that the other principal members of the body might aid digestion and refine the food, sending it on to replenish individual bodily parts according to their need. This happens all the time by natural heat working continuously on the humidity in bodily matter to accomplish the necessary restoration.

In man digestion is more refined, for, in accordance with his nature, which is most excellent among all living things, there are many digestive operations. In the second digestion in man the food is refined and divested of its own form, and then takes on another form, and the coarse matter is separated from the finer. Some of this substance, which is now soft and porous, is sent on to the liver where it is refined even further by its own heat, and is assimilated by its own proper action together with the natural heat of the blood. When the matter thus produced by this digestion is drawn in by any and all members as nourishment, then replenishment is accomplished through nourishment, growth, and reparation of losses.

We should note that this loss takes place in individual members by means of heat continually acting upon humidity, and consumes it by this action, making it evaporate. Animal life is made up of the hot and the humid, as we see in the writings of medical authorities and in many philosophical writings as well, especially in the book *On Death and Life*.[131] Therefore it is necessary that an animal make use of nourishment or food, for otherwise he would be corrupted, for heat always acts on the humid making it evaporate, as we see written in the book *On Youth and Old Age*.[132]

Commentary A

Note that man has the best and most subtle digestion because he possesses great heat, and because of these many labors he digests and consumes humidity, for heat acts on humidity as a subject and causes the radical humidity to evaporate. There must be a readjustment of this heat lest it consume the radical humidity and cause death, for no medicines can help when the radical humidity in which life consists is consumed.[133] Note, however, that an individual can live for a year or longer without food through the healing art, as has been experienced, but this cannot be done except according to the common course.

Commentary B

Note that according to everyone, doctors and natural philosophers alike, animal life is like a burning lamp or a candle, and there are two things required in order that they burn, namely the heat of fire and oil or some other fatty substance. For as long as the oil or other fat on which the fire continually acts lasts, it burns, unless perchance it is impeded by something outside which extinguishes it. In a similar manner, animal life lasts as long as the radical humidity, which is continually consumed by natural heat, endures, unless the individual is violently killed by a sword or something similar.

Text

A question arises from what we have described, namely when the heat acts upon the humid by consuming it, is this an operation of the heat, insofar as it is heat, or insofar as it is virtual, or insofar as it is natural? In reference to this we should note that according to Albert in his commentary on the fourth book of the *Metaphysics*, or in the *Meteorology*, in the chapter on the operation of active qualities, heat has a threefold operation.[134] The first operation of heat in its capacity as heat is to dissolve; to compress and bring together what is homogeneous and to separate what is heterogeneous.[135] This can be seen if we take a mass composed of gold and silver and place it in a fire; the heat of the fire will make the gold flow from the silver and the silver from the gold. Aristotle spoke to this effect in the second book *On Generation* when he said that heat accomplishes less than instruments.[136] The operation of heat in its capacity as virtual heat contains in itself the formative power of each nature whose heat it is said to be. Thus there is contained in this heat the power of the heaven and of the celestial movers, and the power of the complexion or the form of that nature, both of which give it its form. In the same way, doctors claim to see [the form] in the heat of the seed of a plant or an animal, where there is located what is called the formative power of the plant. I believe that the same thing is true of men.

Finally, heat in its capacity as natural heat must digest the humid duly subjected to it according to the requirement of the particular species. Therefore, since it does not draw out the humid by consuming it, heat in digestion is to be understood not in its capacity as heat but rather in its capacity as natural heat because in this digestion the humid is brought to its end in the species of that of which it is the humid [matter], for example, as species of a part of a plant or an animal or a woman. It would not be able to do this in its capacity as heat, for in this case it would give a new form to everything which terminates dryness.

Having discusssed this topic, now let us return to our basic proposition and say that sperm is nothing other than excess food which has not been transformed into the substance of the body. From the above remarks we can see more clearly the definition of sperm according to terms which we previously did not understand. When in man, digestion (especially in its third stage) of so much takes place that not everything is used to replace what has been lost and becomes restoration, the surplus is sent in the color of fine clear blood to the seminal receptacles or genitalia, where it is fermented and whitened by the power of the testicles. Therefore male sperm is of a white color on account of the last refining process which is attributed to the testicles.

Once this sperm has been ejected by the man, the body becomes exceedingly dry because sperm has the power of humidifying and heating. When the body is dried up and its humidity extracted, its life is weakened, and as a consequence its powers are weakened and death takes place. This is the reason why those who have a great deal of sexual intercourse do not live for a long time because their bodies are deprived of their natural humidity, and this drying out is the cause of death. Having given the cause, therefore the effect follows as well.

This agrees with what Aristotle said in his book *On the Length and Shortness of Life* that the body dries out when sperm is ejaculated, and he adds that this is the reason why a mule lives longer than the horse or the donkey from whom he is generated, and why females live longer than males if the males have sexual intercourse.[137] He further adds that male sparrows live shorter lives than females, and he comments that it is generally true that males live longer than females if they do not have sexual intercourse, as we see in the book *On the Length and Shortness of Life*.[138] Therefore we see the meaning of the philosopher that life consists in the hot and the humid, and fundamentally so, although other qualities help instrumentally in vital functions. Therefore it appears that coitus dries out men and many other animals.

Commentary B

Note that someone can engage in so much sexual intercourse that he emits not only sperm, which is a superfluity of nature, but also those substances which are necessary for life, such as blood. This can cause death.

Text

We must mention other things about the nature of sperm, namely that the sperm of a man is sometimes hard and well cooked by the testicles with the result that the parts adhere to one another just as the parts of pitch cohere, and this sperm resembles white milk that has congealed to a great degree. Nevertheless, it is fluid in nature, not in its individual parts, but in the genital receptacles, for otherwise it would not be expelled from these receptacles into the vulva of women, and from this type of sperm, as medical authorities testify, is produced a strong and robust individual. However when the sperm is somewhat thin and fluid in its individual parts such that it has not been well cooked, if it is ejaculated and received by the womb a fetus of thin and fragile nature is made from it, and the sperm resembles thin, watery milk.[139]

Commentary B

The sperm of those who rarely have sexual intercourse is well digested. Those who are having sexual intercourse for the first time are quick to generate, and especially to beget males, because the sperm has been cooked for a long time in the testicles.

Text

Now, to be complete, let us review what has been said in this book. First we treated the generation of the embryo; second, the progressive formation of the fetus in accordance with celestial influences; third, the influence of the planets with respect to both the body and the mind; fourth, the generation of animals without seed; fifth, the formation of the embryo; sixth, the generation of monsters; seventh, the signs of corruption; eighth, the signs of chastity; ninth, the malady of the womb that is known as suffocation; tenth, the impediments to conception; eleventh, aids to conception; twelfth and last, the generation of the sperm.[140]

The manner in which these chapters have been arranged in orderly succession is apparent throughout this book, and these are all the topics that I thought pertained to the subject in question. I would say with the commentator on the third book *On the Soul* that if this book does not appear to be complete, it is, nevertheless, a beginning of completeness.[141] Thus I request that all my brothers who read this essay record their questions, and perhaps in this way they will find some truth in what I have written; if it seems incomplete, let the search go on through further questions.

Let us therefore bring this work to an end, and give thanks to God who has enlightened our understanding and that of our readers beyond the understanding of those who never read this work, for they are like those who do not know what they want, as is evident enough from the second book of the *Metaphysics*.[142]

NOTES

INTRODUCTION

1. Lynn Thorndike, "Further Consideration of the *Experimenta, Speculum astronomiae* and *De secretis mulierum* ascribed to Albertus Magnus," *Speculum* 30 (1955): 427–43.

2. Brigitte Kusche, "Zur 'Secreta mulierum' Forschung," *Janus* 62 (1975): 103–23.

3. Margaret Rose Schleissner, *Pseudo-Albertus Magnus: Secreta Mulierum cum Commento, Deutsch. Critical text and Commentary.* (Ph.D. diss., Princeton University, 1987), p. 9.

4. In 1922 Ernest Wickersheimer gave an incomplete list of fifty-five manuscripts containing this work. Ernest Wickersheimer, "Henri de Saxe et le 'De secretis mulierum,'" in the *Proceedings of the Third International Congress of the History of Medicine* London 17–22 July 1922 (Antwerp, 1923), 253–54. The list was supplemented by Lynn Thorndike, *A History of Magic and Experimental Science,* vol. II (New York: Columbia University Press, 1923), pp. 749–50, and by Lynn Thorndike and Pearl Kibre, *Catalogue of Incipits of Medieval Scientific Writings in Latin,* (Cambridge, Mass.: Mediaeval Academy of America, 1963).

5. For a full discussion of the term *vulva* and its translation, see Danielle Jacquart and Claude Thomasset, *Sexuality and Medicine in the Middle Ages,* tr. Matthew Adamson (Princeton: Princeton University Press, 1988), p. 24.

6. Ernest Wickersheimer has shown that Henry of Saxony did not compose one of them, as some early editions claim, but he does not identify the author. See Wickersheimer, "Henri de Saxe," pp. 253–58.

7. See, for example, f. 2r where the term *menstruorum passiones* is substituted for *nocturna pollutio* and three of the reasons for this phenomenon are included in the text.

8. This point is elaborated on in Benedict M. Ashley, "St. Albert and the Nature of Natural Science," in James A. Weisheipl, ed., *Alber-*

tus Magnus and the Sciences: Commemorative Essays 1980 (Toronto: Pontifical Institute, 1980), pp. 73–102.

9. See Ashley, "St. Albert and Nature," p. 93.

10. Albertus Magnus's contribution to medieval western awareness of the discrepancies between Aristotle and Galen is discussed by Nancy Siraisi in "The Medical Learning of Albertus Magnus," in Weisheipl, *Albertus Magnus and the Sciences:* pp. 399–401.

11. Luke Demaitre and Anthony A. Travill, "Human Embryology and Development in the Works of Albertus Magnus," in Weisheipl, *Albertus Magnus and the Sciences*, p. 408.

12. M. Anthony Hewson, *Giles of Rome and the Medieval Theory of Conception. A Study of the De formatione corporis humani in utero* (London: Athlone, 1975), pp. 51, 153.

13. Chapter XII: Concerning Impediments to Conception.

14. On this point see Jacquart and Thomasset, *Sexuality,* Chapter I: Anatomy, or the Quest for Words.

15. See Ilza Veith, *Hysteria: The History of a Disease,* (Chicago: University of Chicago Press, 1965), p. 2.

16. On this topic see Vern Bullough, "Medieval Medical and Scientific Views of Women," *Viator* 4 (1973): 496; Helen Rodnite Lemay, "William of Saliceto on Human Sexuality," *Viator* 12 (1981): 177–78.

17. Anthonius Guainerius, *Tractatus de matricibus* in *Opera Omnia* (Pavia, 1481), f. x4r.

18. *Dilecto sibi in Christo socio et amico N. clerico de tali loco,* Strasbourg (Argentine), 1510, edition. Lynn Thorndike discusses various versions of this dedication in "Further Consideration," p. 428.

19. Chapter Two: On the Formation of the Fetus.

20. Chapter Four: On the Generation of Imperfect Animals.

21. Thorndike, "Further Consideration," p. 437.

22. On the connection between Thomas of Cantimpré and Albertus Magnus, see S. D. Wingate, *The Mediaeval Latin Versions of the Aristotelian Corpus, with Special Reference to the Biological Works* (London: Courier, 1931; repr. Wm. Brown, Dubuque, Iowa), p. 78, p. 107 n. 72.

23. Giovanni Romagnoli, "Una questione multisecolare: L'opera 'De secretis mulierum' attribuita comunemente ad Alberto Magno è

autentica o apocrifa?" in *Atti del XXIV Congresso Nazionale di Storia della Medicina*, Taranto-Bari, 25–28 Settembre 1969, pp. 407–8.

24. Monica Helen Green, *The Transmission of Ancient Theories of Female Physiology and Disease through the Early Middle Ages*, Ph.D. dissertation, Princeton University, 1985, p. 202.

25. On this point, see Helen Rodnite Lemay, "Women and the Literature of Obstetrics and Gynecology," in Joel T. Rosenthal, ed., *Medieval Women and the Sources of Medieval History* (Athens: University of Georgia Press, 1990), pp. 189–209.

26. Et suo modo accidit forte quod si vir eiecerit urinam ad radios lune citus coitum et statim de hinc cum mulier cohyerit si concepit ipsa abhorriciet post hoc non formam humanam sed quandam massam solidam carneam in cuius egressu adeo laborare poterit ut in partu quod a quadam honesta femella didici in confessione sociali et quod pluries quam semel acciderit affirmabat. MS Paris B.N. lat. 7148, f. 4v. The phrase "in confessione sociali" is ambiguous. It may refer to a form of pastoral counseling, and therefore provide further evidence for the clerical nature of this treatise.

27. Christoph Ferckel, *Die Gynäkologie des Thomas von Brabant* (Munich: Carl Kuhn, 1912), p. 10.

28. Bartholomaeus Anglicus, *De genuinis rerum coelestium, terrestrium et infernarum proprietatibus* (Frankfurt: Wolfgang Richter, 1601; repr. Frankfurt: Minerva, 1964), pp. 234–35. On Bartholomaeus Anglicus see R. James Long, *Bartholomaeus Anglicus on the Properties of Soul and Body (De proprietatibus rerum, Libri III et IV)* (Toronto: Pontifical Institute, 1979), Introduction.

29. Vincentius Bellovacensis, *Speculum naturale* (Duaci: Baltazaris Belleri, 1624; repr. Graz: Akademische Druck-u. Verlagsanstalt, 1964).

30. Vincentius Bellovacensis, *Speculum naturale*, cap. XXXIX, cols. 2321–22.

31. Brian Lawn, *The Salernitan Questions: An Introduction to the History of Medieval and Renaissance Problem Literature*, (Oxford: Clarendon, 1963), pp. 3, 80.

32. Brian Lawn, *Salernitan Questions*, pp. 229, 230.

33. Lorenzo Minio-Paluello, "Aristotle," in *Dictionary of Scientific Biography*, vol. I (New York: Scribners, 1970), p. 250b.

34. Aristotle (pseudonym), *The Problems of Aristotle with Other Philosophers and Physicians*, (London: printed for W. K., 1670).

35. Albertus Magnus, *Quaestiones super De animalibus*, ed. E. Filthaut (Monasterii Westfalorum in Aedibus Aschendorff, 1955), pp. 204–07.

36. See Schleissner, *Pseudo-Albertus*, p. 97 n. 22.

37. See Jacquart and Thomasset, *Sexuality*, p. 127.

38. Aristoteles (pseudonym), *Secretum secretorum*, (Venice, 1553).

39. Michael Scotus, *De secretis naturae* (Lyons: Quadratus, 1580), p. 263.

40. Thorndike, *History of Magic*, vol. II, p. 741.

41. See M. D. Chenu, "*Exemplaria* universitaires des XIIIe et XIVe siècles," *Scriptorium* VII (1953): 68–80.

42. Michael Johnson, "Science and Discipline: The Ethos of Sex Education in a Fourteenth-Century Classroom," in Helen Rodnite Lemay, ed., *Homo Carnalis: The Carnal Aspect of Medieval Human Life*, ACTA, vol. XIV (1987) (SUNY Binghamton: CEMERS, 1990), pp. 162–64..

43. Jacquart and Thomasset, *Sexuality*, p. 129.

44. Citations of Aristotle in the *De secretis mulierum* do not correspond to the standard editions. Pseudo-Albert often refers, for example, to "the sixteenth book on animals." Benedict Ashley has pointed out that Albertus Magnus used the Michael Scot translation of Aristotle's works in which the nineteen books of the *Historia animalium, De partibus animalium*, and *De generatione animalium* are all lumped together. Presumably pseudo-Albert relied on this translation as well. See Ashley, "St. Albert and Nature," p. 94.

45. Albertus attributes this information to Empedocles. Albertus Magnus, *Physicorum*, ed. A. Borgnet, II, iii, tex. 82, p. 168.

46. See notes to the text for details.

47. Chapter IV: On the Generation of Imperfect Animals. See also Commentary B, Preface.

48. Avicenna, *De caelo et mundo, De animalibus*, in *Opera philosophica*, Venice, 1508.

49. Avicenna (ps.) *Avicennae ad Hasen regem epistola de re recta*; *Tractatulus de Alchimia* in *Praecipuos selectorum auctorum tractatus de Chemiae et Lapidis Philosophici...* vol. IV (Argentorati: Zetzner, 1659). The *De congelatione et conglutione lapidum*, also in this volume, does not discuss spontaneous generation.

50. Thorndike, *History of Magic*, vol. II, p. 137.

51. Thorndike, *History of Magic*, vol. III, p. 479.

52. *G.A.* II, 4; 738b 20.

53. Ibid., II, 4; 738b 20. For a discussion of the implications of Aristotle's doctrines for medieval medicine see Anne-Liese Thomasen, "'Historia animalium' contra 'Gynaecia' in der Literatur des Mittelalters," *Clio Medica* 15 (1980): 5–24.

54. *G.A.* II, 3; 737a 10ff.

55. See Nancy Siraisi, "Medical Learning," p. 392, and Luke Demaitre and Anthony A. Travill, "Human Embryology," p. 415, both in Weisheipl, *Albertus Magnus and the Sciences.*

56. Joseph Needham, *A History of Embryology* (New York: Abelard-Schuman, 1959), pp. 70–73.

57. Needham, *History of Embryology,* pp. 70–73.

58. See Wingate, *Mediaeval Latin Versions,* p. 72ff.

59. Siraisi, "Medical Learning," pp. 391–93, Demaitre and Travill, "Human Embryology," pp. 408–9.

60. "Et putant homines quod Aristoteles putaverit quod sperma viri non esset pars pueri neque immixta cum materia pueri, sed hoc non fuit eius consilium. Sed suum consilium fuit quod involvatur cum materia et profundatur in materia ut sit operator membrorum; educat idoneam materiam ad membra, et erit illud sperma materia spiritus in creatura quia efficitur multum subtile et habile ut transeat in spiritum. Et Galienus et sui sequaces obviant Aristotelem et dimittamus istam explanationem, licet sit vera. Et dicamus etiam quod sperma sine profundatione operator sit in menstruo sanguine et non sit sperma mulieris operans sed materia, et videamus quid dixit ille medicus contra Aristotelem putans se aliquid dicere cum nihil dixerit; licet sciverit multum de ramis, ignorans radices scientie." Avicenna, *De animalibus* in *Opera Philosophica*, Venice, 1508, f. 41.

61. "Et nos mirati sumus supra illud quid olfacit medietatem cuiuslibet rei, et dixit se scire phylosophiam." Avicenna, *De animalibus*, f.

41rb. "Et stultus est quod dicit quod eo modo operatur matrix." f. 41va. "Et mentiebatur ille quod dixit quod causa forme fuit aut sperma aut sanguis." f. 41 vb. "...in isto syllogismo divisivo est falsitas." f. 41vb.

62. Avicenna, *De animalibus*, f. 42.

63. "Et preterea ad quid facti sunt testiculi in muliere, et vasa spermatis si non sint utilia ad creaturam. Dixit et nos iam invenimus vasa spermatis in muliere plena humiditate spermentali, nisi quod illud sperma est magis humidum quam sperma maris. Dixit et iam vidimus mulierem patientem suffocationem matricis propter abstinentiam a viro et eius coitu, deinde evacuabatur a spermate multo." Avicenna, *De animalibus*, f. 41rb.

64. "Sed ille qui dixit quod sperma propter sui viscositatem fuit generans ossa et nervos bonus esset quod diceret." Avicenna, *De animalibus*, f. 41va.

65. Demaitre and Travill, "Human Embryology," p. 411; Needham, *History of Embryology*, p. 86.

66. Demaitre and Travill, "Human Embryology," p. 417. Danielle Jacquart and Claude Thomasset also point out Albertus Magnus's inconsistency on the role of male and female seed. See "Albert le Grand et les problèmes de la sexualité," *History and Philosophy of the Life Sciences* 3 (1981): 80.

67. "Est enim unum de accidentibus dolor inguinis ex multa constrictione matricis et tunc ex calore spermatis pellis generatur circa duos humores, et quia virtus quae operatur, est in spiritu, non est improbabile quin totum vel maior pars spermatis virilis convertatur in spiritum propter sui subtilitatem, et ingrediatur in humorem muliebrem sicut in suam materiam: et tunc infra pellem dictam format eum et distinguit in membra: ad humorem enim muliebrem convertitur quando propter circumdantem pellem et cooperturam matricis coartatur. Primum ergo quod distinctum ante omnia generatur ex spermate, est pellis circumdans et custodiens sperma, ne diffluat, et custodiens spiritum et calorem ne evaporet.... Impossibile est enim naturam non maximam habere sollicitudinem de spiritu tali et loco ipsius, quia aliter ipso dissoluto vel debilitato periret totum opus." Albertus Magnus *De animalibus*, ed. Hermann Städler in *Beiträge zur Geschichte der Philosophie und Theologie des Mittelalters* 15 (1916): 719–720.

68. Petrus de Abano, *Conciliator*, Diff. xxxvi (Venice: Luceantonij de Giunta, 1522), f. 51vb. Discussion of some later treatments of the opposition between Aristotle and Galen may be found in my "Mas-

culinity and Femininity in Early Renaissance Treatises on Human Reproduction," *Clio medica* 18 (1983): 21–32.

69. The family to which the Lyons, 1580, edition belongs consists of those editions containing Commentary A.

70. "Istis autem visis accepta via una Aristotelis et alia medicorum nihil hic determino." *De secretis mulierum* (Venice, 1508), f. A6vb. This statement is found in editions that contain Commentary B, e.g. Venice: Jo. Alvisium de Varisio, 1501; Vienne: Joannes Winterburg, before 1506; Liptzk: Melchior Lotter, 1500.

71. The noncommittal stance is found in MS Utrecht 723, f. 50v; MS Munich CLM 22297, f. 23; MS Munich CLM 22300, f. 62.

72. "Aristoteles autem voluit et alii phylosophi quod semen ipsius patris non cedit in substantiam foetus; sed disponit semen ipsius matris ad formationem embrionis, et postea dicunt ipsum evaporabiliter exhalare et ista est sententia auctoris." Commentary B (Venice, 1508), f. A6ra. See also the Venice, 1501, edition, f. A6ra.

73. See Richard Lemay, "Origin and Success of the Kitāb Ṭamara of Abū Jaʿfar Aḥmad ibn Yūsuf ibn Ibrāhīm," in *Proceedings of the First International Symposium for the History of Arabic Science, 5–12 April, 1976* (University of Aleppo, Institute for the History of Arabic Science, 1978), vol. II, 91–107.

74. Instead of the printed text's "antiqui vocaverunt deos naturae" in Chapter III, MS Paris B.N. lat. 7148 states: "Arabes, tractantes de constellationibus, dominos naturae vocaverunt." f. 4v.

75. Avicenna, *The Metaphysics of Avicenna*, tr. Parviz Morewedge (New York: Columbia University Press, 1973), ch. 9, p. 26.

76. "Notandum est quod dicit Avicenna in ii. sue sufficientie quod accidentia sunt in triplici genere." MS Munich CLM 22230 f. 63v. "Nota quod dicitur Avicenna in suo sufficientie...." MS Munich CLM 22297, f. 25v.

77. See the earlier section entitled "Sources."

78. "Quod autem lumen sic incorporatum diversas induat qualitates vel, quod melius dicitur, qualitatum virtutes, probatur in luna, cuius lumen scitur esse receptum a sole, et tamen quando diffunditur a luna, tunc est frigidum et humidum, cum bene sciamus idem lumen in sole esse calidum et siccum." Albertus Magnus, *De caelo et mundo*, ed. P. Hossfeld, in *Opera Omnia* VI, 1, ed. B. Geyer (Monasterii Westfalorum in aedibus Aschendorff, 1971), p. 29.

79. See Richard Lemay, *Abū Ma'shar and Latin Aristotelianism in the Twelfth Century: The Recovery of Aristotle's Natural Philosophy through Arabic Astrology*, American University of Beirut, Publications of the Faculty of Arts and Sciences, Oriental Series, no. 38 (Beirut, 1962), xxxix–xl.

80. "Porro Luna cum fuerit in prima quarta mensis erit calida humida, et in secunda quarta erit calida sicca, in tertia vero quarta erit frigida sicca, et in quarta erit frigida humida." Abū Ma'shar, *Introductorium maius in astronomiam* IV, 5, tr. John of Seville, ed. Richard Lemay (Naples: Istituto Universitario Orientale, in press). "Nam corpora animalium in tempore augmentationis Lune...fiunt fortiora, eritque in eis calor et humiditas, effectus quoque et incrementum vincet in eis. Post impletionem vero fiunt corpora debiliora et frigus vincet in eis, eruntque commixtiones que sunt in corpore hominis, ut sanguis et flecma et cetera, quamdiu duraverit in augmentatione luminis sui in superficie corporum ac venarum, et augebunt exteriora corporum...humiditatem et pulcritudinem; cum vero minuitur lumen Lune, fiunt hi humores in profundo corporis ac venarum, et augebit superficies corporis siccitatem." Abū Ma'shar, *Introductorium*, III, 9.

81. "Verbum 20. Dixit Ptholomeus. Tangere membrum ferro et Luna in signo illius membri verendum. Expositio. Iam convenerunt astrologi quod Luna auget humiditatem in omni membro [MS membrum] ad cuius signum mutatur. Et tangere membra ferro est illa vulnerare, et addere vulneri humiditatem multiplicat nocumentum." Aḥmad ibn Yūsuf, *Centiloquium*, MS Paris B.N. lat. 7307, f. 5v. I am grateful to Richard Lemay for citations from the *Centiloquium*.

82. "Quia dum prolixius sederit homo aut dormierit in lumine Lune in nocte, generatur in corpore suo pigritia et laxatio et excitatur in eo catharrus et dolor capitis." Abū Ma'shar, *Introductorium*, III, 9.

83. See Richard Lemay, "The True Place of Astrology in Medieval Science and Philosophy: Towards a Definition," in Patrick Curry, ed., *Astrology, Science and Society* (Woodbridge, England: Boydell and Brewer, 1987), pp. 71–72.

84. "Verbum 1. Scientia stellarum ex te et illis est. Astrologus non debet dicere rem specialiter sed universaliter, ut qui eminus videt rem aliquam.... Expositio.... *Astrologus non debet dicere rem specialiter sed universaliter*, ideo dixit quia hec scientia non est nisi secundum probationem et oppinionem. Et quia materia ad quam pertinet totum opus stellarum convertibilis est ad unum et ad aliud, ideo dixit: *non specialiter sed universaliter*; ut ignis effectum calorem vocamus, sic et

effectum aliarum rerum calorem efficientium, licet ignis effectu proprie dicatur combustio." Ahmad ibn Yūsuf, *Centiloquium*, f. 1.

85. Averroes held that the stars exert particular effects upon things of this world, but they are hidden from us. Revolutions in the course of the sun and stars "give each being the nature by which it is particularized...." Averroes, *Epitome on Aristotle's De generatione et corruptione* II, 10, 336a, tr. Samuel Kurland (Cambridge, Mass.: Mediaeval Academy, 1958), pp. 133–34.

86. See Lemay, "The True Place," p. 72.

87. See Thorndike, *History of Magic*, vol. II, Chapter LXII; Lemay, *Abū Ma'shar*, pp. xxiii–xxiv, n. 1; Albertus Magnus, *Speculum astronomiae*, ed. Caroti, Pereira, and Zamponi under the direction of Paola Zambelli, *Quaderni di Storia e Critica della Scienza*, new series, 10 (Pisa: Domus Galilaeana, 1977). On the authorship of the *Speculum astronomie* see Richard Lemay, "De la scolastique à l'histoire par le truchement de la philologie: itinéraire d'un médiéviste entre Europe et Islam," in *La diffusione nelle scienze Islamiche nel medio evo Europeo*, Convegno Internazionale, Roma 2–4 ottobre 1984 (Rome: Accademia Nazionale dei Lincei, 1987), p. 487.

88. Galen (ps.), *Microtegni seu De spermate,* tr. Vera Tavone Passalacqua (Rome: Istituto di Storia della Medicina, 1959), p. 10.

89. Galenus (ps.), *De spermate*, in *Opera* (Lyons, 1528). This treatise begins, "Incipit alius liber de spermate Galeni ascriptus," and follows another *De spermate* which does not discuss planetary influences. The first treatise begins, "Incipit liber Galeni de spermate qui dicitur de zogonia, id est de animalium generatione." The second *De spermate* also exists in an Italian translation by Vera Tavone Passalacqua (see note 88).

90. Lemay, "The True Place," pp. 57, 64–65, 70.

91. Ibid., pp. 60–62.

92. Trotula of Salerno, *The Diseases of Women*, tr. Elizabeth Mason-Hohl (Los Angeles: Ward Ritchie Press, 1940), p. 2.

93. Trotula, *Diseases of Women*, pp. 1–2.

94. I am using the term "Trota" broadly here; John Benton and Monica Green have pointed out that there are actually three treatises comprising the Trota texts, the *Ut de curis, Cum auctor*, and *De ornatu*. I have not attempted to distinguish among them in this discus-

sion. See Green, *Transmission of Ancient Theories,* p. 269ff. Monica Green is preparing an edition of these writings.

95. See, for example, MS Lille 334, Nicholus, *De passionibus mulierum,* a fifteenth-century manuscript that lists in its chapter headings the topics of the complexion of the womb, sterility, conception, the fetus, pregnancy, birth, abortion, disorders of the womb (mole, suffocation, ulcers), and the menstrual period.

96. For further discussion on this point see Helen Rodnite Lemay, "Women and the Literature of Obstetrics," pp. 189–209; Monica Green, "Women's Medical Practice and Health Care in Medieval Europe," *Signs* 14 (2) (1989): 434–73.

97. See Green, "Women's Medical Practice," p. 457ff.

98. Green, *Transmission of Ancient Theories,* p. 472.

99. Edward J. Kealey, *Medieval Medicus: A Social History of Anglo-Norman Medicine* (Baltimore: Johns Hopkins University Press), p. 319; Nancy Siraisi, *Taddeo Alderotti and His Pupils: Two Generations of Italian Medical Learning* (Princeton: Princeton University Press, 1981), pp. 279–82.

100. See Helen Rodnite Lemay, "Anthonius Guainerius and Medieval Gynecology," in Julius Kirshner and Suzanne Wemple, eds., *Women of the Medieval World* (Oxford: Basil Blackwell, 1985), pp. 319–23; "Women and the Literature of Obstetrics," pp. 190–91.

101. On legal proceedings against women who practiced medicine in the middle ages, see Régine Pernoud, "La femme et la médecine au moyen-age," *Colloque Internationale d'Histoire de la Médecine Médiévale,* Orléans, 4–5 mai, 1985 (Orléans: La Société, 1985), pp. 38–39. For attitudes of male doctors toward female physicians, see Renate Blumenfeld-Kosinski, *Not of Woman Born: Representations of Caesarean Birth in Medieval and Renaissance Culture* (Ithaca: Cornell University Press, 1990), ch. 3: "The Marginalization of Women in Obstetrics."

102. For details see Helen Rodnite Lemay, "Women and the Literature of Obstetrics," pp. 197–98.

103. See Janice Delaney, Mary Jane Lupton, and Emily Toth, *The Curse: A Cultural History of Menstruation,* rev. ed. (Urbana: University of Illinois Press, 1988).

104. Green, *Transmission of Ancient Theories.*

105. Ibid., pp. 17, 27, 96.

106. Ibid., p. 227.

107. Ibid., pp. 158, 262.

108. For this period Lynn Thorndike lists in his classic *History of Magic*, I, pp. 594–640, "pseudo-" literature (pseudo-Pliny, pseudo-Apuleius, interpolated and pseudo-Dioscorides, etc.), and Boethius, as well as Isidore, Bede, and Gregory the Great. "Pseudo-" literature poses unique problems of its own and is not really germane to this discussion. Boethius can in one sense be said to have divorced philosophy from religion, since he does not mention Christianity in the *Consolation of Philosophy*, however many historians consider him to be a late classical and not a medieval figure. Thorndike, *History of Magic*, I, 619–20.

109. Ernest Bréhaut, *An Encyclopedist of the Dark Ages: Isidore of Seville* (New York: Columbia University Press, 1917; Burt Franklin reprint 1964), pp. 33, 34.

110. "Menstrua supervacuus mulierum sanguis. Dicta autem menstrua a circuitu lunari luminis, quo solet hoc venire profluvium; luna enim Graece *selene* dicitur. Haec et muliebria nuncupantur; nam mulier solum animal menstruale est. Cuius cruoris contactu fruges non germinant, acescunt musta, moriuntur herbae, amittunt arbores fetus, ferrum rubigo corripit, nigrescunt aera. Si qui canes inde ederint, in rabiem efferuntur. Glutinum asphalti, quod nec ferro nec aquis dissolvitur, cruore ipso pollutum sponte dispergitur." Isidore of Seville, *Etymologiae*, ed. Jose Oroz Reta and Manuel A. Marcos Casquero (Madrid: Editorial Catolica, 1983), vol. II, lib. XI, 1, 140–41, pp. 36–38.

111. Monica Green, *Transmission of Ancient Theories*, chapters II and IV. For more information on the Arabic sources, see Manfred Ullmann, *Die Medizin im Islam* (Leiden/Köln: Brill, 1970), pp. 140–49 and Fuat Sezgin, *Geschichte des Arabischen Schrifttums* (Leiden: Brill, 1970), vol. III, pp. 304–7, 320–22.

112. Green makes the remark with reference to al-Majusi, Constantine's source. Green, *Transmission of Ancient Theories*, p. 112.

113. Green, *Transmission of Ancient Theories*, pp. 258–262.

114. Ibid., p. 284.

115. *Cum auctor* cited by Monica Green, ibid., p. 282.

116. *Erotis medici liberti Iuliae quem aliqui Trotulam inepte nominant muliebrium liber....* in *Harmoniae Gynaeciorum sive de morbis muliebribus liber ex Prisciano Cleopatra Moschione libro Matricis dicto et Theodoro Prisciano collectus* (Argentinae: Zetzner, 1597), p. 42.

117. Trotula of Salerno, *Diseases of Women*, p. 2.

118. Barbara Newman, *Sister of Wisdom: St. Hildegard's Theology of the Feminine* (Berkeley and Los Angeles: University of California Press, 1987), p. 133. Nancy Siraisi states, however, that Hildegard "drew on medical material only recently made available in Latin for [her description] of the physical universe, including human physiology." Nancy Siraisi, *Medieval and Early Renaissance Medicine: An Introduction to Knowledge and Practice* (Chicago: University of Chicago Press, 1990), p. 15.

119. In Book VI of the *Dragmaticon*, for example, he states that he will give Constantine's description of the cerebrum. William of Conches, *Dragmaticon (Dialogus de Substantiis Physicis, ante annos ducentos confectus a Vuilhelmo Aneponymo philosopho)*, ed. Guillelmus Gratarolus (Argentorati: Rihelius 1557; reprint Minerva, 1967), p. 275.

120. On William of Conches' developing awareness of the Aristotelian idea of the quintessence see Helen Rodnite Lemay, "Science and Theology at Chartres: The Case of the Supracelestial Waters," *British Journal for the History of Science* 10 (1977): 226–36, esp. 232.

121. Joan Cadden, "It Takes All Kinds: Sexuality and Gender Differences in Hildegard of Bingen's 'Book of Compound Medicine,'" *Traditio* 40 (1984): 151, 155.

122. "Et cum etiam in quibusdam feminis de superfluitate infirmitatum earum humores, qui in eis sunt, in diversum et contrarium malum superhabundant et effluunt, venas, quae rivulos sanguinis portant, in ipsis constringunt, ita quod menstrua earum deficiunt, quia tempestates humorum iniustum frigus et diversitatem caloris parant, ita quod sanguis earum interdum frigidus est et quod interdum fervet; unde etiam diverso modo in eis hac et illac discurrit; et tunc venae, quae tempore suo effluere debebant, propter ariditatem, quam in se habent, obligantur et non effluunt." Hildegard of Bingen, *Causae et Curae*, ed. Paul Kaiser (Leipzig: Teubner, 1903), lib. II, p. 107.

123. "Sed sicut arbor in aestate de sole floret et frondet, ita etiam menstrua mulierum de laetitia multotiens aperiuntur, et ut frigidus ventus et gelu et hiems folia et ramos arborum arefacit, sic etiam rivuli sanguinis, qui de muliere manare debebant, per tristitiam saepe arescunt." Hildegard of Bingen, *Causae*, lib. II, p. 107.

124. "Sed et aliae quaedam feminae sunt, quae infirmas carnes et crassas habent, quae magis de debilitate et de foeditate earum crescunt, quam de recta viriditate illarum." Ibid., p. 107.

125. "Sed interdum quaedam mulieres dolorem diversarum febrium habent et dolorem stomachi et lateris ac renum, et dolores isti calvariae resistunt, et iusto tempore suo claudatur, velut quaedam procellae inundando loca obstrusa transeunt, et ita rivuli sanguinis in muliere illa in iniusto tempore inordinate effluunt. Et tunc mulier illa in dolore est velut aliquis vir, qui ferro vulneratus est, et ideo eo tempore cum cautela se observet, ne inde plus laedatur, quia etiam medicina cum timore ei adhibenda est." Ibid., p. 108.

126. "Nam a quinquagesimo anno aut aliquando in quibusdam feminis a sexagesimo menstrua cessant et matrix implicari et contrahi incipit ita quod amplius prolem concipere non possunt, nisi interdum eveniat, ut aliqua ex qualibet superfluitate vix semel interim usque ad octogesimum annum prolem concipiat, in qua tamen aliquis defectus interdum continget, velut in illis multotiens evenit, quae infra vicesimum annum tenerae iuvenculae exsistentes in illa teneritudine concipiunt et pariunt." Ibid., p. 106.

127. For a discussion of the ages of menstruation in the middle ages, see Charles T. Wood, "The Doctors' Dilemma: Sin, Salvation, and the Menstrual Cycle in Medieval Thought," *Speculum* 56 (4) (1981): 710–11; Vern Bullough and Cameron Campbell, "Female Longevity and Diet in the Middle Ages," *Speculum* 55 (2) (1980): 323–25; Vern Bullough, "Sexology and the Medievalist," in Helen Rodnite Lemay, ed., *Homo Carnalis,* pp. 37–39; Darrel W. Amundsen and Carol Jean Diers, "The Age of Menarche in Medieval Europe," *Human Biology* 45 (1973): 363–68.

128. "Omnes autem venae mulieris integrae et sanae permansissent, si Eva in pleno tempore paradisi perstitisset." Hildegard of Bingen, *Causae,* lib. II, p. 103.

129. "D. Quomodo fiunt menstrua, et quare post conceptum cessant? P. Cum mulier, ut praediximus, naturaliter frigida sit, perfecte cibum decoquere non potest; remanentque superfluitates quaedam, quas natura per singulos menses expellit, unde nominantur menstrua, sed facta conceptione, calor ex foetu augmentatur, sicque melius cibus decoquitur, nec tantae superfluitates oriuntur, et ex eis quae restant, partus in utero nutritur." William of Conches, *Dragmaticon,* pp. 244–45.

130. "Nil, quod sit naturale, turpe est, est enim creationis donum." Ibid., p. 244.

131. Ibid., pp. 238, 241.

132. On theology and gynecology, see R. Howard Bloch, "Medieval Misogyny," *Representations* 20 (fall 1987): 1–24, esp. p. 20, n.1; and Wood, "Doctors' Dilemma," 710–27.

133. Siraisi, "Medical Learning," p. 392.

134. See Joan Cadden, "Medieval Scientific and Medical Views of Sexuality: Questions of Propriety," *Medievalia et Humanistica*, n.s. 14 (1986): 161.

135. "Menstrua temperata in quantitate et qualitate suo et in tempore suo currente secundum consuetudinem suam naturalem in omni spacio sunt causa sanitatis mulieris et mundificationis corporis eius ab omni nocumento in quantitate et qualitate, et faciunt ipsam acquirere castitatem et paucitatem desiderii." Avicenna, *Liber canonis* (Venice, 1507; reprint Hildesheim: Georg Olms, 1964), lib. III, fen xxi, tractatus iii, cap. i: De iudiciis menstruorum, f. 371ra.

136. "Retentio autem menstruorum et paucitas eorum commovent in ea egritudines repletionis omnes, et preparant eam ad apostemata, et dolores capitis et reliquorum membrorum et tenebrositatem visus et perturbationem sensus et fe[brem] et multiplicatur cum ea repletio vasorum spermatis eius quare fit desiderans non casta et non suscipiens filium ex impregnatione propter corruptionem matricis eius et spermatis ipsius." Ibid.

137. Green, *Transmission of Ancient Theories*, pp. 20, 115.

138. "Et huiusmodi quidem mulierum nature virorum similes existunt naturis et sunt potentes super digestionem ultimam et distributionem necessariam et expulsionem superfluitatum secundum modum quo expellunt eas viri, et iste sunt pingues nervose lacertose, de quibus sunt fortes viragines quarum anche ipsarum pectoribus sunt strictiores et ipsarum extremitates sunt pingues plus, et sunt multarum evacuationum cum medicinis et exercitiis et proprie sanguis fluentes per nares aut emorroydas aut plagas aut alia." Avicenna, *Liber canonis*, lib. III, fen xxi, tract. iii, cap. xxv, f. 373rb–373va.

139. Aristotle, *De hist. animal.* l. 7 c. 4 (584b 6–9).

140. See Helen Rodnite Lemay, "William of Saliceto on Human Sexuality," *Viator* 12 (1981): 165–81.

141. Guilielmus de Saliceto, *Summa conservationis et curationis* (Venice, 1489), f. h8rb (cap. clxiii, De retentione menstruorum).

142. Guilielmus de Saliceto, *Summa conservationis*, f. 48rb.

143. Bernardus de Gordonio, *Lilium medicinae* (Paris, 1542), lib. VII, cap. viii, f. 324. In this edition "lx" is corrected in the margin to "quinquagesimum."

144. Pseudo-Albert states that young women normally have their menses in the beginning of the month because they are very humid, and older women in the end, because they are less so. Commentator B holds that women with a sanguine complexion bleed during the first quarter; choleric and melancholic during the middle two; and phlegmatic during the last. Chapter I.

145. Bernardus de Gordonio, *Lilium medicinae*, lib. VII, cap. viii, f. 324v.

146. "Septima notandum quod menstrua veniunt naturaliter in tempore determinato, quia natura aliquo modo intendit se iuvare ex eis, et non est ita impurum, aliae autem superfluitates non sunt ita iuvativae, et sunt magis immunde et impurae, ideo non servant ordinem nec periodum." Ibid., f. 326.

147. "Octavo intelligendum, quod in retentione menstruorum, mulieres magis appetunt propter titillicum et pruritum quae inducunt, ista autem non sunt sic in fluxu, vel post. Nono advertendum, quod retentio menstruorum diminuit appetitum cibi, quia replet et provocat coitum, quia stimulat." Ibid.

148. See the earlier section entitled "Human Generation" and note 60 for the text.

149. See Helen Rodnite Lemay, "Masculinity and Femininity," 27–29.

150. Siraisi, *Taddeo Alderotti*, pp. 195–202.

151. Albertus Magnus, *Quaestiones*, lib. IX, Q. 9, pp. 206–7.

152. Ibid., p. 207.

153. Ibid., p. 215.

154. "Utrum mas habilior sit ad mores quam femina.... Ad istud dicendum, quod femina minus est habilis ad mores quam mas. Complexio enim feminae magis est humida quam maris, sed humidi est de facili recipere et male retinere. Humidum est enim de facili mobile, et ideo mulieres sunt inconstantes et nova semper petentes. Unde cum est in actu sub uno viro, si esset possibile, in eodem tempore vellet esse sub alio. Unde nulla fides est in muliere.
Crede mihi: si credis ei, tu decipieris;
Experte crede magistro.

Cuius enim signum est, quod sagaces viri consilia et facta sua uxoribus suis minime propalant. Mulier etiam est vir occasionatus et habet naturam defectus et privationis respectu maris...." Ibid., p. 265 (lib. XV, Q. xi).

155. "Oppositum dicitur in IX HUIUS [ETHICORUM] et manifestum est. Dicitur enim communiter et proverbialiter et vulgariter, quod mulieres sunt magis mendaces et fragiles, diffidentes, inverecundae, eloquentes deceptorie, et breviter mulier nihil aliud est quam diabolus specie humana effigiatus. Unde vidi quandam Coloniae, quae videbatur esse sancta et tamen breviter omnes in amorem suum illaqueabat." Ibid.

156. "...et ideo quod non potest acquirere per se, nititur acquirere per mendacia et diabolicas deceptiones. Unde, ut breviter dicam, ab omni muliere est cavendum tamquam a serpente venenoso et diabolo cornuto, et si fas esset dicere, quae scio de mulieribus, totus mundus stuperet." Ibid., p. 266.

157. Michael Scot provides us with a good illustration. He states, for example, that *maleficia* can be made from menses. For a discussion see Helen Rodnite Lemay, "Some Thirteenth- and Fourteenth-Century Lectures on Female Sexuality," *International Journal of Women's Studies* I (4) (1978): 398–99.

158. An example of Thomas's misogyny is given by R. Howard Bloch, who cites Thomas Aquinas, *Summa Theologiae* (New York, 1963) Ia, Q. 92 and IIIa, Q. 32 in "Medieval Misogyny," p. 20, n.1. Charles Wood argues that Thomas, along with Augustine, looked upon women more favorably than did most medieval theologians because they both believed that sexual relations had from the beginning been part of the divine plan. See Wood, "Doctors' Dilemma," p. 712. Thomas's discussion of this point is found in *Summa Theologiae* Ia, Q. 92: De productione mulieris. See St. Thomas Aquinas, *Summa Theologiae*, vol. 13 (New York and London: Blackfriars and McGraw Hill, 1963), pp. 34–37.

159. On Albertus Magnus's life see James A. Weisheipl, "The Life and Works of St. Albert the Great," in *Albertus Magnus and the Sciences: Commemorative Essays 1980* (Toronto: Pontifical Institute of Mediaeval Studies, 1980), pp. 13–51. On university practices, see Cadden, "Medieval Scientific and Medical Views," 162.

160. Siraisi, *Medieval and Early Renaissance Medicine*, p. 79; Mary Frances Wack, *Lovesickness in the Middle Ages: The Viaticum*

and Its Commentaries (Philadelphia: University of Pennsylvania Press, 1990), p. 173.

161. Tertullian, *De cultu feminarum*, in Julia O'Faolain and Lauro Martines, eds., *Not in God's Image: Women in History from the Greeks to the Victorians* (New York: Harper and Row, 1973), p. 132. Although not all Church fathers unrestrainedly censure women, there is a strong theme of the female as potential seducer running through many patristic writings. Some citations can be found in Katherine M. Rogers, *The Troublesome Helpmate: A History of Misogyny in Literature* (Seattle: University of Washington Press, 1966), pp. 14–22 cited in Susan Groag Bell, ed., *Women: From the Greeks to the French Revolution* (Belmont, Cal.: Wadsworth, 1973), pp. 84–89. Recent scholars have pointed to some of the positive aspects of women and sex that are mentioned in the fathers, but these do not negate the overwhelmingly misogynistic tone. For a discussion see Vern Bullough, Brenda Shelton, and Sarah Slavin, *The Subordinated Sex: A History of Attitudes toward Women* (Athens: University of Georgia Press, 1988), Chapter 5: Christianity, Sex and Women.

162. Helen Rodnite Lemay, "Some Thirteenth- and Fourteenth-Century Lectures," 391–400.

163. "Duodecimo queritur utrum vir magis appetat coytum quam mulier aut econverso, aut quia mulier magis appetat. Videtur quia secundum philosophum primo philosophorum materia appetit formam sicut mulier virum et turpe bonum, sed magis et multo praestancius perfectibile appetit perfectionem et turpe bonum quam econverso, ergo mulier magis appetit virum.

"Sed contra, appetitus et eius cohitus est ex calore, sed secundum Avicennam frigidissimus virorum calidior est calidissima muliere, ergo respondetur et dicendum quod vir magis appetit cohitum quam mulier quia naturaliter vir principalior est in generatione que est propter salvacionem speciei ut patet 2° de anima et Avicenna. Sicut ergo vir in generacione est principalior sic et in appetitu coitus." MS Paris B.N. lat. 7148, f. 2v.

164. Heinrich Kramer and James Sprenger, *Malleus maleficarum*, tr. Montague Summers (New York: Dover, 1971), pp. 44–47.

165. Medieval ideas on menstruation are discussed in Charles Wood, "Sin, Salvation and the Menstrual Cycle in Medieval Thought," *Speculum* 56 (4) (1981): 710–27.

166. Kramer and Sprenger, *Malleus maleficarum*, p. 47.

167. Ibid., pp. 136–37.

168. I have not been able to locate this passage in Avicenna. See the section entitled "Sources."

169. Kramer and Sprenger, *Malleus maleficarum*, p. 48.

170. Monica Green makes the point that old women, and not midwives, were persecuted as witches by the inquisition. She acknowledges the denunciation of midwives in the *Malleus*, however. See Green, "Women's Medical Practice," 451. On midwives and the inquisition see Blumenfeld-Kosinski, *Not of Woman Born,* pp. 106ff., 117.

171. Kramer and Sprenger, *Malleus maleficarum*, p. 17.

172. Lynn Thorndike refers to Commentary A as the "leading commentary." Thorndike, "Further Consideration," p. 429.

173. Kramer and Sprenger, *Malleus maleficarum*, p. 17. The theme of a camel cast into a ditch by fascination is not unique to the *Secrets* and the *Malleus*. Bert Hansen provides us with a list of medieval examples of this story in *Nicole Oresme and the Marvels of Nature: A Study of His De causis mirabilium with Critical Edition, Translation and Commentary* (Toronto: Pontifical Institute of Medieval Studies, 1985), p. 314 n. 71. What is significant here is the order in which the ideas are presented in both the *Secrets* and the *Malleus*. Although the *Malleus*, in accordance with the Parisian condemnation, uses the more generic term *incantator* which can apply to a male or female enchanter, the parallel remains significant.

174. Condemnations of 1277, Proposition 112: "Quod intelligentie superiores imprimunt in inferiores, sicut anima una imprimit in aliam, et etiam in animam sensitivam; et per talem impressionem incantator aliquis prohicit camelum in foveam solo visu." *Chartularium Universitatis Parisiensis*, eds. Henricus Denifle and Aemilio Chatelain, vol. I (Paris, 1899; reprint, Bruxelles, 1964), p. 549.

175. Kramer and Sprenger, *Malleus maleficarum*, pp. 17–18.

176. Ibid., p. 18.

177. Ibid., p. 44.

178. Ibid., p. 121.

179. Ibid., p. 66.

180. Thorndike, "Further Consideration," p. 438, n. 80.

181. For a recent discussion of abortion in the early medieval medical tradition, see Monica H. Green, "Constantinus Africanus and the Conflict between Religion and Science," in G. R. Dunstan, ed., *The Human Embryo: Aristotle and the Arabic and European Traditions* (Exeter: University of Exeter Press, 1990), pp. 47–69.

DE SECRETIS MULIERUM
(ON THE SECRETS OF WOMEN)

1. Leviticus 15:19.

2. *Met.* I, 1; 980a 1.

3. *G.A.* II, 1; 731b–732a.

4. *De anima*, II, 4; 415a 26.

5. Averroes, *Commentarium magnum in Aristotelis De anima libros*, ed. F. Stuart Crawford (Cambridge, Mass.: Medieval Academy, 1953), pp. 182–83.

6. Albert discusses generation in terms of forms in the first book of the *Posterior Analytics*, but he does not bring up spontaneous generation. See Albertus Magnus, *Posteriorum Analyticorum*, ed. Augustus Borgnet, in Opera Omnia II (Paris: Lodovicum Vivès, 1890), I, 1, 5; p. 19.

7. *De gen. et corr.* II, 11; 338b 5ff.

8. cf. Hippocrates, *De la génération*, ed. and trans. Robert Joly (Paris: Les Belles Lettres, 1970), II, 2, p. 45; Hippocrates, *Airs, Waters, Places*, chap. 22 in *The Medical Works of Hippocrates*, tr. J. Chadwick and W. Mann (Oxford: Blackwell, 1950), p. 108.

9. *De anima* II, 3; 414a 29 – 414b 25.

10. Boethius, *Consolation of Philosophy*, tr. Richard Green (Indianapolis: Bobbs-Merrill, 1962), Book Two, Prose 5, p. 32.

11. Cf. *Met.* XII, 7; 1072a–1073a; *Phys.* II, 7; 198a 35ff.

12. The Lyons, 1580, edition reads "mobilitate." The Venice, 1508, edition states "nobilitate."

13. The Lyons, 1580, edition reads "Non" instead of "Nota." "Nota" is found in the Strasbourg, 1510, edition (f. A5) and in the Liptzk, 1500 edition (f. A5).

14. This material is not found in the pseudo-Avicennan *De caelo*

et mundo. For a discussion of this citation, see the section of the Introduction entitled "Sources."

15. Averroes discusses human generation briefly in Book II, Chapter I and in detail in Book II, Chapter X ("Quod est de iuvamentis membrorum officialium que sunt instrumenta virtutis generatione"). He does not raise the issue of spontanteous generation here. Averroes' opinions on generation without seed are discussed later in Chapter IV of the *De secretis mulierum.*

16. Some of the editions add here, "I make no determination on the question." For a discussion of this point, see the section of the Introduction entitled "Human Generation."

17. Avicenna, *Liber Canonis,* tr. Arnoldus de Villanova, lib. III, fen xxi, tractatus i (Venice 1507, repr. Hildesheim: Olms, 1964), f. 360vb.

18. Averroes, *Colliget* (Venice, 1549), f. 53vb.

19. The Venice, 1508, edition reads here: "in balneo ganelli." This reading or a similar one is also found in other editions; e.g., Frankfurt, 1615, says: "in balneo Ganelli." I am taking here the reading of the Venice 1562 edition: "in balneo lavelli." The word *labellum* or *lavellum* means a bathtub according to *Novum Glossarium Mediae Latinitatis,* vol. II (Hafniae: Ejnar Munksgaard, 1958).

20. The text of Commentary B from the Venice, 1508, edition reads, "mala matricis."

21. Galen discusses the penis in *De locis affectis* (Naples, 1548), VI, 6; *De utilitate particularum,* XIV, 10; XV, 3. He does not give these measurements in any of these passages. See Galen, *Oeuvres anatomiques, physiologiques et médicales,* tr. Charles Daremberg (Paris: J. Baillière, 1886), vol. II, 116, 136, 698. A short treatise attributed to Galen, *De anathomia vivorum Galeni ascriptus,* states that normal penile size is between six and eleven inches: "Longitudinem naturalem habet inter vi et xi digitos ut possit attingere ad locum sibi destinatum in proiectione spermatis." See Galenus, *Opera* (Lyons, 1528), f. 77v.

22. Aristotle mentions pleasure in sexual intercourse in *G.A.* 727b 9ff; 728a 10ff, 34ff. None of these passages discusses delectation in a manner that even resembles this text of Commentary B.

23. On extensive and intensive pleasure in sexual intercourse see Mary Frances Wack, *Lovesickness in the Middle Ages: The Viaticum and Its Commentaries* (Philadelphia: University of Pennsylvania Press, 1990), pp. 19–20.

24. On the ages of menstruation in the middle ages see Vern Bullough and Cameron Campbell, "Female Longevity and Diet in the Middle Ages," *Speculum* 55 (2) (1980): 323–24; Charles T. Wood, "The Doctors' Dilemma: Sin, Salvation and the Menstrual Cycle in Medieval Thought," *Speculum* 56 (4) (1981): 710–11.

25. On the chambers of the uterus see Danielle Jacquart and Claude Thomasset, *Sexuality*, pp. 35, 42.

26. In book II of his *Colliget*, Averroes describes the vulva and its blood vessels, but he does not discuss the hymen, nor does he bring up the topic of virginity. Cf. Averroes, *Colliget* (Venice: Junta, 1562), lib. II, f. 23v.

27. Note that according to Commentator B, menses is a superfluity of the third digestion. Commentator A maintains that it is a product of the second digestion.

28. Averroes, *Colliget*, II, 10, f. 54rb: "Et sunt alique mulieres que non possunt impregnari dum lactant."

29. Cf. Aristotle, *Meteor.* IV, 4; 382a 11.

30. Aristotle, *De caelo* I, 4; 271a 30.

31. On this point see Ian Maclean, *The Renaissance Notion of Woman* (Cambridge: Cambridge University Press, 1980), p. 34.

32. This opinion is found in Vincent of Beauvais: "Sed dices mihi, Cum calidi et humidi conveniant huic operi, pueritia vero sit calida et humida, quare non coeunt pueri maxime? Respondeo, Quoniam in hac aetate stricti sunt meatus per quos habet semen discurrere." Vincentius Bellovacensis, *Speculum naturale* (Duaci: Baltazaris Belleri, 1624; repr. 1964), lib. XXI, cap. v, c. 2294.

33. A more complete listing of substances that help and hinder coitus can be found in *Liber minor de coitu*, composed before ca. 1250. See Enrique Montero Cartelle, *Liber minor de coitu: Tratado Menor de Andrologia, Anonimo Salernitano* (Valladolid: Universidad de Valladolid, 1987), pp. 87–97.

34. Macer does not list lentils in his *De virtutibus herbarum*. He treats lettuce, stating that it relieves heat when it is thoroughly boiled, but does not mention sexual desire in this section. See Bruce Pepper Flood, *Macer Floridus: A Medieval Herbalism*, (Ph.D. diss., 1968, University Microfilms, 1969), pp. 159–60. Cf. Macer, *Macri philosophi de virtutibus herbarum*, (Venice, 1508), f. c verso.

35. Of all animals the woman and the mare are most inclined to receive the commerce of the male during pregnancy; while all other animals when they are pregnant avoid the male, save those in which the phenomenon of superfoetation occurs, such as the hare. Aristotle, *H.A.* VII, 4, 585a, tr. D'Arcy Wentworth Thompson (Oxford: Clarendon, 1910).

36. This account of the development of the fetus is found in Augustine, *De diversis quaestionibus*, lxxxiii, referred to in Anthony Hewson, *Giles of Rome and the Medieval Theory of Conception* (London: Athlone, 1975), p. 167. Luke Demaitre and Anthony Travill have pointed out that Albertus Magnus presents the same information in his *Commentary on the Sentences* (In IV Sent. dist. 31, art 18; Borgnet 30: 251), based on material from the Salernitan collection (*Flos medicinae scholae Salerni* IV, 7; ed. Salvatore de Renzi in *Collectio Salernitana* 5; Naples, 1859, 51, 1, vv. 1795–1798). See Luke Demaitre and Anthony A. Travill, "Human Embryology and Development in the Works of Albertus Magnus," in James A. Weisheipl, ed., *Albertus Magnus and the Sciences* (Toronto: Pontifical Institute, 1980), pp. 424–25.

37. Cf. Hippocrates, *Aphorisms*, tr. W. H. S. Jones (Cambridge and London: Harvard University Press and William Heinemann, 1953), V, 31: "Miscarriage follows bloodletting in pregnant women, especially if the fetus be large."

38. Cf. *G.A.* 741a 23ff.

39. Cf. Avicenna, *The Metaphysics of Avicenna*, tr. Parviz Morewedge (New York: Columbia University Press, 1973), chap. 9, p. 26. Avicenna states here that there are two kinds of accidents.

40. Cf. Aḥmad ibn Yūsuf, *Centiloquium*, MS Paris B.N. lat. 7307, verbum 86.

41. Ibid.

42. For a discussion of this topic in ancient and medieval thought, see C. S. F. Burnett, "The Planets and the Development of the Embryo," in G. R. Dunstan, ed., *The Human Embryo* (Exeter: University of Exeter Press, 1990), pp. 95–112.

43. *Meteor.* I, 2; 339a 21ff.

44. Cf. Averroes, *Aristotelis Stagiritae metaphysicorum libri xiiii cum Averrois Cordubensis commentariis* (Venice: Junta, 1562; repr. Minerva, 1962), lib. II, f. 30ra.

45. Cf. Averroes, *Middle Commentary on Aristotle's De genera-*

tione et corruptione, tr. Samuel Kurland (Cambridge, Mass.: Mediaeval Academy, 1958), I, 6, 2, p. 45; Averroes, *Epitome on Aristotle's De Generatione et Corruptione,* II, 10, pp. 133–35.

46. cf. Averroes, *Aristotelis Stagiritae metaphysicorum,* lib. XII, f. 297, 310v–311.

47. Cf. Aristotle, *De gen. et corr.* II, 10; 336b 5–10.

48. Cf. Averroes, *Aristotelis Stagiritae metaphysicorum,* lib. II, f. 32va.

49. Aḥmad ibn Yūsuf, *Centiloquium,* verbum 9.

50. *G.A.* II, iv; 740a 20ff.

51. Aḥmad ibn Yūsuf, *Centiloquium,* verbum 86.

52. The translation of this verse is taken from the English translation of the *De secretis mulierum* by John Quincy, published in London in 1725. In the Augsburg edition (Hans Forschauer, about 1500) the verse is found in the commentary instead of in the body of the text.

53. Abū Ma'shar, *Introductorium maius in astronomiam,* tr. John of Seville, ed. Richard Lemay (Naples: Istituto Universitario Orientale, in press), differentia XII: "In divisione membrorum que sunt unicuique signo de membris corporis humani."

54. The text reads "zodia."

55. Galen (ps.), *De spermate,* in *Opera* (Lyons, 1528), vol. I, f. 66rb: "De conceptione pueri alterata a stellis et non a parentibus." Note that this treatise begins "Incipit alius liber de spermate Galeni ascriptus," and that it follows another *De spermate* which does not discuss planetary influences. This first treatise begins: "Incipit liber Galeni de spermate qui dicitur de zogonia, id est de animalium generatione."

56. "Philosophi dubitantur vero asserunt teste Hippocrate quoniam omnis substantia corporea animata iuncta sit et ligata in planetis et signis, quattuor elementorum nexibus." Galen (ps.), *De spermate,* in *Opera,* f. 66rb.

57. Aḥmad ibn Yūsuf, *Centiloquium,* verbum 20.

58. Cf. Albertus Magnus, *De caelo et mundo,* ed. P. Hossfeld, in *Opera Omnia* VI, 1, ed. B. Geyer: Monasterii Westfalorum in aedibus Aschendorff, 1971, lib. I, tract. i, cap. ii, p. 29.

59. Aḥmad ibn Yūsuf, *Centiloquium,* verbum 20.

60. Leviticus 15:19

61. John Riddle of North Carolina State University has kindly informed me that although the form "Diasidus" may bring to mind "Dioscorides," he has not found the substance of the quotation in Dioscorides, and the type of statement is uncharacteristic of the way the ancient author related data. (Private communication, 30 March 1990).

62. Hippocrates does not make this statement in the *De natura hominis*, nor does he discuss menstruation in this writing. His discussions of menstruation in his writings on intercourse and pregnancy do not contain statements about its foulness corrupting the air. See Hippocrates, *On Intercourse and Pregnancy: An English Translation of On Semen and On the Development of the Child*, tr. Tage U. H. Ellinger (New York: Henry Schuman, n.d.), chaps. 15, 30, pp. 51–53, 101.

63. Aḥmad ibn Yūsuf, *Centiloquium*, verbum 20, commentary.

64. Abū Maʻshar, *Introductorium*, III, 9.

65. Cf. Averroes, *Metaphysicorum Aristotelis opus re ipsa divinum iuxta novam Bessarionis translationem...accessit operi et id commodi quod libri singuli per commentariorum Averrois numeros...* *(Leipzig: Vuolffgangus Monacensis, 1519), lib. XII, cap. viii, f. 100v–102.*

66. Galen, *De complexionibus*, in *Burgundio of Pisa's Translation of Galen's PERI KRASEON "De complexionibus"*, ed. Richard J. Durling (Berlin and New York: Walter de Gruyter, 1976), 2, 6.

67. *Met.* XII, 8; 1074a–b.

68. Cf. Aristotle, *Phys.* VIII, 6; 259b 30.

69. Aḥmad ibn Yūsuf, *Centiloquium*, verbum 8.

70. The Lyons, 1580, edition gives the *Metaphysics* as a reference. However, *Met.* VII, 7; 1032a is much less specific than *Meteor* IV, 2; 379b 5. Therefore, the reading of the Venice, 1508, edition (*"Methau."*) is used here.

71. This material is not found in pseudo-Avicenna's *De caelo et mundo*. Avicenna's treatment of the generation of animals in the *De animalibus* focuses only on generation with seed. See Avicenna, *De caelo et mundo, De animalibus* in *Opera philosophica* (Venice, 1508). For a discussion of this point see the section of the Introduction entitled "Sources."

72. Cf. Aristotle, *Phys.* VIII, 4; 254b 7. Cf. *Met..* VII, 3; 1028b–1029a; IX, 8; 1050a.

73. *Met.* VII 7; 1032a 20, VII 9; 1034a 8ff. The Lyons, 1580, edition reads here "8 *Phys.*"

74. *Meteor.* I, 14; 351a–353a. The text from the beginning of the previous sentence, "But in this..." until this point is taken from MS Munich CLM 22297, f. 33r: "Sed in hoc differt ab Avicenna, quia perfecta animalia nunquam sine semine fiunt secundum philosophum, Avicenna autem oppositum voluit indifferenter in omnibus, ut visum est. Differt etiam ab eo quia secundum eius doctrinam primo *Meth....*" The Lyons, 1580, edition is confusing here.

75. The text here assumes that water from the flood is necessary in order for spontaneous generation to occur. Thus, for all beings (both perfect and imperfect) to be generated without seed, a universal flood would have to take place, covering all areas, so that animals could be generated in every place. If a "universal flood" is impossible, it is impossible that all beings could be generated without seed. Some areas would remain dry, and in these areas animals would have to arise by another method—generation with seed.

76. Cf. Aristotle, *Meteor.* IV, 2–3; 379b 22.

77. Cf. Aristotle, *Met.* VII, 8; 1033b 30ff. The Lyons, 1580, edition reads here "*Meteororum.*"

78. In the *De animalibus*, Albert tells of a noblewoman in Germany who bore 60 children, and another who aborted 150 at the same time (*De animalibus* ed. Augustus Borgnet in *Opera Omnia* XI [Paris: Vivès, 1891], lib. IX, tract. 1, cap. 5, p. 509). This point is discussed in Demaitre and Travill, "Human Embryology," p. 438.

79. Aristotle describes the womb in *G.A.* I, 3, 716b, and *H.A.* III, 1, 510b. In both cases he states that it is two-horned. In the pseudo-Galenic *De spermate*, however, there is a clear statement about the seven-chambered uterus: "Sunt autem in matrice receptacula septem, et tot creantur pueri in quod ex illis ceciderit sperma." Galen (ps.), *De spermate* in *Opera*, vol. I, f. 64va. Danielle Jacquart and Claude Thomasset discuss the chambers of the uterus in *Sexuality*, pp. 35, 42.

80. Aristotle, *De anima* II, 4; 415a 23.

81. Cf. *H.A.* VIII, 1; 588b.

82. For a recent discussion of abortion in the medical tradition, see Monica H. Green, "Constantinus Africanus and the Conflict between Religion and Science," in G. R. Dunstan, ed., *The Human Embryo* (Exeter: University of Exeter Press, 1990), pp. 54–61.

83. On this point see Michael McVaugh, "The 'Humidum Radicale' in Thirteenth-Century Medicine," *Traditio* 30 (1974): 259–83.

84. Albertus Magnus, *Liber Meteororum*, ed. Augustus Borgnet, in *Opera Omnia IV* (Paris: Vivès. 1890), lib. 3, tract. 3, cap. 19, p. 659.

85. In the chapter on monsters in the second book of the *Physics* Albert does not discuss lightning as a cause of monstrosity, although he does cite the corrupting influence of celestial constellations on the seed. Albertus Magnus, *Physicorum Libri VIII*, ed. A. Borgnet, in *Opera Omnia III* (Paris: Vivès, 1890), lib. II, tract. iii, cap. iii, text. 82, p. 168.

86. Aristotle, *G.A.*, II, 3, 737a. "For the female is, as it were, a mutilated male...." tr. Arthur Platt, in *The Works of Aristotle*, vol. V (Oxford: Clarendon, 1912), II, 3, 737a.

87. On this topic see Maclean, *Renaissance Notion of Woman*, 30–31.

88. This point is made by Michael Scot: "Vir natus clama oa, foemina vero oe, quasi masculus dicat o Adam quare peccasti? quia pro te patior miseriam infinitam, et foemina dicat in suo lamentabilis cantu, o Eva quare peccasti? nam tuo peccato sum passura miserabilem vitam in hoc mundo." Michael Scotus, *De secretis naturae* (Lyons, 1580), p. 273.

89. All the editions that I have seen add "q. mater" after "secundina." This may mean "the secundine or the mother." It may also be a textual error.

90. Cf. Constantinus Africanus, *De communibus locis...*, in *Opera* (Basileae, 1536), lib. II, cap. 15: De pelliculis et cute, p. 46; *De omnium morborum qui homini accidere possunt, cognitione et curatione*, in *Opera* (Basileae, 1536), lib. VI, cap. xviii: De secundinae exitu, p. 134.

91. Aristotle does not discuss the umbilicus specifically in *Met.* Book V. In 1014a, 20–21, he states that embryos derive increase by contact and organic adhesion. The umbilicus and blood vessels are described in *G.A.* 745b 20f.

92. See Isidore of Seville, *Etymologiae*, ed. Jose Oroz Reta and Manuel A. Marcos Casquero (Madrid: Editorial Catolica, 1983), XI, 1, 99, vol. II, p. 32: "Umbilicus est medius locus corporis, dictus quod sit umbus illorum. Unde et umbo appellatur locus in medio clypei, a quo pendet. Ex eo enim infans in utero pendet, ex eo etiam et nutritur." See also the discussion by Danielle Jacquart in "Medical Explanations of Sexual Behavior in the Middle Ages," in Helen Rodnite Lemay, ed., *Homo Carnalis*, p. 9 and n. 28.

93. Aristotle discusses milk in *H.A.* VII, 5, 585a; VII, 10, 587b; and most extensively in *G.A.* IV, 7, 776a ff. There is no discussion in any of these passages of the superiority of the milk of a black woman.

94. *Phys.* II, 8; 199a 32.

95. Aristotle, *Meteor.* I, 10.

96. Cf. *De gen. et corr.* II, 7, 334b. The reading here is taken from the Venice edition; the Lyons edition refers to the first book *On Generation.*

97. For a discussion of the six things nonnatural, see Nancy Siraisi, *Medieval and Early Renaissance Medicine* (Chicago: University of Chicago Press, 1990), p. 101.

98. Galen (ps.), *De spermate,* in *Opera* (Lyons, 1528), f. 66rb: "De conceptione pueri alterata a stellis et non a parentibus."

99. Albert does not include this story in the *Physica,* although he does discuss the possibility of a celestial cause for such a monster. He attributes the information to Empedocles. See Albertus Magnus, *Physicorum Libri VIII,* ed. A. Borgnet in *Opera Omnia III* (Paris: Vivès, 1890), lib. II, tract. iii, cap. iii, text. 82, p. 168.

100. Avicenna, *Liber canonis* lib. III, fen xxi, tract. l, cap. xli: De causis masculinitatis, f. 364b.

101. Aristotle, *De anima,* II, 2; 414a 25. This passage is based on Albertus Magnus, *De motibus animalium* I, 1, 3, cited in Lynn Thorndike, "Further Consideration of the 'Experimenta,' ...," *Speculum* 30 (1955): 436.

102. Aristotle, *De caelo,* II, 2; 284b 27–28.

103. Albertus Magnus states in the *De mineralibus,* ed. A. Borgnet, in *Opera Omnia* vol. 5 (Paris: Vivès, 1890), II, tr. 3, c. 2, that constellations are capable of producing images in stones. See John M. Riddle and James A. Mulholland, "Albert on Stones and Minerals," in James A. Weisheipl, ed., *Albertus Magnus and the Sciences* (Toronto: Pontifical Institute, 1980), p. 215. The author seems to be referring here to fossil forms of animals which Albert believed to be impressed in stones by the heavenly bodies.

104. Cf. Avicenna, *Metaphysics of Avicenna,* Chapter 57, pp. 106–7.

105. Albertus Magnus discusses signification by stones in *De mineralibus.* See lib. II, tract. III, pp. 48–57: "De sigillis lapidum, et qualiter est dicendum de sigillis, et quot sunt modi sigillorum, et de expertis."

106. Aḥmad ibn Yūsuf, *Centiloquium*, verbum 9.

107. See Aristotle, *Met.* V, 22; 1022b 20ff; *Categ.* 10; 12a 26ff.

108. Constantinus Africanus, *De communibus medico cognitu necessariis locis*, in *Opera* (Basileae: apud Henricum Petrum, 1539), lib. III, cap 33: De genitalibus, et primum de matrice, p. 74.

109. These signs are identical with those found in Abū Mashar, *Introductorium maius in astronomiam*, I, 2.

110. Hippocrates, *Aphorisms*, V, xli, p. 169.

111. Some editions spell this "pappel de mane," e.g. Strasbourg (Argentine), 1510, f. E3v. I have not been able to locate any identification of this substance.

112. This may be a reference to Chapter I of the *De secretis mulierum* where the topic of the menstrual period is discussed. Albertus Magnus treats the menstrual period in *De animalibus*, Book XVI, tract. 1, cap. 15 and does not state that menstruous women are poisonous. See Albertus Magnus, *De animalibus*, ed. Hermann Städler, 1920, in *Beiträge zur Geschichte der Philosophie und Theologie des Mittelalters* 16 (1920), 1102–1106.

113. Aristotle does not make this statement in *On Sleep and Waking*. He discusses infants and sleep in this treatise only cursorily. See *De somno et vigilia* III; 457a 2ff.

114. Aristotle, *G.A.* II, 6; 744a 5. Cf. *De anima*, III, 1; 425a 4. The text reads "De anima" and it is not clear whether this stands for *De anima* or *De animalibus*. Aristotle makes this point in numerous places.

115. "Sicut quidam cum usitati sunt comedere venenum in tantum quod erat eis cibus, sic accidit modernis dicentibus quod generatio fuit ex non ente, et causa istius existimationis fuit consuetudo." Averroes, *Aristotelis Stagyritici [sic] libri physicorum octo...Averroeque eius exactis [sime] interprete* (Papie, 1520), f. 84v.

116. Avicenna, *Liber canonis*, lib. IV, fen vi, tract. l, cap. ii, f. 470v.

117. Galen, *De locis affectis*, fols. 459v–466v. For an English translation see *Galen on the Affected Parts*, tr. Rudolph E. Siegel (Basel: S. Karger, 1976).

118. Cf. Aristoteles (pseudonym), *Secretum Secretorum Aristotelis ad Alexandrum Magnum*, (Venice, 1555), f. G: "De his quae Macre faciunt corpus."

119. Avicenna discusses the womb expelling superfluities in two places in the *Canon*. Book III, fen. xx, tract. 11, cap. 1 deals with the expulsion of the menses: "Et in ea [matrice] est meatus oppositus ori matricis extrinseco ex quo deglutit sperma et expellit menstrua et parit fetum." Cap. 23 treats the topic of putrid humidities: "Quandoque accidit mulieribus ut currant ex matricibus earum humiditates purime putride et currat ex eis iterum sperma." In neither case is the sewer analogy used. See Avicenna *Liber canonis*, fols. 360vb, 373rb.

120. On the treatment of suffocation of the womb, see Helen Rodnite Lemay, "William of Saliceto on Human Sexuality," *Viator* 12 (1981): 177–78; Wack, *Lovesickness*, p. 131.

121. Cf. *De anima*, I, 4; 408a 7f.

122. The Lyons, 1580, edition adds here: "id est, de generatione." This may be a reference to Aristotle's work on generation. Cf. *De gen. et corr.* II, 2–3; 330a, 25ff.

123. Hippocrates, *Aphorisms*, V, 62.

124. The Venice, 1508, edition reads "quia semen in eis concipitur." The reading "comburitur" used here is taken from the edition of Vienne, 1506, f. 32va.

125. Albertus Magnus, *De animalibus*, ed. Hermann Städler in *Beiträge zur Geschichte der Philosophie und Theologie des Mittelalters* 15 (1916), lib. X, tract. 2, cap. 1, p. 748. This passage discusses only a penis that is too short: "In veretro etiam sunt causa [sterilitatis]: nimia brevitas quae ad os matricis non attingit, sive haec brevitas contingat ex pinguedine corporis carnem ad se trahente, sive sit naturalis aut ex abscisione facta." Other passages that discuss the organ (I, 2, 24; XVI, 1, 2) do not mention penile size.

126. Averroes, *Commentarium magnum in Aristotelis De anima*, ed. F. Stuart Crawford (Cambridge, Mass.: Mediaeval Academy of America, 1953), II, 34, p. 182.

127. *H.A.* VII, I; 581a–b.

128. The Lyons, 1580, edition reads *"frizari."* The translation is based on *"fricari,"* from the Amsterdam, 1662, edition.

129. Hippocrates, *Aphorisms* V, 60.

130. For a discussion of medieval theories of digestion see Hewson, *Giles of Rome*, pp. 75–78.

131. Aristotle, *De iuventute et senectute, De vita et morte,* VI, 470a, 20ff.

132. Ibid.

133. On this point see McVaugh, "The 'Humidum Radicale,'" pp. 259–83.

134. Cf. Albertus Magnus, *Metaphysica,* ed. Bernhardus Geyer in *Opera Omnia* XVI, 1. (Monasterii Westfalorum in aedibus Aschendorff, 1960), lib. IV, tract. 3, cap. 9, p. 200. This reference may simply represent the confusion between "*Met.*" and "*Meth.*" that exists elsewhere in the treatise. The *Meth.* (or *Meteor.*) reference is much more specific. Albertus Magnus, *Liber Meteororum,* ed. A. Borgnet in *Opera Omnia* IV (Paris: Vivès, 1890), lib. 4, tract. 1, cap. 3: De prima operatione activarum qualitatum que est generatio mixti secundum quod mixtum est, pp. 710–711.

135. *Meteor.* IV, 2; 329b 24ff.

136. Cf. *De gen. et corr.,* II, 2; 329b.

137. *De longitudine et brevitate vitae,* V; 466b 8.

138. *De longitudine et brevitate vite,* V; 466b 14.

139. The text adds here: "It sometimes happens that the fetus is of a weakened nature when pregnant women nurse another child born previously. The cause of this weakness is that the matter from which the child existing in the uterus should be nourished goes to the one born earlier whom the mother is nursing. This happens often at present." This is undoubtedly an interpolation, since the subject is treated here completely out of context.

140. This account of the chapter arrangement does not correspond exactly to the numbering in this volume. I have relied on the Lyons, 1580, edition, which does not contain a complete text of this last chapter on sperm. The headings here correspond to those of the Venice, 1508, edition.

141. This statement attributed to the commentator is not found in the modern edition of Averroes' commentary. See Averroes, *Commentarium magnum in Aristotelis De anima libros,* ed. F. Stuart Crawford (Cambridge, Mass.: Mediaeval Academy of America, 1953). It is also not present in other editions of the *De secretis mulierum*: Frankfurt, 1615, Venice, 1508.

141. *Met.* III, 1; 995a 35ff.

BIBLIOGRAPHY

PRIMARY SOURCES

Manuscripts

MANUSCRIPTS OF THE *DE SECRETIS MULIERUM*:
Munich CLM 22297, fols. 21v–50v, a. 1320 (Bayerische Staats-Bibliothek, Munich)
Munich CLM 22300, fols. 61v–76r, 14c. (Bayerische Staats-Bibliothek, Munich)
Paris B.N. lat. 7148, fols. 1r–16r, 15c. (Bibliothèque Nationale, Paris)
Utrecht 723, fols. 46r–78r (commentary), a. 1353. (Bibliotheek der Rijksuniversiteit, Utrecht)
Vat. lat. 4456, f. lr–25r (commentary), 15c. (Bibliotheca Apostolica Vaticana)

OTHER MANUSCRIPT SOURCES:
Abū Ja'far Aḥmad ibn Yūsuf ibn Ibrāhīm (Haly), *Centiloquium*, MS Paris B.N. lat. 7307, fols. 1–20, 14c. (Bibliothèque Nationale, Paris)
Nicholus, *De passionibus mulierum*, MS Lille 334, f. 1–221, 15c. (Bibliothèque Municipale, Lille)

Printed Editions

PRINTED EDITIONS OF THE *DE SECRETIS MULIERUM*:
Albertus Magnus (pseudonym). *Secreta mulierum et virorum*. Argentorati: apud H. Knoblochzer, n.d. (about 1480). Paris, Bibliothèque Nationale, res. R822; contains Commentary A.
———. *Secreta mulierum et virorum nuperrime correpta et emendata*. Paris: J. Petit, n.d. Paris, Bibliothèque Nationale, res. 1908; contains Commentary A.
———. *De secretis mulierum et virorum*. Augsburg: Hans Forschauer, about 1500. National Library of Medicine, Bethesda, Maryland; contains Commentary A.
———. *De secretis mulierum et virorum*. Liptzk: impressum per Melchiorem Lotter, 1500. National Library of Medicine, Bethesda, Maryland; contains Commentary A.

————. *De secretis mulierum cum commento*. Venice: Jo. Alvisium de Varisio, 1501. National Library of Medicine, Bethesda, Maryland; contains Commentary B.

————. *De secretis mulierum cum commento*. Vienne: Joannes Winterburg, before 1506. National Library of Medicine, Bethesda, Maryland; contains Commentary B.

————. *De secretis mulierum cum commento*. Venice: Petri Bergomatis, 1508. New York Academy of Medicine Library; contains Commentary B.

————. *De secretis mulierum et virorum*. Argentine: Mathiam Hüpfuff, 1510. National Library of Medicine, Bethesda, Maryland; contains Commentary A.

————. *Alberti cognomento magni libellus qui inscribitur De formatione hominis in utero materno, vel ut notiori titulo, Secreta mulierum*. Antwerp: ex officina viduae M. Caesaris, 1538. Paris, Bibliothèque Nationale R10704; contains Commentary A.

————. *Secreta mulierum et virorum*. Paris: in domo P. Sergent, 1539. Paris, Bibliothèque Nationale R10703; contains Commentary A.

————. *Alberti cognomento magni De secretis mulierum libellus*. Lugduni, 1566. Paris, Bibliothèque Nationale 8°R5304; New York Academy of Medicine Library; contains Commentary A.

————. *De secretis mulierum*. Lyons: Quadratus, 1580. New York Academy of Medicine Library; contains Commentary A.

————. *De secretis mulierum*. Lyons: Antonius de Harsy, 1598. New York Academy of Medicine Library; contains Commentary A.

————. *De secretis mulierum libellus*. Lugduni, 1615. Paris, Bibliothèque Nationale V21770; contains Commentary A.

Tractatus Henrici de Saxonia, Alberti magni discipuli, De secretis mulierum, in Germania nunquam editus. Frankfurt: Iohannes Bringerus, 1615. National Library of Medicine, Bethesda, Maryland; Paris Bibliothèque Nationale R10753; contains Commentary B.

Albertus Magnus (pseudonym). *De secretis mulierum libellus*. Amsterdam: apud Iodocum Ianssonium, 1643. National Library of Medicine, Bethesda, Maryland; contains Commentary A.

TRANSLATIONS OF THE *DE SECRETIS MULIERUM*:

Albertus Magnus (pseudonym). *De secretis mulierum, or The Mysteries of Human Generation Fully Revealed*, tr. John Quincy. London: E. Curll, 1725.

Les Admirables Secrets d'Albert le Grand. Cologne: chez le dispensateur des secrets, 1706.

OTHER PRIMARY SOURCES:

Abū Ma'shar. *Introductorium maius in astronomiam*, tr. John of Seville, ed. Richard Lemay. Naples: Istituto Universitario Orientale, in press.

Aetios of Amida. *The Gynaecology and Obstetrics of the VIth Century,* A.D., tr. James V. Ricci. Philadelphia and Toronto: Blakiston Company, 1950.

Albertus Magnus. *De animalibus libri XXVI,* ed. Augustus Borgnet, in *Opera Omnia* XI, XII. Paris: Vivès, 1891.

———. *De animalibus libri XXVI,* ed. Hermann Städler. *Beiträge zur Geschichte der Philosophie und Theologie des Mittelalters,* 15 (1916), 16 (1920).

———. *De caelo et mundo,* ed. P. Hossfeld in *Opera Omnia* VI, 1, ed. B. Geyer. Monasterii Westfalorum in aedibus Aschendorff, 1971.

———. *De metaphysica* in *Naturalia ac supra naturalia opera per Marcum Antonium Zimaram...* Venice: Haeredum Octaviani Scoti, 1517–1518.

———. *De mineralibus,* ed. A. Borgnet, in *Opera Omnia* V. Paris: Vivès, 1890.

———. *Liber Metaurorum* in *Naturalia ac supra naturalia opera per Marcum Antonium Zimaram....* Venice: Haeredum Octaviani Scoti, 1517–1518.

———. *Liber Meteororum* ed. Augustus Borgnet, in *Opera Omnia* IV. Paris: Vivès, 1890.

———. *Metaphysica,* ed. Bernhardus Geyer in *Opera Omnia* XVI, 1. Monasterii Westfalorum in aedibus Aschendorff, 1960.

———. *Metheororum,* in *Tabula tractatuum Parvorum naturalium.* Venice: Octavianus Scotus, 1517.

———. *Physicorum libri VIII,* ed. A. Borgnet, in *Opera Omnia* III. Paris: Vivès, 1890.

———. *Posteriorum Analyticorum,* ed. A. Borgnet, in *Opera Omnia* II. Paris: Vivès, 1890.

———. *Quaestiones super De animalibus,* ed. Ephrem Filthaut. Monasterii Westfalorum in aedibus Aschendorff, 1955.

———. *Speculum astronomie,* eds. Caroti, Pereira, and Zamponi, under the direction of Paola Zambelli. *Quaderni di Storia e Critica della Scienza,* new series, 10. Pisa: Domus Galilaeana, 1977.

Albertus Magnus (pseudonym). *De homine,* ed. Marcus Antonius Zimara in *Due partes summe.* Venice: Haeredes Octaviani Scoti, 1519.

Aquinas, Thomas. *Summa Theologiae,* Ia pars, volume 13. New York and London: Blackfriars and McGraw Hill, 1963.

Aristoteles (pseudonym) *Secretum secretorum.* Venice, 1553.

———. (pseudonym) *Secretum secretorum Aristotelis ad Alexandrum magnum.* Venice, 1555.

Aristotle. *Categories,* tr. J. L. Ackrill, in *The Complete Works of Aristotle,* vol. I, ed. Jonathan Barnes. Princeton: Princeton University Press, 1985.

———. *Historia animalium,* tr. D'Arcy Wentworth Thompson in *The*

Works of Aristotle Translated into English. Volume VI. Oxford: Clarendon, 1910.

————. *Metaphysica,* tr. W. D. Ross, in *The Works of Aristotle Translated into English,* volume VIII. Oxford: Clarendon, 1930.

————. *Meteorologica,* tr. E. W. Webster; *De Anima,* tr. J. A. Smith; *Parva naturalia,* tr. J. I. Beane and G. R. T. Ross in *The Works of Aristotle Translated into English,* volume III. Oxford: Clarendon, 1931.

————. *Physica, De caelo, De generatione et corruptione,* tr. W. D. Ross, in *The Works of Aristotle Translated into English,* volume II. Oxford: Clarendon, 1931.

————. *The Generation of Animals,* tr. A. L. Peck. Cambridge: Harvard University Press, 1953.

————. *The Generation of Animals,* tr. Arthur Platt, in *The Works of Aristotle,* vol. V. Oxford: Clarendon, 1912.

————. (pseudonym) *The Problems of Aristotle with Other Philosophers and Physicians.* London: printed for W. K., 1670.

Averroes. *Aristotelis Stagiritae metaphysicorum libri xiiii cum Averrois Cordubensis commentariis.* Venice: Junta, 1562; reprinted, Frankfurt/Main: Minerva, 1962.

————. *Aristotelis Stagyritici [sic] libri physicorum octo...Averroeque eius exactis[sime] interprete.* Papie, 1520.

————. *Colliget.* Venice, 1549.

————. *Colliget* in Joannes Arculanus, *In fen primam quarti canonis Avicennae.* Venice, 1552.

————. *Colliget.* Venice: Junta, 1562.

————. *Commentarium magnum in Aristotelis De anima libros,* ed. F. Stuart Crawford. Cambridge, Mass.: Mediaeval Academy, 1953.

————. *Commentarium medium in Aristotelis De generatione et corruptione libros,* ed. Samuel Kurland. Cambridge, Mass.: Mediaeval Academy, 1956.

————. *Metaphysica,* in Albertus Magnus, *Summa philosophiae.* Leipzig, 1513.

————. *Metaphysicorum Aristotelis opus re ipsa divinum iuxta novam Bessarionis translationem...accessit operi et id commodi quod libri singuli per commentariorum Averrois numeros....* Leipzig: Vuolfgangus Monacensis, 1519.

————. *Middle Commentary and Epitome On Aristotle's De generatione et corruptione,,* tr. Samuel Kurland. Cambridge, Mass.: Mediaeval Academy, 1958.

Avicenna. *De animalibus,* tr. Michael Scotus. Venice: Joannes and Gregorius de Gregoriis, de Forlivio, ca. 1500. (National Library of Medicine, Bethesda, Maryland, incun. 24).

————. *De caelo et mundo, De animalibus*, tr. Dominicus Gundissalinus in *Opera philosophica*. Venice, 1508; microfilm, Columbia University Library.

————. *Liber canonis* tr. Arnoldus de Villanova. Venice, 1507; reprint Hildesheim: Georg Olms, 1964.

————. *Metaphysica sive Prima philosophica*. Venice, 1495; reprint Frankfurt/Main: Minerva, 1966.

————. *The Metaphysics of Avicenna (ibn Sina)*, tr. Parviz Morewedge. New York: Columbia University Press, 1973.

Avicenna (pseudonym). *Avicennae ad Hasen regem epistola de re recta. Tractatulus de alchiminia. De congelatione et conglutione lapidum* in *Praecipuos selectorum auctorum tractatus de chemiae et lapidis philosophici...*, volume IV. Argentorati: Zetzner, 1659.

Bartholomaeus Anglicus. *De genuinis rerum coelestium, terrestrium et inferarum proprietatibus*. Frankfurt: Wolfgang Richter, 1601; reprinted Frankfurt: Minerva, 1964.

Bernardus de Gordonio. *Lilium medicinae*. Paris, 1542.

Boethius. *Consolation of Philosophy*, tr. Richard Green. Indianapolis: Bobbs-Merrill, 1962.

Caelius Aurelianus. *Gynaecia*, ed. Miriam Drabkin and Israel Drabkin. Baltimore: Johns Hopkins University Press, 1951.

Cartelle, Enrique Montero. *Liber minor de coitu: Tratado menor de Andrologia, Anonimo Salernitano*. Valladolid: Universidad de Valladolid, 1987.

Chartularium universitatis Parisiensis, eds. Henricus Denifle and Aemilio Chatelain, volume I. Paris, 1899; reprinted, Bruxelles: Culture et Civilisation, 1964.

Constantinus Africanus. *De communibus locis...*, in *Opera*. Basileae, 1536.

————. *De communibus medico cognitu necessariis locis*, in *Opera*. Basileae: apud Henricum Petrum, 1539.

————. *De omnium morborum qui homini accidere possunt, cognitione et curatione*, in *Opera*. Basileae, 1536.

Ferckel, Christoph. *Die Gynäkologie des Thomas von Brabant*. Munich: Carl Kuhn, 1912.

Flood, Bruce Pepper. *Macer Floridus: A Medieval Herbalism*. Ph.D. diss., 1968; University Microfilms, 1969.

Galen. *De complexionibus* in *Burgundio of Pisa's Translation of Galen's PERI KRASEON "De complexionibus,"* ed. Richard J. Durling. Berlin and New York: Walter de Gruyter, 1976.

————. *De locis affectis [ed.: affectibus] libri sex*. Naples: ex officina Ioannis Pauli Sugganappi, 1548. Translated as *Galen on the Affected Parts*, tr. Rudolph E. Siegel. Basel: S. Karger, 1976.

————. *Oeuvres anatomiques, physiologiques, et médicales,* tr. Charles Daremberg. Paris: J. Baillière, 1886.

————. *Opera.* Lyons, 1528.

———— (pseudonym). *Microtegni seu De spermate,* tr. Vera Tavone Passalacqua. Rome: Istituto di Storia della Medicina, 1959.

Guainerius, Anthonius. *Tractatus de matricibus,* in *Opera Omnia.* Pavia, 1481.

Guilielmus de Saliceto. *Summa conservationis et curationis.* Venice, 1489.

Hansen, Bert. *Nicole Oresme and the Marvels of Nature: A Study of his De causis mirabilium with Critical Edition Translation, and Commentary.* Toronto: Pontifical Institute of Mediaeval Studies, 1985.

Hildegard of Bingen. *Causae et curae,* ed. Paul Kaiser. Leipzig: Teubner, 1903.

Hippocrates. *Aphorisms,* tr. W. H. S. Jones. Cambridge and London: Harvard University Press and William Heinemann, 1953.

————. *De la génération,* ed. and trans. Robert Joly. Paris: Les Belles Lettres, 1970.

————. *On Intercourse and Pregnancy: An English Translation of On Semen and On the Development of the Child,* tr. Tage U. H. Ellinger. New York: Henry Schuman, n.d.

————. *The Medical Works of Hippocrates,* tr. J. Chadwick and W. Mann. Oxford: Blackwell, 1950.

Isidore of Seville. *Etymologiae,* ed. Jose Oroz Reta and Manuel A. Marcos Casquero. Madrid: Editorial Catolica, 1983.

Kramer, Heinrich, and James Sprenger. *Malleus maleficarum,* tr. Montague Summers. New York: Dover, 1971.

Macer. *Macri philosophi de virtutibus herbarum.* Venice, 1508.

Michael Scotus. *De secretis naturae.* Lyons: Quadratus, 1580.

Petrus de Abano. *Conciliator.* Venice: Luceantonij de Giunta, 1522.

Soranus of Ephesus. *Soranus' Gynecology,* tr. Owsei Temkin. Baltimore: Johns Hopkins Press, 1956.

Trota. *Erotis medici liberti Iuliae quem aliqui Trotulam inepte nominant muliebrium liber...,* in *Harmoniae gynaeciorum sive de morbis muliebribus liber ex Prisciano Cleopatra Moschione Libro matricis dicto et Theodoro Prisciano collectus.* Argentinae: Zetzner, 1597.

Trotula of Salerno. *The Diseases of Women,* tr. Elizabeth Mason-Hohl. Los Angeles: Ward Ritchie Press, 1940.

Vincentius Bellovacensis. *Speculum naturale.* Duaci: Baltazaris Belleri, 1624, reprinted Graz: Akademische Druck-u. Verlagsanstalt, 1964.

William of Conches. *Dragmaticon (Dialogus de substantiis physicis, ante annos ducentos [sic] confectus a Vuilhelmo Aneponymo philo-*

sopho), ed. Guillelmus Gratarolus. Argentorati: Rihelius, 1557; reprint Minerva, 1967.

SECONDARY WORKS:

Allen, Prudence. *The Concept of Woman: The Aristotelian Revolution.* Montreal: Eden, 1985.

Amundsen, Darrell W., and Carol Jean Diers. "The Age of Menarche in Medieval Europe," *Human Biology* 45 (3) (September 1973): 363–69.

Ashley, Benedict M. "St. Albert and the Nature of Natural Science," in James A. Weisheipl, ed., *Albertus Magnus and the Sciences: Commemorative Essays 1980.* Toronto: Pontifical Institute, 1980.

Baader, Gerhard. "Frauenheilkunde und Geburtshilfe im Frühmittelalter," in *Frauen in der Geschichte, VIII: Interdisziplinäre Studien zur Geschichte der Frauen im Frühmittelalter.* Düsseldorf: Schwann, 1986.

Bazala, Vladimir. "Astrologische Diagnose und Prognose," *Neue Münchner Beiträge zur Geschichte der Medizin und Naturwissenschaften* (Medizinhistorische Reihe-Munich) 7–8 (1978): 177–84.

Bell, Susan Groag, ed. *Women: From the Greeks to the French Revolution.* Belmont, Cal.: Wadsworth, 1973.

Bloch, Howard. "Medieval Misogyny," *Representations* 20 (fall 1987): 1–24.

Blumenfeld-Kosinski, Renate. *Not of Woman Born: Representations of Caesarean Birth in Medieval and Renaissance Culture.* Ithaca: Cornell University Press, 1990.

Bréhaut, Ernest. *An Encyclopedist of the Dark Ages: Isidore of Seville.* New York: Columbia University Press, 1917. Burt Franklin reprint, 1964.

Bullough, Vern. "Medieval Medical and Scientific Views of Women," *Viator* 4 (1973): 485–501.

———. "Sexology and the Medievalist," in Helen Rodnite Lemay, ed., *Homo Carnalis: The Carnal Aspect of Medieval Human Life.* ACTA, volume XIV, 1990 (for 1987). State University of New York at Binghamton: CEMERS, 1990, pp. 23–44.

Bullough, Vern, Brenda Shelton, and Sarah Slavin. *The Subordinated Sex: A History of Attitudes toward Women.* Athens: University of Georgia Press, 1988.

Bullough, Vern, and Cameron Campbell. "Female Longevity and Diet in the Middle Ages," *Speculum* 55 (2) (1980): 317–25.

Burnett, C. S. F. "The Planets and the Development of the Embryo," in G. R. Dunstan, ed., *The Human Embryo: Aristotle and the Arabic and European Traditions.* Exeter: University of Exeter Press, 1990, pp. 95–112.

Cadden, Joan. "It Takes All Kinds: Sexuality and Gender Differences in Hildegard of Bingen's 'Book of Compound Medicine,'" *Traditio* 40 (1984): 149–74.

———. "Medieval Scientific and Medical Views of Sexuality: Questions of Propriety," *Medievalia et Humanistica* new series, 14 (1986): 157–71.

Chenu, M. D. "*Exemplaria* universitaires des XIIIe et XIVe siècles," *Scriptorium* VII (1953): 68–80.

Delaney, Janice, Mary Jane Lupton, and Emily Toth. *The Curse: A Cultural History of Menstruation,* revised edition. Urbana: University of Illinois Press, 1988.

Demaitre, Luke E. *Doctor Bernard de Gordon: Professor and Practitioner.* Toronto: Pontifical Institute of Mediaeval Studies, 1980.

———, and Anthony Travill. "Human Embryology and Development in the Works of Albertus Magnus," in James A. Weishepl, ed., *Albertus Magnus and the Sciences: Commemorative Essays 1980.* Toronto: Pontifical Institute, 1980.

Diepgen, Paul. *Frau und Frauenheilkunde in der Kultur des Mittelalters.* Stuttgart: Georg Thieme Verlag, 1963.

Ferckel, Christoph. *Die Gynäkologie des Thomas von Brabant.* Munich: Carl Kuhn, 1912.

———. "Die Secreta Mulierum und ihr Verfasser," *Sudhoffs Archiv* 38 (1954): 267–74.

Ferguson, John. *On a Copy of Albertus Magnus' 'De secretis mulierum' Printed by Machlinia.* Westminster: Nichols, 1886, reprinted from *Archaeologia* 49.

Flood, Bruce Pepper. *Macer Floridus: A Medieval Herbalism.* Ph.D. diss., 1968; University Microfilms, 1969.

Green, Monica H. "Constantinus Africanus and the Conflict between Religion and Science," in G. R. Dunstan, ed., *The Human Embryo: Aristotle and the Arabic and European Traditions.* Exeter: University of Exeter Press, 1990, pp. 47–69.

———. "The *De genecia* attributed to Constantine the African," *Speculum* 62 (2) (1987): 299–323.

———. *The Transmission of Ancient Theories of Female Physiology and Disease through the Early Middle Ages.* Ph.D. diss., Princeton University, 1985.

———. "Women's Medical Practice and Health Care in Medieval Europe," *Signs: Journal of Women in Culture and Society* 14 (2) (1989): 434–73.

Hansen, Bert. *Nicole Oresme and the Marvels of Nature: A Study of His De causis mirabilium with Critical Edition, Translation and Commentary.* Toronto: Pontifical Institute of Medieval Studies, 1985.

Hewson, M. Anthony. *Giles of Rome and the Medieval Theory of Conception: A Study of the De formatione corporis humani in utero.* London: Athlone Press, 1975.

Horowitz, Maryanne Cline. "Aristotle and Women," *Journal of the History of Biology* 9 (2) (1976): 183–213.

Jacquart, Danielle."Medical Explanations of Sexual Behavior in the Middle Ages," in Helen Rodnite Lemay, ed., *Homo Carnalis. ACTA*, volume XIV, 1990 (for 1987). State University of New York at Binghamton: CEMERS, 1990, pp. 1–21.

――――, and Claude Thomasset. "Albert le Grand et les problèmes de la sexualité," *History and Philosophy of the Life Sciences* 3 (1981), 73–93.

――――, and Claude Thomasset. *Sexualité et savoir médical au moyen âge.* Paris: Presses Universitaires de France, 1985.

――――, and Claude Thomasset. *Sexuality and Medicine in the Middle Ages*, tr. Matthew Adamson. Princeton: Princeton University Press, 1988.

Johnson, Michael. "Science and Discipline: The Ethos of Sex Education in a Fourteenth-Century Classroom," in Helen Rodnite Lemay, ed., *Homo Carnalis: The Carnal Aspect of Medieval Human Life. ACTA*, volume XIV, 1990 (for 1987). State University of New York at Binghamton: CEMERS, 1990, pp. 157–72.

Kealey, Edward J. *Medieval Medicus: A Social History of Anglo-Norman Medicine.* Baltimore: Johns Hopkins University Press, 1981.

Keil, Gundolf. "Die Frau als Ärztin und Patientin in der Medizinischen Fachprosa des Deutschen Mittelalters," *Oesterreichische Akademie der Wissenschaften. Philosophisch-Historische Klasse, Sitzungsberichte* 473 (1986): 157–211.

King, Lester. "Friedrich Hoffman and Some Medical Aspects of Witchcraft," *Clio Medica* 9 (4) (1974): 299–309.

Kusche, Brigitte. "Zur 'Secreta Mulierum' Forschung," *Janus* 62 (1975): 103–23.

Lawn, Brian. *The Salernitan Questions: An Introduction to the History of Medieval and Renaissance Problem Literature.* Oxford: Clarendon, 1963.

Lemay, Helen Rodnite. "Anthonius Guainerius and Medieval Gynecology," in Julius Kirshner and Suzanne Wemple, eds., *Women of the Medieval World.* Oxford: Basil Blackwell, 1985, pp. 317–36.

――――. "Guido Bonatti: Astrology, Society and Marriage in Thirteenth-Century Italy," *Journal of Popular Culture* (1984): 79–90.

―――, ed. *Homo Carnalis: The Carnal Aspect of Medieval Human Life. ACTA*, volume XIV, 1990 (for 1987). State University of New York at Binghamton: Center for Medieval and Early Renaissance Studies (CEMERS), 1990.

―――. "Human Sexuality in Twelfth- Through Fifteenth-Century Scientific Writings," in Vern Bullough and James Brundage, eds., *Sexual Practices and the Medieval Church*. Buffalo: Prometheus Books, pp. 187–205.

―――. "Masculinity and Femininity in Early Renaissance Treatises on Human Reproducion," *Clio Medica* 18 (1983): 21–31.

―――. "Science and Theology at Chartres: The Case of the Supracelestial Waters," *British Journal for the History of Science* 10 (1977): 226–36.

―――. "Some Thirteenth- and Fourteenth-Century Lectures on Female Sexuality," *International Journal of Women's Studies* 1 (4) (1978): 391–400.

―――. "William of Saliceto on Human Sexuality," *Viator* 12 (1981): 165–81.

―――. "Women and the Literature of Obstetrics and Gynecology," in Joel T. Rosenthal, ed., *Medieval Women and the Sources of Medieval History*. Athens: University of Georgia Press, 1990, pp. 189–209.

Lemay, Richard. *Abū Ma'shar and Latin Aristotelianism in the Twelfth Century; The Recovery of Aristotle's Natural Philosophy through Arabic Astrology*. American University of Beirut, Publications of the Faculty of Arts and Sciences, Oriental Series, no. 38. Beirut, 1962.

―――. "De la Scolastique à l'histoire par le truchement de la philologie: Itinéraire d'un médiéviste entre Europe et Islam," in *La diffusione nelle scienze Islamiche nel medio evo Europeo*, Convegno Internazionale, Roma 2–4 ottobre 1984. Rome: Accademia Nazionale dei Lincei, 1987, pp. 399–535.

―――. "Origin and Success of the Kitāb Ṭamara of Abū Ja'far Aḥmad ibn Yūsuf ibn Ibrahim from the Tenth to the Seventeenth Century in the World of Islam and the Latin West," in *Proceedings of the First International Symposium on the History of Arabic Science*, 5–12 April 1976. University of Aleppo, Institute for the History of Arabic Science, 1978, volume II, pp. 91–107.

―――. "The Late Medieval School of Astronomy at Cracow and the Copernican System," in *Science and History: Essays in Honor of Edward Rosen. Studia Copernicana* XVI, 337–54.

―――. "The Teaching of Astronomy in the Universities of the Fourteenth–Fifteenth Century, Principally in Paris," *Essays in Honor of Pearl Kibre. Manuscripta* 20 (1976): 197–217.

————. "The True Place of Astrology in Medieval Science and Philosophy: Towards a Definition," in Patrick Curry, ed., *Astrology, Science and Society*. Woodbridge, England: Boydell and Brewer, 1987, pp. 57–73.

Levey, Martin, and Safwat S. Souryal. "Galen's On the Secrets of Women and On the Secrets of Men: A Contribution to the History of Arabic Pharmacology," *Janus* 55 (1968): 208–19.

Long, R. James. *Bartholomaeus Anglicus on the Properties of Soul and Body (De proprietatibus rerum, libri III et IV)*. Toronto: Pontifical Institute of Mediaeval Studies, 1979.

Maclean, Ian. *The Renaissance Notion of Woman: A Study in the Fortunes of Scholasticism and Medical Science in European Intellectual Life*. Cambridge: Cambridge University Press, 1980.

McVaugh, Michael. "The 'Humidum Radicale' in Thirteenth-Century Medicine," *Traditio* 30 (1974): 259–83.

Meyerhof, M., and D. Joannides. *La Gynécologie et l'Obstétrique chez Avicenne (ibn Sina) et leurs rapports avec celles des Grecs*. Cairo: R. Schindler, 1938.

Minio-Paluello, Lorenzo. "Aristotle," in *Dictionary of Scientific Biography*, volume I. New York: Scribners, 1970, pp. 266–81.

Naibielek, Rainer. "Sexualerziehung im Werk des Avicenna. Ein Beitrag zur arabisch-islamischen Sexualgeschichte," *NTM: Schriftenreihe für Geschichte der Naturwissenschaft, Technik, und Medizin* 13 (2) (1976): 82–87.

Needham, Joseph. *A History of Embryology*. New York: Abelard-Schuman, 1959.

Newman, Barbara. *Sister of Wisdom: St. Hildegard's Theology of the Feminine*. Berkeley and Los Angeles: University of California Press, 1987.

Novum Glossarium Mediae Latinitatis. Hafniae: Ejnar Munksgaard, 1958.

O'Faolain, Julia, and Lauro Martines, eds. *Not in God's Image: Women in History from the Greeks to the Victorians*. New York: Harper and Row, 1973.

Pernoud, Régine. "La femme et la médecine au moyen-âge," *Colloque International d'Histoire de la Médecine Médiévale*, Orléans, 4–5 mai 1985. Orléans: La Société, 1985, pp. 38–43.

Pinto, Lucille. "The Folk Practice of Gynecology and Obstetrics in the Middle Ages," *Bulletin of the History of Medicine* 47 (5) (1973): 513–23.

Preus, Anthony. "Galen's Criticism of Aristotle's Conception Theory," *Journal of the History of Biology* 10 (1977): 65–85.

Riddle, John M., and James A. Mulholland. "Albert on Stones and Minerals," in James A. Weisheipl, ed., *Albertus Magnus and the Sciences*. Toronto: Pontifical Institute, 1980.

Rogers, Katherine M. *The Troublesome Helpmate: A History of Misogyny in Literature*. Seattle: University of Washington Press, 1966.

Romagnoli, Giovanni. "Una questione multisecolare: L'opera 'De secretis mulierum" attributa comunemente ad Alberto Magno è autentica o apocrifa?" in *Atti del XXIV Congresso Nazionale di Storia della Medicina*, Taranto-Bari, 25–28 settembre 1969, pp. 402–16.

Salvat, Michel. "L'accouchement dans la littérature scientifique médiévale," in *L'enfant au moyen-age. (Littérature et Civilisation), Sénéfiance* 9 (1980): 87–106.

Schleissner, Margaret Rose. *Pseudo-Albertus Magnus: Secreta Mulierum cum Commento, Deutsch. Critical Text and Commentary*. Ph.D. diss., Princeton University, 1987.

Schoffler, Heinz Herbert. "Zur Mittelalterlichen Embryologie," *Sudhoffs Archiv* 57 (1973): 297–314.

Sezgin, Fuat. *Geschichte des Arabischen Schrifttums*, volume III. Leiden: Brill, 1970.

Shaw, James Rochester. "Scientific Empiricism in the Middle Ages: Albertus Magnus on Sexual Anatomy and Physiology," *Clio Medica* 10 (1975): 53–64.

Siraisi, Nancy. *Medieval and Early Renaissance Medicine: An Introduction to Knowledge and Practice*. Chicago: University of Chicago Press, 1990.

———. *Taddeo Alderotti and His Pupils: Two Generations of Italian Medical Learning*. Princeton: Princeton University Press, 1981.

———. "The Medical Learning of Albertus Magnus," in James A. Weisheipl, ed., *Albertus Magnus and the Sciences: Commemorative Essays 1980*. Toronto: Pontifical Institute, 1980.

Thomasen, Anne-Liese. "'Historia animalium' contra 'Gynaecia' in der Literatur des Mittelalters," *Clio Medica* 15 (1980); 5–24.

Thomasset, Claude. "Quelques principes de l'embryologie médiévale (de Salerne à la fin du XIIIe siècle), in *L'enfant au moyen-âge (Littérature et Civilisation), Sénéfiance* 9 (1980): 107–21.

Thorndike, Lynn. "Further Consideration of the *Experimenta, Speculum astronomiae*, and *De secretis mulierum* ascribed to Albertus Magnus," *Speculum* 30 (1955): 413–43.

Thorndike, Lynn. *A History of Magic and Experimental Science*, volumes II and III. New York: Columbia University Press, 1923, 1934.

Thorndike, Lynn, and Pearl Kibre. *Catalogue of Incipits of Medieval Scientific Writings in Latin*. Cambridge, Mass.: Mediaeval Academy of America, 1963.

Ullmann, Manfred. *Die Medizin im Islam*. Leiden/Köln: Brill, 1970.

Veith, Ilza. *Hysteria: The History of a Disease*. Chicago: University of Chicago Press, 1965.

Wack, Mary Frances. *Lovesickness in the Middle Ages: The Viaticum and Its Commentaries*. Philadelphia: University of Pennsylvania Press, 1990.

Weisheipl, James A., ed. *Albertus Magnus and the Sciences: Commemorative Essays 1980*. Toronto: Pontifical Institute of Medieval Studies, 1980.

Wickersheimer, Ernest. *Dictionnaire Biographique des médecins en France au moyen-age*. 1936; reprint Genève: Droz, 1979. Two volumes with supplement by Danielle Jacquart.

———. "Henri de Saxe et le 'De secretis mulierum,'" in the *Proceedings of the Third International Congress on the History of Medicine*. London, 17–22 July 1922. Antwerp, 1923, pp. 253–54.

———. *Les manuscrits latins de médecine du haut moyen age dans les bibliothèques de France*. Documents, etudes et répertoires publiés par l'Institut de Recherche et d'Histoire des Textes, vol. XI. Paris, 1966.

Wingate, S. D. *The Mediaeval Latin Versions of the Aristotelian Scientific Corpus, with Special Reference to the Biological Works*. London: Courier Press, 1931; reprint Wm. Brown, Dubuque, Iowa.

Wood, Charles T. "The Doctors' Dilemma: Sin, Salvation and the Menstrual Cycle in Medieval Thought," *Speculum* 56 (4) (1981): 710–27.

INDEX

Abortion, 33, 57–8, 79, 101–4, 169n.181, 175n.82.
Aḥmad ibn Yūsuf, 26–7,
Al-Majūsī, 38.
Albertus Magnus: and Aristotelian ideas, 47; and astrology, 31; and human generation 21–4, 64; and menses, 46, 129; *Metaphysics*, comm. 20, 146, 149; *Meteorology*, 20, 30, 146; misogyny, 47–51; *On Animals* 24; *On Generation* 20; *On the Generation of Animals*, 138; *On the State of the Sun and Moon*, 20, 28, 87; philosophical level, 9, 13–4, 40, 47; *Physics*, 17, 105, 116; *Posterior Analytics*, comm., 61; and pseudo–Albert, 1, 3, 20, 23; *Questions on Animals*, 12, 48, 54; *Speculum astronomie*, 30, 159n.87; and Thomas of Cantimpré, 8.
Albumasar, 10–11, 26–9.
Aquinas, Thomas, 14, 50, 166n.158.
Aristotle, 155n.44, and astrology, 11, 13, 31, 91; *Book on Animals*, 79, 101, 106, 111, 130, 139; condemns women, 47–50; and doctors, 3, 155n.53; *Ethics* 49; and human generation, 10, 21–6, 78, 80, 85; and medieval science, 15, 37, 40; *Metaphysics*, 60, 94, 97–8, 109; *Meteorology*, 26, 30, 74, 81, 95, 97–8; *On Death and Life*, 145; *On Generation and Corruption*, 62, 82, 113, 146; *On Heaven and Earth*, 74, 91, 118; *On Sleep and Waking*, 54, 129; *On the Genera-*

tion of Animals, 18, 22, 60, 68, 77; *On the Length and Shortness of Life*, 147; *On the Soul*, 60, 63, 101, 118, 136; *On Youth and Old Age*, 145; *Physics*, 91, 97, 111; source for *De secretis mulierum*, 4, 17–20; 59; and women, 43–4, 47–9, 51.
Aristotle, pseudonym, *Book on Sperm*, 99–100; *Problems*, 11, 42; *Secret of Secrets*, 12–13, 132.
Astrology: and Catholic doctrine, 7, 11, 29, 31; determinism, 9, 29–30; emphasized in *De secretis mulierum*, 13–14, 18, 26–32; and natural philosophy, 3, 26, 40; popular astrology, 32.
Averroes, and astrology, 30, 159n.85; *Colliget*, 19, 65–7, 70; *On Generation and Corruption*, 82; *Metaphysics*, 81–3, 91; *On the Soul*, 60, 139, 148; *Physics*, 130; and pregnancy, 71; source for *De secretis mulierum*, 4, 13–4, 17, 19–20, 30.
Avicenna: and accidents, 27, 80; *Book on Floods*, 19, 65, 95; *Canon of Medicine*, 19, 22, 43–4, 131; and hermaphrodites, 116–7; and human generation, 23–5; *Metaphysics (Sufficientie)*, 17, 27, 119; *On Animals*, 19, 22, 23; and menses, 44–6; and monsters, 120; and principal members, 61; and spontaneous generation, 96–7; source for *De secretis mulierum*, 17–20, 53; sympathethic to women, 47; and womb, 66, 133.

195

Made in the USA
San Bernardino, CA
07 February 2014